SCHWATKA'S SEARCH

SLEDGING IN THE ARCTIC IN QUEST OF THE FRANKLIN RECORDS

By

WILLIAM H. GILDER

First published in 1880

Read &' Co.

Copyright © 2021 Read & Co. History

This edition is published by Read & Co. History,
an imprint of Read & Co.

This book is copyright and may not be reproduced or copied in any
way without the express permission of the publisher in writing.

British Library Cataloguing-in-Publication Data
A catalogue record for this book is available
from the British Library.

Read & Co. is part of Read Books Ltd.
For more information visit
www.readandcobooks.co.uk

CONTENTS

SIR JOHN FRANKLIN
By John Knox Laughton 7

INTRODUCTION. 21

CHAPTER I
NORTHWARD 29

CHAPTER II
THE WINTER CAMP 41

CHAPTER III
OUR DOGS 59

CHAPTER IV
IN THE SLEDGES. 70

CHAPTER V
NATIVE WITNESSES 84

CHAPTER VI
THE MIDNIGHT SUN 96

CHAPTER VII
RELICS 103

CHAPTER VIII
IRVING'S GRAVE. 116

CHAPTER IX
ARCTIC COSTUMES 125

CHAPTER X
OVER MELTING SNOWS. 133

CHAPTER XI
AMATEUR ESQUIMAUX 147

CHAPTER XII
WALRUS DIET 159

CHAPTER XIII
THE RETURN.....................................168

CHAPTER XIV
FAMINE...186

CHAPTER XV
ESQUIMAU HOME-LIFE............................202

CHAPTER XVI
HOMEWARD.....................................218

CHAPTER XVII
THE GRAVES OF THE EXPLORERS.................233

APPENDIX

INUIT PHILOLOGY..............................239

GLOSSARY.......................................249

ILLUSTRATIONS

Lieutenant Schwatka 20

The Overland Route of the Exploring
Expedition of Lieut. Schwatka to and from
King William's Land. 1879-1880 27

Lieut. Schwatka's Exped. to King William
Land to Discover the Remains of the
Franklin Expedition.. 28

Camp Daly in Summer 40

Esquimaux Going to the Hunting-Ground. 43

A Cairn 50

Cairn Marking Deposit of Provisions 52

The Ships in Winter Quarters 56

Esquimau Playing the Ki-Lowty 62

Camp Daly in Winter 72

Down-Hill with the Sledges. 77

Hunting Musk-Oxen. 79

The Great Bend in Hayes River 81

The Sources of the Hayes River 82

The Lower Portion of Back's or Great Fish River 83

Meeting with the Ookjooliks. 86

The Netchillik Ambassadress. 89

The Council with the Netchilliks 93

Snow-Huts on Cape Herschel 109

Crossing Erebus Bay 113

Curious Formation of Clay-Stone. 136

Clay-Stone Mounds. 137

The Breaking up of the Ice. 142

The March Southward. 143

Schwatka's Permanent Camp. 169

Henry Klutschak's Camp. 170

View on Back's River. 181

The Dangerous Rapids, Back's River. 183

The March in Extreme Cold Weather. 189

View on Connery River. 192

Esquimaux Building a Hut. 212

Section and Plan of Esquimau Hut. 213

Esquimau Woman Cooking. 216

SIR JOHN FRANKLIN

By John Knox Laughton

Arctic explorer, the twelfth and youngest son of Willingham Franklin of Spilsby in Lincolnshire, was born on 16 April 1786. It had been intended to bring him up for the church, but a holiday visit to the seashore excited a strong desire to go to sea, which his father vainly endeavoured to overcome by sending him for a voyage in a merchant vessel as far as Lisbon. On his return he entered the royal navy on board the Polyphemus, then just sailing for the Baltic, where she played a leading part in the battle of Copenhagen. Two months later Franklin was appointed as a midshipman to the Investigator, under the command of his cousin, Matthew Flinders, and on the point of sailing for Australia. While in the Investigator Franklin distinguished himself by his remarkable aptitude for nautical and astronomical observations; he was employed at Sydney as assistant in a little observatory which Flinders established, and won the notice of Captain King, the governor, who used to address him familiarly as Mr. Tycho Brahe. When the ship's company was broken up after the wreck of the Porpoise, Franklin accompanied Lieutenant Fowler to China in the Rolla, and, taking a passage home in the East India Company's ship Earl Camden, was with Commodore Dance in his extraordinary engagement with Linois (15 Feb. 1804), on which occasion Fowler commanded on the lower deck and Franklin took charge of the signals. On arriving in England Franklin was appointed to the Bellerophon, in which he was present in the battle of Trafalgar, again having charge of the signals, and being one of the few on

7

the Bellerophon's poop who escaped unhurt. Two years later he joined the Bedford, and, continuing in her after his promotion to lieutenant's rank (11 Feb. 1808), was employed on the home station till the peace in 1814, when the ship was ordered to North America, to form part of the expedition against New Orleans. In a boat attack on some gunboats in Lac Borgne Franklin was slightly wounded; and he had besides a full share in the laborious duties of the campaign. Its failure may account for the fact that no attention was paid to the strong recommendation of Sir John Lambert, in command of the troops with which he had been serving, and that he remained a lieutenant, serving on board the Forth frigate, with Sir William Bolton, Nelson's nephew. With Franklin's appointment in January 1818 to command the hired brig Trent, fitting out to accompany Captain Buchan in the Dorothea, Franklin's career as an Arctic explorer commenced. Their instructions were to pass between Spitzbergen and Greenland, use their best endeavours to reach the pole, and thence, if possible, to shape a course direct for Behring's Straits. The two ships sailed on 25 April, sighted Spitzbergen on 26 May, and passed without difficulty along its western coast; they were then stopped by the ice, and, being driven into the pack on 30 July, the Dorothea received so much damage as to be in momentary danger of foundering. They got into Dane's Gat, where such repairs as were possible were executed, but it was still very doubtful whether she could live through the passage home, and further contact with the ice was clearly out of the question. Buchan's instructions fully authorised him in this contingency to move into the Trent and send the Dorothea home; but he was unwilling to appear to desert his shipmates in a time of great danger. The Dorothea's state was such as to forbid her being sent home unattended, and Franklin's request that he might be allowed to go on rendered the task of superseding him the more disagreeable. So Buchan judged rightly that his proper course was to take the Dorothea home, with the Trent in close attendance on her. They arrived in England on 22 Oct.

Early in the following year Franklin was appointed to the command of an exploring expedition to be sent out with the general idea of amending the very defective geography of the northern part of America, and with more particular instructions 'to determine the latitudes and longitudes of the northern coast of North America, and the trendings of that coast from the mouth of the Coppermine River to the eastern extremity of that continent.' The details of the route from York Factory, named as a starting-point, were left to Franklin's judgment, guided by the advice he should receive from the agents of the Hudson's Bay Company, who would be instructed to co-operate with the expedition, and to provide it with guides, hunters, clothing, and ammunition. The small party, including Dr. (afterwards Sir John) Richardson, Hood and Back, midshipmen, the last of whom had been with Franklin in the Trent, two seamen, and four Orkney boatmen, landed at York on 30 Aug. 1819, and started on 9 Sept. The scheme was, with portable boats or canoes, to follow the line of rivers and lakes, beginning with the Nelson and Saskatchewan, and ending with the Elk, Slave, and Coppermine. At Cumberland House, a long-established station on the Saskatchewan, it was found that further progress that season was impossible. One of the seamen and the Orkneymen were sent back, and, leaving Hood and Richardson to bring on the boats when the way should be open, Franklin and Back started on foot for Fort Chipewyan on the shore of Lake Athabasca, which they reached on 26 March 1820. It was Franklin's intention to make all arrangements for an onward march as soon as the boats should arrive. He now found that owing to the rivalry, amounting almost to war, between the two trading companies which disputed the territory, no supplies were available; and, when the boats came on, the expedition left Fort Chipewyan on 18 July with little more than one day's provisions and with a scanty supply of powder. On 2 Aug. they left Fort Providence on the northern shore of Great Slave Lake, the party consisting, what with Canadian voyageurs and interpreters, of twenty-eight men, besides three women and three children. The next day they were joined by a large party of Indian hunters, under a chief Akaitcho. The progress was very slow, and the winter came on earlier than usual. By 25 Aug. the pools were beginning to freeze, and, though Franklin was anxious at all hazards to push on to the sea and establish himself for the winter at the mouth of the Coppermine, he yielded to the very urgent remonstrances of Akaitcho, and wintered in a hut which is still shown on the map as Fort Enterprise. It was not till 14 June 1821 that the ice gave way sufficiently for them to launch their canoes on the Coppermine, and to bid farewell to Akaitcho and his Indians. By 14 July they came within sight of the sea, and on the 21st embarked for their voyage in the Arctic Ocean. And so to the eastward in a tedious navigation along the coast, naming Cape Barrow and Cape Flinders, as far as Cape Turnagain, which they reached on 18 Aug.; when Franklin, finding that his resources would admit neither of going on nor of going back to the Coppermine, determined to take his way by a river to which he gave the name of his young companion, Hood. Hood's river was soon found to be impracticable for navigation. They took the large canoes to pieces, built two small ones which they could carry with them, reduced their baggage as much as possible, and began their march for Fort Providence through the country which has the distinction of being labelled, even in the Arctic, as 'Barren Grounds.' The story of their sufferings is one of the most terrible on human record. Cold, hunger, and fatigue broke down even the strongest of the party. Some died, some were murdered—poor Hood among the number, one was put to death as the murderer. In their last extremity Franklin and Richardson fell in with Akaitcho, who fed them, took care of them, and brought them in safety to Fort Providence on 11 Dec. Back and the miserable remnant of their party joined a few days later. They rested there for some months, and reached York again on 14 June 1822. 'Thus terminated,' wrote Franklin, 'our long, fatiguing, and disastrous travels in North America,

10

having journeyed by water and land (including our navigation of the Polar Sea) 5,550 miles.'

In the following October Franklin, with his companions, arrived in England. He had already, during his absence (1 Jan. 1821), been made a commander; he was now (20 Nov.) advanced to post rank, in recognition of his labours and sufferings; he was also elected a fellow of the Royal Society. Richardson was appointed surgeon of the Chatham division of marines, and Back, who had been promoted to be a lieutenant, after three Arctic winters was sent out to the West Indies to be thawed. Franklin employed his time in England in writing the narrative of his journey, which was published early in the following year, and at once took its place among the most classic of books of travel. He also wooed and, in August 1823, was married to Miss Porden. Early in 1824 Franklin laid before the admiralty a scheme for another expedition, which might benefit by his previous experience, and possibly co-operate with the more purely naval expedition then fitting out under the command of Captain Parry. Franklin proposed that during the course of 1824 and the early months of 1825 stores, together with a party of English seamen, should be sent on in advance as far as possible; that he himself, starting in the spring, should go from New York to Lake Huron, and take on from the naval establishment there such further supplies as were available; and so, picking up his party as he proceeded, make his way to the Great Bear Lake, down the Mackenzie river, and along the coast westward as far as Kotzebue Sound, where a ship might be sent to meet him. In accordance with this the instructions were drawn out; the Blossom was commissioned for the service in Behring's Straits; and the previous arrangements having been made, Franklin, again with Back and Richardson, and with Mr. Kendall, a mate, as a third colleague, sailed from Liverpool on 16 Feb. 1825.

His wife, who had some months before given birth to a daughter, was now in an advanced decline; but he had probably persuaded himself that her illness was not necessarily mortal, and was much shocked by the news of her death, which reached him at the station on Lake Huron. He pushed on to join his advanced party with the boats, which he found near Fort Methy on 29 June. On 7 Aug. they reached Fort Norman on the Mackenzie, and leaving a party to build huts by Great Bear Lake, Franklin himself went down the river, a run of six days, to the sea; and landing on an island—which he named Garry Island, after the deputy-governor of the Hudson's Bay Company—he there planted the British flag, a silk union-jack which had been worked for the express purpose by his deceased wife. 'I will not,' he wrote, 'attempt to describe my emotions as it expanded to the breeze.' For the sake of his companions, however, he endeavoured to simulate cheerfulness; and after examining the archipelago at the mouth of the river, returned to the winter quarters, which he had intended naming Fort Reliance, but which, in his absence, the officers had named Fort Franklin.

The winter passed not unpleasantly; they had a sufficiency of clothing and food, and were able to keep open their communications with the posts of the Hudson's Bay Company, and to get occasional letters from home. As the summer approached, their preparations for the coming voyage were made, and they started on 24 June 1826, with the boats provisioned for eighty days at full allowance. At the head of the delta on 3 July they separated, Richardson and Kendall going eastwards as far as the Coppermine River and returning to Fort Franklin overland; while Franklin and Back went westwards, examining the coast as far as Point Beechey, in longitude 149° 37′ W. It was then 16 Aug.; there appeared no possibility of fetching Kotzebue Inlet; the hazard of shipwreck increased each day; wintering on the coast, as was suggested in their instructions, was out of the question; and a winter journey overland to Fort Franklin was an alternative which Franklin's past experience warned him against. One of the Blossom's boats

12

had at this time advanced to the immediate neighbourhood of Point Barrow, but of this Franklin was of course ignorant; fortunately so, he thought afterwards; for otherwise he would have advanced, but would, in all probability, have been unable to overtake the Blossom's party. As it was, he returned to Fort Franklin by the way he had come. Richardson had been before him and had started again on a geologising expedition to Great Slave Lake. Franklin, remaining at the fort till 20 Feb. 1827, set out on foot for Fort Chipewyan, whence on 18 June he reached Cumberland House. There he rejoined Richardson, and the two, returning by way of Montreal and New York, where they were splendidly fêted, arrived in Liverpool on 26 Sept. The rest of the expedition, which had lost only two men, arrived at Portsmouth a fortnight later in charge of Captain Back. The journey, not so exciting nor so tragic as the former, had been even richer in geographical results, as was fully shown when the narrative was published in 1828. The Geographical Society of Paris awarded Franklin their gold medal; on 29 April 1829 he received the honour of knighthood; and at the summer convocation, the university of Oxford conferred on him the honorary degree of D.C.L. It was also during this period of relaxation that, on 5 Nov. 1828, he married Miss Griffin.

From August 1830 to December 1833 Franklin commanded the Rainbow frigate on the Mediterranean station, and during most of the time was employed on the coast of Greece, a service for which he received the order of the Redeemer of Greece, and afterwards (25 Jan. 1836) the Hanoverian Guelphic order. In the summer of 1836 he was appointed lieutenant-governor of Van Diemen's Land, and arrived at Hobart Town on 6 Jan. 1837. The period of his government, extending over nearly seven years, was marked by many measures for the social and moral improvement of the colony, then still, to a great extent, a convict station. The condition of the convicts more especially was a subject which much occupied his attention, and his endeavours for humanising them were strenuously aided by the exertions and the liberal expenditure of his wife. For the better class of colonists he established a scientific society which has developed into the present Royal Society of Hobart Town; and not only founded but largely endowed a college, for which, at his request, Dr. Arnold of Rugby selected a head-master. By the colonists, as a body, he was much beloved. At the close of his period of service he embarked at Hobart Town on 3 Nov. 1843, 'amidst,' he wrote, 'a burst of generous and enthusiastic feeling.' After visiting several places on the coast, he crossed over to Port Phillip, then a very recent settlement, from which he sailed 10 Jan. 1844, and arrived at Portsmouth in the following June.

Arctic exploration was exciting special interest. The Erebus and Terror had come home from a remarkable voyage to the Antarctic, so that suitable ships were at once available there was, too, a stagnation in the shipping interest, and seamen were everywhere clamouring for employment. Back and Dease and Simpson and Ross had traced the northern coast-line of America almost in its entirety; little remained to be done to solve the problem of the north-west passage. Few capable men any longer doubted its actual existence; though whether, under any circumstances, it could be available for navigation was still problematical. The admiralty resolved on a naval expedition. There was at first some hesitation about the commander; but Franklin claimed the post, as being the senior officer of Arctic experience then in England. The first lord of the admiralty pointed out to him that he was sixty years of age. 'No, no, my lord,' answered Franklin, 'only fifty-nine.' 'Before such earnestness all scruples yielded; the offer was officially made and accepted', and on 3 March 1845 Franklin commissioned the Erebus for 'particular service,' the Terror being at the same time commissioned by Captain Crozier.

The two ships, fitted, for the first time in the annals of Arctic exploration, with auxiliary screws, and provisioned (as it was believed) for three years, sailed together from Greenhithe on 18 May, with instructions to make their way to about 74°

N., 98° W., in the vicinity of Cape Walker, and thence to the southward and westward in a course as direct to Behring's Straits as ice and land might permit. 'It was well known,' wrote Sherard Osborn in 1859, 'that this southern course was that of Franklin's predilection, founded on his judgment and experience. There are many in England who can recollect him pointing on his chart to the western entrance of Simpson Strait and the adjoining coast of North America and saying, "If I can but get down there, my work is done; thence it's plain sailing to the westward."' In the beginning of July the ships were at Disco, and Fitzjames, the commander of the Erebus, wrote on the 12th 'that Sir John was delightful;' that both officers and men were in good spirits and of excellent material (Osborn, p. 286). On 26 July the ships parted from an Aberdeen whaler off the entrance of Lancaster Sound; a fair wind bore them away westward, and they vanished into the unknown. Over their movements a dark curtain settled down, which was raised slowly and with difficulty, nor was it fully lifted for fourteen years.

As early as the winter of 1846-7 there were gloomy anticipations; and though it was maintained at the admiralty that, as the ships were provisioned for three years, there were no grounds for anxiety, popular feeling so far prevailed that in the summer of 1847 large supplies, under the charge of Sir John Richardson and Dr. Rae, were sent out to Hudson's Bay to be conveyed by the inland water route to the mouth of the Mackenzie or of the Coppermine, or to other stations on the coast. As the winter of 1847-8 passed by without any news of the ships, a very real uneasiness was felt. With the spring of 1848 began a series of relief and search expeditions, both public and private, English and American, which has no parallel in maritime annals, and which, while prosecuting the main object of the voyages, turned the map of the Arctic regions north of America from a blank void into a grim but distinct representation of islands, straits, and seas. These expeditions, of which a complete list is given by Richardson (Polar Regions,

p. 172), may be summarised thus: One in 1847, that already mentioned from Hudson's Bay under Richardson and Rae; five in 1848; three in 1849; ten in 1850, including those sent out by the admiralty under Austin, Ommanney, Collinson, and McClure; two in 1851; nine in 1852, including the one under Sir Edward Belcher; five in 1853, including one in boats and sledges by Dr. Rae, and one into Smith's Sound by Dr. Kane of the United States Navy; two in 1854; one in 1855; and one, that of the Fox, in 1857.

In 1850 Captain Ommanney discovered on Beechey Island the traces of the missing ships having there passed their first winter, and at the same time vast stacks of preserved meat canisters, which, there was only too much reason to believe, had been found to be filled with putrid abomination, and had been there condemned by survey, thus fatally diminishing the three years' provisions which were supposed to be on board (ib. p. 163). Nothing further was learned till April 1854, when Dr. Rae, a factor of the Hudson's Bay Company, in a boat expedition carried on at the company's expense, gathered intelligence of a party of white men having been seen, four winters before, travelling over the ice near King William's Land, and of their bodies having been afterwards seen on the main land in the neighbourhood of a large river, presumably Back's Great Fish River. From the Eskimos who told him of this, Rae also obtained numerous small articles, silver spoons, &c., the marks on which clearly identified them as having belonged to officers of the Erebus and Terror; among others a small silver plate engraved 'Sir John Franklin, K.C.H.' (*Journal of the Royal Geographical Society*, 13 Nov. 1854, xxv. 250).

By these visible tokens the substantial truth of the story seemed to be fully confirmed, and the admiralty declined to enter on any further search. Others, however, were fain to hope that some survivors might still remain, and, chiefly by the personal exertions and at the personal cost of Lady Franklin, the Fox yacht was fitted out in 1857, under the command of

Captain (now Admiral Sir) Leopold McClintock. She failed through the accident of the seasons to get into the prescribed locality in the first or second year. It was not till the early months of 1859 that McClintock and his colleagues, Lieutenant Hobson of the navy, and Captain (now Sir) Allen Young of the mercantile marine, came on distinct traces of the lost expedition. Numerous relics were then found: a boat, a few skeletons, chronometers, clothing, instruments, watches, plate, books; and at last, towards the end of May, a written paper, the contents of which, together with what was told by the Eskimos or could be argued by induction, comprise the sum of all that can be known. The paper, which was one of the official forms issued to be left for transmission by any casual finder, had been in the first instance filled up in the customary manner, but carelessly and with a wrong date: '28 May 1847—H.M. ships Erebus and Terror wintered in the ice in lat. 70° 05o'N., long. 98° 23o W. Having wintered in 1846-7 [a mistake for 1845-6] at Beechey Island in lat. 74° 43o'28' N., long. 91° 39o'15' W., after having ascended Wellington Channel to lat. 77° and returned by the west side of Cornwallis Island. Sir John Franklin commanding the expedition. All well. . . .'

In 1846 they proceeded to the south-west, and eventually reached within twelve miles of the north extreme of King William's Land, when their progress was arrested by the approaching winter; and there they remained. The rest of the story was written on the margin of the same form by Captain Fitzjames: '25 April 1848—H.M. ships Terror and Erebus were deserted on 22 April, 5 leagues N.N.W. of this, having been beset since 12 Sept. 1846. The officers and crews, consisting of 105 souls, under the command of Captain F. R. M. Crozier, landed here in lat. 69° 37o 42" N., long. 98° 41o W. Sir John Franklin died on 11 June 1847, and the total loss by deaths in the expedition has been to this date 9 officers and 15 men.' To which was added, in Crozier's writing, 'and start on to-morrow, 26th, for Back's Fish River.' And this was all. From the Eskimos

McClintock learned that one of the ships sank in deep water, and that, to their grief, they got nothing from her; the other, much broken, was forced on shore, and from her they obtained the wood and iron which he saw in their possession. But there was no further news of the men. It was too certain that every soul of the party perished miserably; some earlier on King William's Land; some 'falling down and dying as they walked,' as an old woman told McClintock; many on the mainland by the Great Fish River. Most fortunate then in his end was Franklin, who died before this terrible fate fell on his men; died, proud in the consciousness of having seen, even if he had not fully travelled over the north-west passage, the strait separating King William's Land from Victoria Land; the strait which, if the ice would have permitted, would have led him into the known waters already explored by Dease and Simpson.

Since the finding of this written record Franklin has been recognised as the discoverer of the north-west passage, and is so styled on the pedestal of the statue to his memory erected at the public cost in Waterloo Place, London. This statue 'gives a tolerably faithful representation of him.' There are other statues at Hobart Town and Spilsby. A portrait painted by T. Phillips, R.A., about the time of his first marriage, has been photographed. Another portrait by John Jackson, R.A., lent by Mr. John Murray, was exhibited in the loan exhibition at South Kensington in 1868. Another portrait by Derby is engraved for Jerdan's 'National Portrait Gallery' (vol. ii.), and there is a capital lithograph by Negelen. A monument in Westminster Abbey, erected by his widow, was uncovered a fortnight after her death in 1875.

Franklin was a man not only of iron resolution and indomitable courage, but of a singular geniality, uprightness, and simplicity, which kindled into the warmest affection his influence over his comrades and subordinates. He left but one child, the daughter of his first wife. She married in 1849 the Rev. John Philip Gell, the head of an old Derbyshire family, who, as a young man, had been selected by Dr. Arnold's advice to be principal of the college in Hobart Town, and was long rector of Buxted in Sussex. Mrs. Gell died in 1860, leaving several children.

A BIOGRAPHY FROM
Dictionary of National Biography, 1885-1900

Lieutenant Schwatka

INTRODUCTION

On the 25th of September, 1880, the leading English newspaper published the following words:—

"Lieutenant Schwatka has now resolved the last doubts that could have been felt about the fate of the Franklin expedition. He has traced the one untraced ship to its grave beyond the ocean, and cleared the reputation of a harmless people from an undeserved reproach. He has given to the unburied bones of the crews probably the only safeguard against desecration by wandering wild beasts and heedless Esquimaux Which that frozen land allowed. He has brought home for reverent sepulture, in a kindlier soil, the one body which bore transport. Over the rest he has set up monuments to emphasize the undying memory of their sufferings and their exploit. He has gathered tokens by which friends and relatives may identify their dead, and revisit in imagination the spots in which the ashes lie. Lastly, he has carried home with him material evidence to complete the annals of Arctic exploration."

The record of Schwatka's expedition is written in these pages. Much of it has already been published in detached letters by the 'New York Herald', which engaged the author to act as its correspondent during the journey. Other hands than his have reduced it to its present shape, for his restless energy has again driven him toward the North, and has enlisted him among the crew of the 'Rodgers', which is seeking the lost 'Jeannette'. Beyond a mere concatenation of the chapters it has been nowhere altered with a view to literary effect or sensational color. The notes from which it is drawn were made from day to day; and if critics find in it facts which are either improbable or unpalatable, they may, at least, have the satisfaction of knowing that it is a faithful narrative of carefully sifted evidence.

This needs to be said because the statements of the writer have already been questioned in one or two details. He says that the party experienced such cold weather as was almost without precedent in Arctic travel, the temperature falling to seventy-one degrees below zero. He says that the party killed more than five hundred reindeer, besides musk-oxen, bears, walrus, and seal, in regions where Rae and McClintock could scarcely find game at all, and where the crews of the 'Erebus' and 'Terror' starved to death. He says that of the last survivors of Franklin's party the majority were officers, arguing that the watches and silver relics found with their skeletons go far to prove their rank. These statements have been doubted. The accuracy of the thermometers being questioned, they were tested and found to be curiously exact. The facilities for procuring game were assisted by the use of improved weapons; and besides, as Sir Leopold McClintock has justly shown, it was merely a tradition, not an ascertained fact, that these sub-arctic regions were destitute of animal life. The method by which the official position of the bodies was determined is indisputably open to objection. "Watches and silver relics," writes Vice-admiral Sir George Richards, "do not necessarily indicate a corresponding number of officers. Such light valuable articles would naturally be taken by the survivors."

But the point which has provoked more criticism than all the rest is the native evidence that the distressed crews were in the last resort reduced to cannibalism. This is set down just as it was heard, being worth neither more nor less than any testimony on an event which happened so many years ago. Between the risk of giving pain to living relatives, and the reproach of having suppressed essential parts of the story, no traveller should hesitate for an instant. Dr. John Rae, the veteran of Franklin search parties, writes to the author in the following words: "As my name is mentioned in connection with the subject of cannibalism, I must state that when I came home in 1854 I felt bound to report in as condensed a form as possible all the information given us by the Esquimaux, including the most painful part. I would have felt it my duty to do this even had my dearest friends been among the lost ones, for had I withheld any part of the sad story, it would have come to light through my men, and I should have been accused, with some show of justice, of garbling my report. I consider it no reproach, when suffering the agony to which extreme hunger subjects some men, for them to do what the Esquimaux tell us was done. Men so placed are no more responsible for their actions than a madman who commits a great crime. Thank God, when starving for days, and compelled to eat bits of skin, the bones of ptarmigan up to the beak and down to the toe-nails, I felt no painful craving; but I have seen men who suffered so much that I believe they would have eaten any kind of food, however repulsive."

On the other hand, Sir George Richards shows strong reasons why the Esquimaux should not be believed. "They are said to give as their reasons," he writes, "that some of the limbs were removed as if by a saw. If this is correct, they were, probably, the operators themselves. We learn from the narrative that they were able to saw off the handles of pickaxes and shovels. At all events the intercourse between the natives and such of Franklin's crews as they met is surrounded by circumstances of grave suspicion, as learned from themselves, and this suspicion gathers strength from various circumstances related on Schwatka's journey. Be this as it may, I take my stand on far higher ground. Of course such things have happened. Strong, shipwrecked mariners, suddenly cast adrift on the ocean, have endeavored to extend life in this way when they were in hourly expectation of being rescued. But how different the case in point! The crews of the 'Erebus' and 'Terror', when they abandoned their ship, were, doubtless, for the most part, suffering from exhaustion and scurvy; death had been staring them in the face for months. The greater part of them probably died from exhaustion and disease long before they got a hundred miles from their ships, and found their graves beneath the ice when it melted in summer, or on the beach of King William Land. It is possible that no more than half a dozen out of the whole crew ever reached the entrance to the Great Fish River. We need not call in starvation to our aid. I fully believe that by far the greater portion perished long before their provisions were consumed. The only thing that would have restored men to convalescence in their condition would have been nursing and the comforts of hospital treatment, not a resort to human flesh."

Apart from these objections, of which the reader is only forewarned, the importance of the results achieved by Lieutenant Schwatka's expedition has not been gainsaid by any one possessing the least acquaintance with Arctic matters. It made the largest sledge journey on record, having been absent from its base of supplies for eleven months and twenty days, and having traversed 2,819 geographical, or 3,251 statute miles. It was the first expedition which relied for its own subsistence and for the subsistence of its dogs on the game which it found in the locality. It was the first expedition in which the white men of the party voluntarily assumed the same diet as the natives. It was the first expedition which established beyond a doubt the loss of the Franklin records. McClintock recorded an opinion that they had perished: Schwatka recorded it as a fact.

The success of this latest Arctic journey has been attributed to small, as well as to greater causes. The advantages of summer exploration were manifest. The Esquimaux of the party gave invaluable aid, building snow-huts with the skill to which none but natives attain, coating the sledge-runners with ice according to a method which only natives understand, and by their good offices enabling the expedition to hold communication and have dealings with the wild tribes with whom they came in contact. The dogs were chosen with the utmost circumspection, and justified this care by their wonderful endurance. Game was abundant. Such minor devices as the use of blue lights proved efficacious in the dispersal of wolves. Woolen foot gear, made by friendly natives, supplied a need which has often proved fatal in the Arctic. Good management kept all the Esquimaux loyal, and Schwatka's strong will helped the travellers to live while the dogs were falling exhausted and dying by the way.

Among the relics that were brought home was the prow of the boat seen by Sir Leopold McClintock in Erebus Bay, the sled on which it had been transported, and the drag-rope by which the sled was drawn. There were also two sheet-iron stoves from the first camp on King William Land, a brush marked "H. Wilkes," some pieces of clothing from each grave, together with buttons, canteens, shoes, tin cans, pickaxes, and every thing that could in any way tend to identify the occupants of the different graves or those who died without burial. They were offered to the British Admiralty, and, having been gratefully accepted, were added to the relics already deposited at the Museum in Greenwich Hospital, and at the United Service Institution in London.

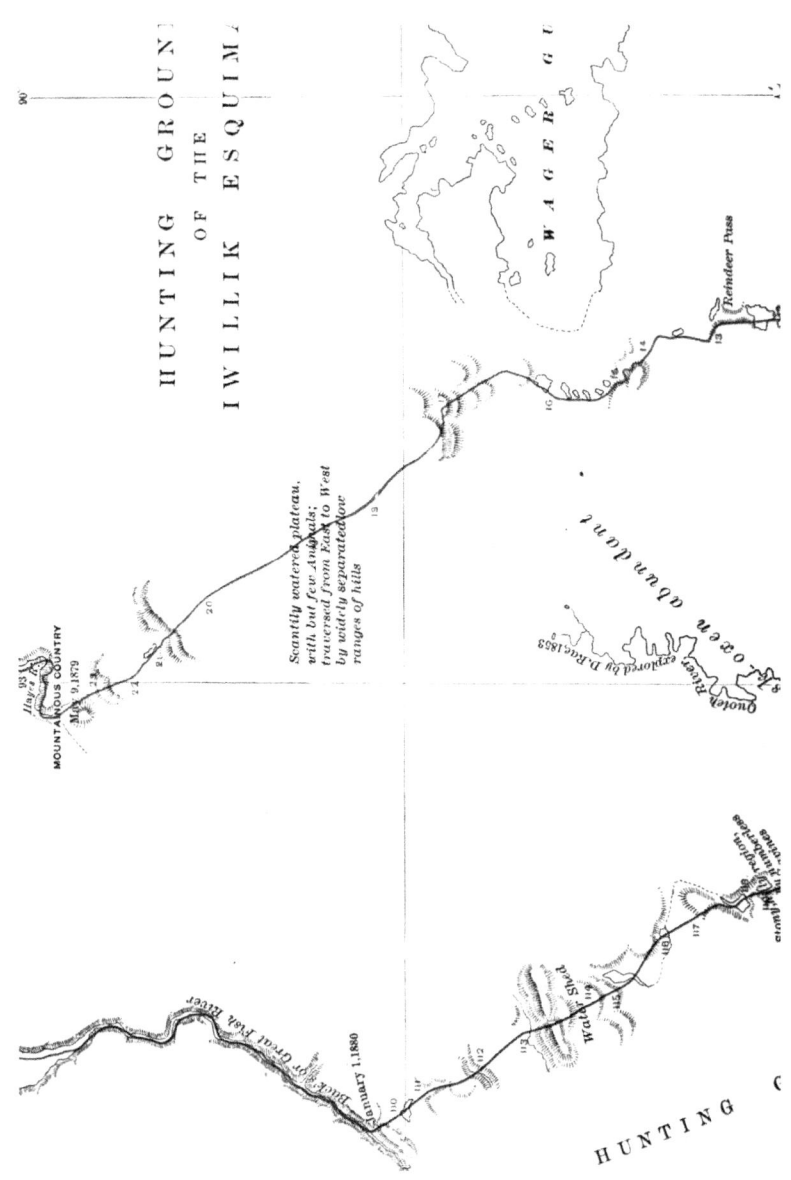

HUNTING GROUN
OF THE
IWILLIK ESQUIM

Scantily watered plateau,
with but few Animals;
traversed from East to West
by widely separated
ranges of hills

MOUNTAINOUS COUNTRY

May 9,1879

Quoter River explored by Dr.Rae 1853

frozen abundant

WAGER G

Reindeer Pass

HUNTING

HUNTING C

Water Shed

January 1,1880

Back of Great Fish River

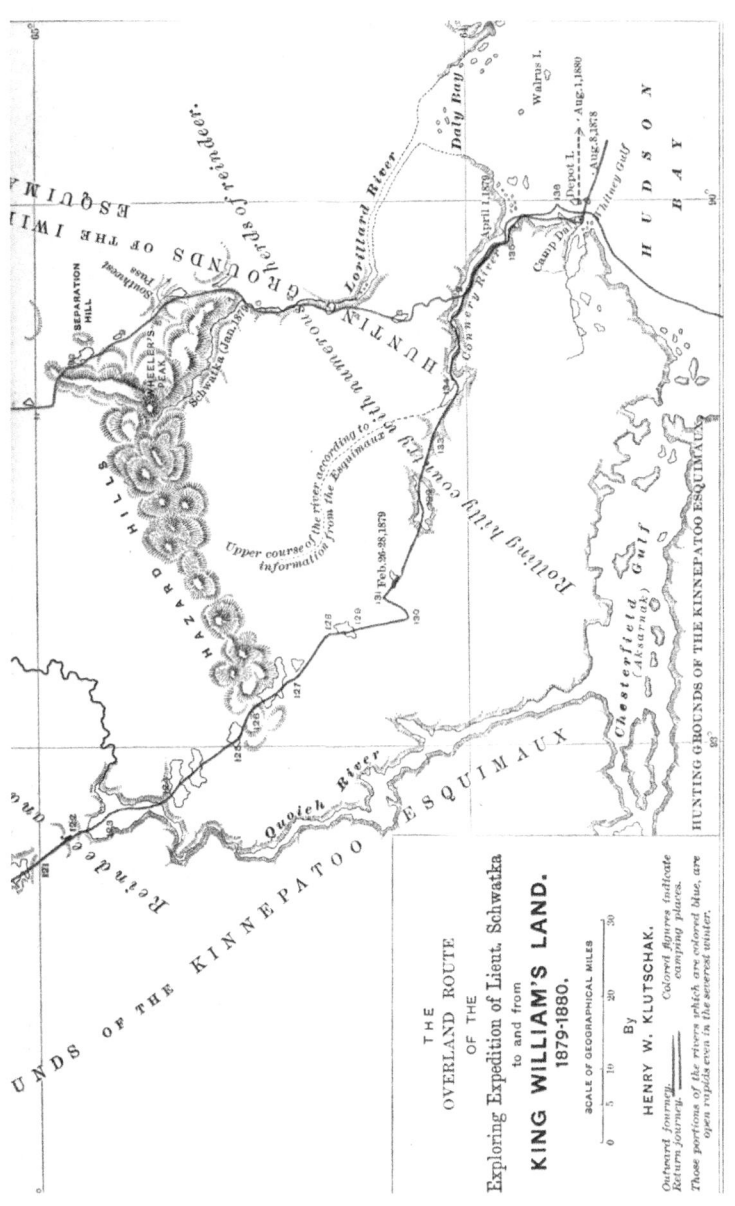

The Overland Route of the Exploring Expedition
of Lieut. Schwatka to and from King William's Land.
1879-1880

Lieut. Schwatka's Exped. to King William Land to Discover the Remains of the Franklin Expedition.

SCHWATKA'S SEARCH

CHAPTER I

NORTHWARD

"Haul in the gang-plank;" "Let go the tow-line," shouted the captain of the 'Fletcher'. Then he signalled the engineer to go ahead, and the little schooner 'Eothen' was abandoned to her own resources and the mercy of the mighty ocean. The last frantic handshaking was over, and only wind-blown kisses and parting injunctions passed back and forth as the distance between the voyagers and their escort kept continually increasing, until nothing could be heard but the hearty cheers that wished for us a pleasant journey and unbounded success. There was no time now for regrets, for if we would be comfortable we must direct our thoughts seaward and get our bunks ready for sleeping. So we were paired off and went immediately to work. As Lieutenant Schwatka was not only the senior officer of the expedition, but at the same time taller than I by several inches, I willingly yielded him the top bunk of our state-room, and waited patiently outside until he had prepared his lair, for it would be impossible for two to work at the same time in such very narrow space. He at last arranged his two buffalo robes to his perfect satisfaction, and I soon spread my humbler blankets to the best advantage. So much accomplished we retired to our first sleep on shipboard.

29

We had left New York on the 19th June, 1878, a party of five, none of us unaccustomed to hardship and adventure. Lieutenant Frederick Schwatka, of the Third United States Cavalry, Polish by descent, American by birth, had been distinguished in the war; and I, who was second in command, had seen a good deal of active service. Henry Klutschak, a Bohemian by birth, a civil engineer by profession, brought us the advantage of his previous experiences in the Arctic; Frank E. Melms was an experienced whaleman; and Joseph Ebierbing, well known as "Esquimau Joe," had been with Captain Hall and Captain Hayes in their journeys, and with the 'Pandora' expedition from England. The 'Eothen', that carried us, was commanded by Captain Thomas F. Barry. Her crew included a first, second, and third mate, a carpenter, blacksmith, cooper, steward and cook, three boat-steerers, and twelve men before the mast. To prepare her for encounters with the ice, the hull had been overlaid to the chain-plates with oak planking an inch and a half thick, and the stem had been covered with oak about two feet thick, over which was iron plating to the depth of three-quarters of an inch. She was a stout vessel of one hundred and two tons. The stock of provisions laid in on board of her for the use of the party included hard bread, Indian-meal, flour, molasses, pemmican, canned meats, preserved vegetables, preserved fruits, coffee, tea, and chocolate. Horseradish was taken as a preventive against scurvy, and tobacco was stored in abundance for the use of such Esquimaux as might have stories to tell or assistance to offer. Arms and ammunition had been generously presented to us by several manufacturers, and to individual bounty we also owed many of our books, night-signals, instruments, and the timber for our sledges.

The commander of the 'Eothen' was, indirectly, the originator of the expedition. Everybody knows that for more than twenty years explorers had been sailing from English and American ports in search of the bodies or the papers of Sir John Franklin and his party. The partial success which attended the investigations of Sir Leopold McClintock had served to whet the public appetite. A story which Captain Barry brought home from the Arctic made the curiosity still greater. He said that in 1871-73, while on a whaling expedition, he was frozen in with the 'Glacier' in Repulse Bay, and was there visited by several Esquimaux who brought their families on board his vessel. They had lost their way while hunting, and were anxious to see the ships of white men. While on board the 'Glacier' they spoke of a stranger in uniform who had visited them some years before, and who was accompanied by many other white men. All of the party had afterward died, but the chief had meanwhile collected a great quantity of papers. He had left these papers behind him in a cairn, where, among other things, some silver spoons had since been found. In the winter of 1876, while the captain was with the bark 'A. Houghton' before Marble Island, another set of Esquimaux visited him, and while looking at his logbook said that the great white man who had been among them many years before had kept a similar book, and having told him this one of them gave him a spoon engraved with the word "Franklin."

This was enough to arrest the attention and stir the adventurous spirit of Lieutenant Schwatka. He became eager to organize a search party and find the cairn where the papers were supposed to be still buried. He obtained leave of absence, went to New York, and proposed to Judge Daly, of the Geographical Society, to take charge of an expedition. After listening to the lieutenant's offer, Judge Daly gave him all the information in his possession concerning the whereabouts of the supposed cairn, so far as its site could be ascertained from the history of the relics already said to be found, and commended him to General Sherman, indorsing his application to be detailed to command the exploring party. The lieutenant also conferred with Messrs. Morrison & Brown, the shipping merchants of South Street, New York, who owned the whaling vessel on which the supposed clew was brought home, and they readily accepted his offer, and with the help of private subscriptions fitted out the 'Eothen'. Their instructions to Lieutenant Schwatka were as follows: "Upon your arrival at Repulse Bay you will prepare for your inland journey by building your sledges and taking such provisions as are necessary. As soon as sufficient snow is on the ground you will start for King William Land and the Gulf of Boothia. Take daily observations, and whenever you discover any error in any of the charts you will correct the same. Whenever you shall make any new discoveries you will mark the same on the charts; and important discoveries I desire to be named after the Hon. Charles P. Daly and his estimable wife, Mrs. Maria Daly. Any records you may think necessary for you to leave on the trip, at such places as you think best, you will mark "Eothen' Franklin Arctic Search Party, Frederick Schwatka in command;' date, longitude, and latitude; to be directed to the President of the American Geographical Society, New York, United States of America. Should you be fortunate in finding the records, remains, or relics of Sir John Franklin or his unfortunate party, as I have hopes you will, you will keep them in your or Joe's control, and the contents thereof shall be kept secret, and no part thereof destroyed, tampered with, or lost. Should you find the remains of Sir John Franklin or any of his party, you will take the same, have them properly taken care of, and bring them with you. The carpenter of the 'Eothen' will, before you start on your sledge journey, prepare boxes necessary for the care of relics, remains, or records, should you discover the same. Whatever you may discover or obtain you will deliver to Captain Thomas F Barry, or whoever shall be in command of the schooner 'Eothen', or such vessel as may be despatched for you. You are now provisioned for eighteen months for twelve men. I shall next spring send more provisions to you, so that in the event of your trip being prolonged you shall not want for any of the necessaries of life. You will be careful and economical with your provisions, and will not allow anything to be wasted or destroyed. Should the expedition for which it is intended prove a failure, make it a geographical success, as you will be compelled to travel over a great deal of unexplored country."

Thus manned, equipped, and instructed, we sailed from New York. It was nearly a month before we saw our first iceberg. During the night of July 11th I heard the order given to wear ship, and was called on deck to see an iceberg dead ahead; but so great was the distance and so foggy the weather that it was some time before I could make it out, and then it appeared only as a thin, faintly bluish line. The eagle eyes of the second mate had discovered it in time to avoid any danger of collision; but the captain thought it more prudent to heave to and wait until dawn before continuing on our course. The following morning a regular old veteran berg could be seen from the deck, about twenty miles away. It was apparently about a mile long, and could have supplied the city of New York with ice for many years, were there any way to preserve it for that purpose. During the 13th we saw four large icebergs, which passed close by the ship. While writing in the cabin, about eleven o'clock of the 15th, the mate on watch called me on deck to see a magnificent aurora, the first we had seen. It was truly a grand spectacle. At the same time the moon was shining brightly and the sea was as smooth as glass. Near by an immense iceberg looked black against the red twilight along the horizon, while in the distance another berg was white in the light of the full moon. The air was filled with the voices of wild-ducks, who could be heard, but not seen. On Friday, the 19th, in latitude 59 deg. 54 min. north, and longitude 60 deg. 45 min. west., thirteen icebergs were to be seen during the morning, and were of the most varied and picturesque description. One appeared like a huge circus tent, with an adjoining side-show booth; while near by another was a most perfect representation of a cottage by the sea, with gables toward the observer, and chimneys rising at proper intervals along the roofs. On the other side of the vessel a huge monster presented a vast amphitheatre, with innumerable columns sparkling in the sunlight and dazzling the spectator with their intense brilliancy. I made a few sketches of the most remarkable in view; but as twenty-three could be seen from the deck at three o'clock I gave up in despair. At six o'clock thirty-three were in sight, and the sun set beautifully, eight minutes past nine, surrounded by fourteen of these monsters of the deep. On the night of the 19th I went on deck to see an iceberg, which was a perfect counterpart of Newstead Abbey. One could almost fancy he saw the ivy creeping over its sides, so deceptive were the shadows that fell upon it from pinnacles and horizontal projections innumerable.

At half-past seven o'clock in the evening we sighted a brigantine off the weather beam, while thirty-one icebergs were around us. The vessel was going the same way that we were bound, and was about fifteen miles away. Sunday night, the 21st, was a splendid night. One could read distinctly on deck throughout the entire night. There were plenty of icebergs around. Those in front and on both sides of the ship were black against the sky, the moon being on the other side of them, while those we passed shone in all their virgin beauty in the bright moonlight. The red twilight still lingered along the horizon, graduating through a pale yellow tint to orange, and then deepening into intense blue that was almost black. The picture was fierce in color and startling in the contrasts it presented.

At a quarter before nine o'clock the next night we sighted Resolution Island in the dim distance. Spy-glasses were at once brought into requisition, and we could see that the mirage had fooled us, though there seemed little doubt of the land's being visible. The next morning the land was in plain sight, about thirty or thirty-five miles off the weather beam, and the water filled with small and dangerous pieces of ice. The land was covered with fog, and looked desolate enough, but nevertheless seemed acceptable after a tedious journey against head winds and calms. The wind was still directly out of the straits, and we had to beat backward and forward from Resolution to Button Island, and it seemed as if the straits were unapproachable. Toward night the wind blew a perfect gale, and added to the usual dangers was the risk of running upon the innumerable pieces of loose ice which appeared on every side, many of them having sharp points projecting below the surface of the water, and heavy enough to pierce the sides of any vessel going at the speed we were compelled to make in order to keep sufficient headway to steer clear of such obstacles as could be seen. The captain and first mate, who were on deck most of the night, said that disaster was imminent; that the danger was constant, and that the night was withal one of the most terrible ordeals they had ever experienced. I was tired and slept soundly, and consequently knew nothing about it until morning, which dawned brightly and with a light breeze, under which we passed up to the first ice-pack I had ever seen. While engaged in conversation an inexperienced hand at the wheel brought us so close to a small cake of ice, about the size of a schooner, that collision was inevitable. A long projection beneath the water had a most dangerous look, but fortunately was so deep that the keel of the 'Eothen' ran up on it and somewhat deadened her headway. Long poles were got out at once, and, all hands pushing, succeeded after a while in getting her clear without damage; but it was a perilous moment.

We worked over toward the south side of the straits, and found a channel through which we could make but slow progress. The wind increased and blew terrifically all night, forcing the vessels to beat back and forth in the mouth of the straits, and we had a similar experience on the night of the 22d, running the gauntlet under reefed mainsail and jib through loose ice and in imminent danger of shipwreck. Next day the ice appeared somewhat open, and Captain Barry concluded to venture into the pack. When we got into clear water we worked up to the bulkhead of ice and passed Resolution Island. We were almost as glad to get rid of it as we had been to see it, nearly a week before. All the icebergs we saw were aground, and several of them had arches cut into their sides, which looked as if our vessel might safely sail inside and secure a harbor. We worked up beyond the Lower Savage Islands, and in sight of the Middle Savage and Saddleback Rock.

When we went to bed the weather was a dead calm, and the water of glassy smoothness. Not a sound was to be heard save the distant thunder of bursting icebergs and the water swashing up against the field-ice that now and then passed with the current. It sounded for all the world like waves upon a rock-bound coast, or like the distant rumbling of a train of cars. About midnight Joe called me to announce that the natives were coming off to the ship in boats. I hastened to put on my clothes; but before I got dressed I could hear the captain's voice shouting "Kimo" (Welcome), from the quarter-deck, and when I joined him I could see two dark objects that seemed to be approaching rapidly, and could hear the confused sounds of voices in conversation coming up from the water. Presently it could be seen that one was a kyack and the other an omien, or women's boat, filled with women and children and a few men. By this time Joe had come on deck, and at Captain Barry's request invited them to come aboard. When they heard their native tongue from the stranger ship their surprise was unfeigned. The men bought a number of corlitangs and kummings (native boots), as well as other articles of apparel, and gave in exchange small pieces of tobacco, a few cases of matches, and articles of clothing that were not worth keeping. Captain Barry got a quantity of whalebone, reindeer and fox skins, walrus ivory, a bear-skin, and about a hundred and fifty pounds of fresh reindeer meat. We also bought three dogs for about a pound of powder, and a kyack for Joe, for which the captain gave an old broken double-barrelled gun and a handful of powder and shot. The owner was in ecstasy over the bargain and Joe was more than happy.

I could not help, however, feeling mortified that such advantage should be taken of their childish ignorance of values. I was not surprised, then, when Joe, who has been long enough in civilized lands to know what values are, came to me and said he thought it was wrong to rob these people. They were his own people, and from the same tribe, in fact, so that his interest was naturally with them. His own uncle was one of the chief men of this tribe, but at the time we arrived had gone inland with most of the men on a hunting expedition. Joe sent him his pocket-knife as a present, and also was liberal with needles among the women, who were very grateful for his generosity. The whalers seriously object to giving things away to the natives, as it renders their system of barter more difficult. It would be a greater benefit to all these tribes to send one or two of their most intelligent young men to the United States or to England for a few years, so that they could protect them against the rapacity of the masters and owners of whaling ships. They could then get something like a fair equivalent for the goods they have to dispose of. The natives are better whalemen than any of the seamen who come to this country, and they should certainly receive more than a handful of powder and a few bullets for hundreds of pounds of bone, worth about $2.50 a pound. Shortly after daylight the natives departed, and a breeze springing up we set sail upon our journey.

Most of the day we were in full sight of the land, which I regarded with keen interest. It certainly seemed the most desolate-looking region I ever saw—a succession of hills of bald rock, with occasional patches of snow and moss; not a house, nor a tree, nor, in fact, any sign of animal or vegetable life—and yet I longed to put my foot upon that barren soil and commence the work we had before us.

One of the principal annoyances of all sailing-masters in the Arctic regions is the sluggish action of the magnetic needle as they approach the magnetic pole, and it was a difficulty from which we were not exempt. The land all looks so much alike that even when running in plain sight of it it requires the greatest familiarity with the principal points to be able to steer by them. During the night of Friday, August 2, we, by some mysterious operation, got in between Nottingham and

Salisbury Islands, when we thought we were beyond the Digges. We found a bad reef, just on a level with the water's edge, about eight miles north-west of the north-west point of Nottingham Island, which is not down upon the charts, and is situated just where a vessel running along at night, "handy to the land," as sailors say, would inevitably run upon it. We put it down upon our charts and called it Trainor's Reef, as it was discovered by the third mate from the mast-head. During a previous voyage Captain Barry discovered a similar reef, about the same distance off the easterly point of Salisbury Island, which we also noted and put down as Barry's Rock.

We reached Whale Point, at the entrance of Rowe's Welcome, during the morning of Wednesday, August 7, just seven weeks from New York, and about six o'clock a whale-boat reached the vessel's side, after having chased us all night. It was loaded with natives of the Iwillie tribe, two or three families of whom still remained at the Point, while the others had gone down to the vicinity of Depot Island, which is half-way between Cape Fullerton and Chesterfield Inlet. The visitors comprised two men, a woman, two boys, a little orphan girl, and a baby. The woman was a daughter of "Prince Albert," a man of considerable influence in his tribe, and I understood that his power was due to superior intelligence and sagacity. In fact, all those whom we met at this time seemed much superior in intelligence to those who came aboard at the Lower Savage Islands. They were cleaner, but by a mere trifle, and showed improvement from contact with civilization. They usually preferred to array themselves in some part of the costume of white people, though not by any means particular in wearing it as white people do. One of the men was a young fellow known as "Jim," who, the captain thought, would be a desirable acquisition to our party to go to King William Land, and Joe made the proposition to him. He regarded the matter favorably, and was particularly interested when he saw some of our fine rifles. His father was an old man, called "The Doctor," who was dependent upon his son. After giving our guests breakfast and a few presents we bade them good-by, and set sail for Depot Island, where we arrived about four o'clock in the afternoon.

The lookout from the mast-head saw some boats coming from the main-land, and presently three kyacks, an omien, and two whale-boats came alongside, bringing about fifty people, including men, women, and children. Among them were Armow and his two half-brothers, Ik-omer (Fire) and Too-goo-lan. "Papa" was there also, and he, too, is one of the few savages that are thoroughly reliable in every respect. He was one of Captain Hall's party when he visited King William Land in 1868. All these people seemed very friendly toward us, and upon a consultation over the charts we decided to go on to the main-land, near Depot Island, to spend the winter. We learned with deep regret that one of the Natchillis, who was said to have spoken to Captain Barry about the existence of books among the Franklin relics, had since died, and that nobody knew what had become of the other. We determined to make every effort to find the latter, for should he know where the books were hidden, and be willing to conduct us there, our labor would have been materially lessened. But in any case, whether we found him or not, we had great faith that, by staying at least one season on King William Land, when the snow was off the ground, we should be able to find the records, and complete the history of Sir John Franklin's last expedition.

Camp Daly in Summer

CHAPTER II

THE WINTER CAMP

Meanwhile we had need of patience. Our camp, which was in latitude 63 deg. 51 min. north and 90 deg. 26 min. 15 sec. west of Greenwich, had been named by Lieutenant Schwatka after the president of the American Geographical Society. The tents that had been provided for the expedition proving quite inadequate for our wants, Captain Barry got Armow (the Wolf), one of the most influential natives, to let us have his tent, one that had been made by the crew of the brig 'A. Houghton', memorable to us as the vessel on which Captain Barry received his spoon. The Iwillie tribe moved up their tupics to the land nearest Depot Island, so as to be near us; but finding they were a considerable distance from any fresh water, moved again to the spot where our stores were landed. We had bidden adieu to the officers and crew of the 'Eothen', and had been rowed ashore by the Inuits. The solitude of our first day on land was enlivened by the visit of a ponderous young Natchilli, named Joe (or Natchilli Joe, to distinguish him from Esquimau Joe). He promised to accompany us in the spring. He was a fine-looking young man, with a big head, and a shock of raven-black hair, as massive-looking as a lion, and with none of the bloodthirsty look which I had been led to expect in the Natchilli features. He had been living with the Iwillie tribe for about two years, and they all liked him very much. We felt that it would tend to assure our favorable reception by his tribe to have one or two of their own people with our party.

Ten days after we landed all went to the hunting-grounds but Armow and his party, who were to go in a boat, but it was so stormy that they did not get off. When the others broke camp and started over the hills it was a novel and interesting spectacle. Each one had his load, the women, in addition to their other burdens, having to carry their children upon their backs. Behind them came their dogs, staggering under loads that almost hid them from view and getting into all kinds of trouble among the rocks. They were accompanied by "Jerry," a native for whom Esquimau Joe had a great liking. He took all his family except his son Koumania, who had been given to me as a body-servant. Koumania was an unusually bright, manly little fellow, and, though so young, had already killed a reindeer. We were all much interested in him, and his parents were much pleased that he had found favor with the Kodlunars. His father was one of Captain Hall's party in his King William Land journey, and was also to accompany us. He seemed like a good, honest, faithful fellow, and had the reputation of being a first-class hunter. Koumania came running to me, before his father's departure, with his face covered with smiles and soapsuds, and I found that Frank had given him some soap and told him I would like him better if he would wash. Poor fellow! he had done the best he could, and had at any rate shown a willing spirit.

It was not until Wednesday that the boat party could get away. Most of the time it rained and blew a perfect gale. We were then alone in the camp, with the exception of a tupic, which contained one old man, two old women, and three children. There were plenty of dogs, though, and we had concerted music every night. I spent some time in making over some civilized clothes for my boy. I had to take them in everywhere except around the waist. There he was as big as I am, though I weigh nearly two hundred pounds.

I returned from a hunting and exploring excursion Saturday night, August 31, and had come to the conclusion by that time, after satisfactory experience, that tuk-too hunting is not a pastime.

Esquimaux Going to the Hunting-Ground

It is good, solid work from beginning to end, with no rest for the weary. If any readers have meditated such a task as a divertisement, I would beg to dissuade them from the undertaking, for they know not what they do. Before attempting to follow tuk-too hunters over these hills and valleys, I would advise a severe course of training. We started on the morning of the 25th, in the midst of a strong gale, which had been blowing all night from the north-west, and was bitter cold. It rained, snowed, and hailed all at the same time, and the pelting hard stones cut our faces nearly all the morning. The party consisted of "Sam," another of Joe's friends, his two younger brothers, Koumania, and myself. I took a blanket and some

43

little provisions, in case I should be out over night. We walked along, without stopping, a distance of about eight miles across the hardest country to travel over I had ever seen, and when we halted to rest I was indeed tired. The rocks and hills were hard enough to walk over, but the worst of all were the moss-covered meadows. Your foot would sink at every step, and it was as much like walking in loose, wet sand as anything with which I could compare it. I wore native boots, or kummings, as they are called, for I knew it would be impossible to get along with anything else; but the sharp edges and points of the stones could be felt through them almost as if one were barefooted. Do not think that the mossy meadows were a relief after the rocks. On the contrary, they were but a delusion and a snare, for beneath the velvet cushion was concealed the sharp and jagged rock that cut the foot all the same, and proved a more deadly, because a hidden foe. Though tired when I sat down to rest, I was more so when I got up to walk again; but, ashamed of my weakness, I kept on, gritting my teeth and determined to do or die.

It was getting late, and still we saw no deer—in fact, I was losing my interest in deer very rapidly, and only hoped I might soon see a tupic. After we had walked about fifteen miles, "Sam" pointed out a mountain that did not seem so very far off, and said, "Io wunga tupic sellow" (My tent is there). This was refreshing, and I plodded along still more determinedly. I would have given anything to have been back in my own tent, but that was out of the question. It was farther to go back than to go ahead, and though every bone in my body ached I plodded along, frequently stopping to rest. I thought we had passed the mountain that "Sam" had pointed out, and finally I ventured to ask him where the tupic was. His answer was invariably, "Con-i-tuk-vo-loo" (A little way), and I began to weary of the monotony of the answer, as probably he did of the question, until at last, in a valley farther off than I had originally thought the mountain, I saw the tupic. The approach was by a circuitous route, the wind still blowing so strongly against us that each took his turn in leading, the others crouching behind the slight shelter thus afforded. And this was a pleasure trip! When we finally did reach the tent, I received the kindly welcome of old "Molasses" and his wife, and dropped down on some deer-skins, completely used up. The hunters were naturally hungry after their long walk, and from a pile of fresh meat on the side of the tent "Sam" seized a large piece, half cooked, and taking a vigorous bite, cut off the mouthful with his disengaged hand and passed the rest to the one standing nearest him, who helped himself in the same way, and thus it kept circulating until it was all gone.

I awoke early the next morning, and went outside the tent and feebly attempted to walk; but it was a most excruciating effort. My hip-joints, that ached like a toothache the night before, now seemed to be made of old rusty iron, and grated and shrieked when I tried to move, as if they rebelled against it. I felt as if there was nothing left for me to do but to walk the soreness off; therefore I kept moving, though I was conscious that my step lacked its wonted firmness and grace. After bathing in the lake that spread out in the valley in front of the tupic, I returned to find the hunters ready for the day's sport. I took up my rifle and started off with the hunters. Presently the pain left my hips, or, more properly speaking, my feet got so sore from the constant walking over sharp rocks that my mind was diverted in that direction solely. While resting on the top of a high bluff overlooking the lakes, I heard a faint "halloo," which seemed to come on the wind from an immense distance. I called "Sam's" attention to it, and he immediately dropped behind a rock, out of the wind, until it was repeated several times, when saying, "Inuit ky-ete" (Somebody says come), he started off down the steep mountain side in the direction of the voice, and the boys and I followed him. We walked nearly three-quarters of an hour before we finally saw the object of our search, and then he appeared perched on a rock against the clear blue sky, but still too far off to be recognized even by my hawk-eyed guides. At last we were near enough to see that it was "Alex Taylor," one of the Inuits from our camp, who had left with the others for the hunting-grounds. He had with him his wife and two children, one a babe in the hood, and two bags packed with tupic and poles. He had a heavy back-load of skins, and his wife another big bundle. They seemed both surprised and pleased to see me. "Alex" told me that he had seen no deer that day, but had previously shot nine, and that there were "ama-suet" (plenty) farther on. He regaled us with some raw meat, and honored me with a nice raw deer tongue, which I ate with great relish after he had skinned it and eaten the skin.

After luncheon and a pipe, we gathered up the bundles and trudged along until nearly sundown, when we arrived at a tupic under a cliff and between two large lakes. Two young married women and an old palsied crone came out to meet us. "Alex Taylor" told me that I was to stay there all night. The next morning, after walking about nine or ten miles without seeing anything in the way of game except some deer tracks, we ascended a high bluff that had been on our right since leaving camp, when, to my infinite delight, I saw a large river, which "Alex," tracing the course with his finger, indicated as emptying into a large bay near our camp, opposite Depot Island. Its course was nearly straight for about three miles below and seven miles north of where we stood; then, as my guide indicated with a wave of his hand, flowed to the east and again to the south. It extended much farther to the west and north, and from what I have since learned from the natives, rises between the head of the Invich and Wager rivers, and is about ninety-five miles in length. To the south and west of where we stood it passed over a broad stony portage, and beyond that swelled out, as do most of the rivers in this country, into a series of broad lakes filled with islands.

This discovery appeared to me of inestimable value, as indicating an entirely new and feasible route to King William Land, and, since my return to camp, Esquimau Joe, who had been away with the hunters for about three weeks, was here for a few hours, and told me that his hunting-camp was on the east bank of this same river, and the inquiry he has already made of the Inuits in his party confirmed my judgment of the feasibility of this route. I named the river after Mr. Thomas B. Connery, of New York.

We resumed our walk, turning back along the bank of the river, which on the east side is high and almost perpendicular. We reached the portage, about three miles to the south, and crossed over to the west side, which is a low, rolling country, covered with moss, which at a distance looked like sun-burned grass. The portage was nearly a quarter of a mile wide, but by the exercise of some agility, where the current ran most swiftly through the large rocks, we got over without wetting our feet, and about a mile from the river bank stopped to rest on a rocky eminence. "Alex" pointed vaguely in the direction of some hills about two or three miles away, and said he thought there were some deer over there; but as I had been walking three days now without seeing a deer, and was desperately tired, I told him to go on if he wanted to, and take my rifle, and I would wait till he came back. He trotted along, and I sat under the lee of a rock, taking advantage of the opportunity to write up my journal and trace the course of the river. In the meantime the sun sank lower and lower, but no signs of "Alex Taylor." About three hours after he left me he reappeared, with his hat in his hand and a heavy bundle over his shoulder, trotting along so nimbly that I envied him. He had shot two deer, a "cooney" and an "isaacer"—that is, a doe and a buck—and he had their warm, bloody skins on his back. He said that there were plenty of deer over there, and to-morrow we would move the camp up to that spot. So we put the skins and some tenderloin in a cairn, and covered it up with heavy stones, and after eating some of the raw tenderloin we started for home. It was long after dark when we reached there, and I was glad to find Sam's tupic already up, with his old father and young mother, and my blankets and a little package of salt, which I had missed very much while eating so much raw meat.

The next day we broke camp at an early hour, and moved bag, and baggage, to the place where "Alex Taylor" had shot the deer the preceding afternoon. Notwithstanding my sore feet and tired limbs, I took a load on my shoulders out of sheer shame, for without that I would have been the only one, old or young, biped or quadruped, without something, so I made a martyr of myself. Just after leaving the spot where "Alex" and I had cached the skins yesterday afternoon, "Sam" dropped his burden from his shoulders, grasped his rifle, and, with the single word "tuk-too," started over the country on a run. Three others joined him, and the rest of us kept on until we reached the lake, where our new camp was to be located. The tents were soon put up, and the boys started off to carry in the two carcasses that "Alex" had shot and buried under stones. Presently the hunters who went off with "Sam" came back, saying they had seen nothing, and later "Sam" came in with the skin of a big buck which he had shot. He is quite young, but one of the best and most indefatigable hunters in the tribe.

I went out in the morning with "Sam" and "Roxy" to find some deer. After some wanderings, in which "Sam" got separated from us, and after several unsuccessful shots at the game, "Roxy" and I returned, I being too weary and footsore to find much interest in the sport, especially as it began to rain and was bitter cold. In fact, the first new ice I have seen this summer was around the shores of the lake that morning, and I had to break it when I went down to bathe. On our way home we passed, on the top of a high, barren hill, a cairn, which "Roxy" at once said had been built by the Kinnepatoos, a tribe which formerly occupied these lands, and the boys soon threw aside the stones to find the dried-up skeleton of a deer killed many years ago. "Sam" did not get back until dark, but he brought with him the skin of an isaacer that he had killed since he left us.

That night I proposed to "Sam" to bring me down to our tent at the salt water, and though I could see that he did not relish leaving the good hunting-grounds just as he had reached them, he consented, and finally seemed delighted when I promised him an old pair of pantaloons for his trouble. "Alex Taylor" also came to the tupic and said he would accompany us, and this made the prospect more cheerful, as I knew it would be at least two days' hard travelling. During the night we were visited by a severe thunder-storm, which frightened my tent-mates because unused to it, and they lighted an ikomer to take the sharp edge off the lightning; but I slept on peacefully while "Old Molasses" held a stick so that the shadow kept the light of the lamp from my eyes. It stopped raining toward morning, but it was still chilly and damp when we started, shortly after daylight, on our long journey.

"Sam" and "Alex" again got separated from us in pursuit of deer, and I became so chilly that we gave up waiting for them to rejoin us, and moved on. At last we could see Picciulok, as the natives call Depot Island, but it was at a considerable distance, and it was getting late. The sun was then below the horizon, and we hastened along to get sight of some familiar ground; but, alas! at every hill-top Picciulok seemed as far, if not farther off, and finally we could not see it all, it was so dark. My guides knew they were lost, and wanted to lie down until morning, but I kept them up, for I could see the stars and could keep the right course; but the walking was terrible. My feet were now so sensitive that I could feel every sharp stone through the soles of my kummings, and the stony portages between the lakes and over the little indentations of the coast seemed to increase in number all the time. It was so dark that I could not see where to step, and my feet would slip down and wedge in the angle between the sharp stones, or the point of a rock would come right in the hollow of my foot, until I stumbled and floundered and almost screamed with pain. And yet no familiar landmarks. I began to despair, or rather to doubt my physical ability to proceed, when the sharp-eyed Netchuk called my attention to the light from a tupic at a considerable distance, and a little to our right. This was indeed refreshing, so we kept on as well as we could, though we often fell, and I staggering with a strained cord in one foot and the skin worn off the sole of the other. But there were the lights ahead, and we kept right straight for them, though no matter how far we walked they seemed just the same distance off. It was certainly discouraging, and I could not help thinking of the will-o'-the-wisp, and wondering if the phenomenon was ever seen in the Arctic. I could not remember any instance in my reading, and determined to reach that light or perish in the effort. At last it did seem nearer. We could make out the shapes of the tents, and finally we could hear dogs barking and snarling, and before long we were there. We found the lights in the tupics that were occupied by the old folks left behind at Camp Daly by the hunters, and found "Alex Taylor," "Sam," and the boy had just got in; so, after learning that "Alex" had killed two deer with my gun, "Sam" and Koumania and I went up to our own tent, which was dark.

A Cairn

These were our diversions. Our business was to inquire into the truth of Captain Barry's story. Pursuing our investigation through the next three months, we learned that there had never been other than three families of Natchillis living with the Iwillik Esquimaux. One of those, the native who had died in the preceding winter, was an aged paralytic called "Monkey," whose tongue was so affected that even his own people could scarcely understand him. The second was Natchilli Joe, known to his own people as Ekeeseek, who was a child in his mother's hood at the time when he lived on King William Land, and only knew the story of the Franklin expedition from hearsay. The third, Nu-tar-ge-ark, a man of about forty-five or fifty years of age, gave us valuable information. His father, many years ago, opened a cairn on the northern shore of Washington Bay, in King William Land, and took from it a tin box containing a piece of paper with some writing on it. Not far from this same spot were the ruins of a cairn which had been built by white men and torn down by Inuits. The cairn had been built upon a large flat stone, which had the appearance of having been dragged to its present location from a stony point near by. The cairn itself was found to be empty, but it was generally believed by the Inuits that there was something buried beneath this stone. It was very heavy, and as they had only been there in parties of two or three at a time, they had never been able to overturn the stone, though they had repeatedly tried. Nutargeark also said he had brought a spoon with him from King William Land, which corresponded in description with the one Barry took to the United States. He said it was given to him by some of his tribe, and that it had come from one of the boat places, or where skeletons had been found on King William Land or Adelaide Peninsula, he could not remember exactly where.

He had not given the spoon to Captain Barry, but to the wife of Sinuksook, an Iwillik Esquimau, who afterward gave it to a Captain Potter. We saw Sinuksook's wife a little later, and she distinctly remembered having given the spoon to Captain

Potter. It was necessary, therefore, to find this officer.

During the first week in January, 1879, we learned that he was wintering at Marble Island, being now second in command on the whaler 'Abbie Bradford'.

Cairn Marking Deposit of Provisions

So Henry Klutschak and I made our way to Marble Island, with the first sled that had crossed from the main-land, being eight days on the road from Depot Island. We had reason to believe that Captain Barry and the 'Eothen' would also be at our destination, and that we could there replenish our stores. The trip was uneventful, except that when four days out I ran out of food through sharing my hard bread and pork with the natives, of whom there were twelve on my sled. They had plenty of tepee walrus meat, which was good food for them, but which I could not at that time eat. So for four days I had not a mouthful to eat, though I walked and ran nearly the whole distance travelled. I did not experience much inconvenience from weakness until the last day, which was that on which we came across the ice from Little Rabbit Island. When nearly half-way over, and moving rapidly over the new ice, the sled on which I was seated broke through, and all its occupants were precipitated into the water. The front part of the sled still hung by the ice, which bent beneath its weight. When I was struggling to get out the ice kept breaking off in huge cakes, and my clothing getting heavier and heavier all the time, I began to think that I would not be able to save myself; but at last I succeeded in rolling out upon the hard ice, and turning around to see if my help was needed in rescuing the women and children, found them already safely landed on the floe. The thermometer ranging thirty-eight degrees below zero, we were not long standing in the wind before our clothes were frozen stiff, so that it was almost impossible to bend a limb.

We succeeded in getting the sled out again, and started once more for Marble Island. I went ahead to pick out a route for the sled, and again the treacherous ice gave way under me, and I sank below the surface. It was with great difficulty that I regained the firm ice, and by this time my clothing was so heavy and stiff that I had to take off my outside tocklings, or trousers, in order to walk at all. It was now about ten o'clock in the morning, and in half an hour we reached about two miles distant from the island, but only to find an impassable channel of open water from a quarter to half a mile wide. We could see some one walking upon the shore of the island, but could hold no conversation with him. The natives who were with me said that when the tide turned perhaps the channel might close, and they proposed to wait; but in the meantime I was afraid I might freeze to death unless I kept moving. In the course of a few hours, during which I found out that I could not get back to Rabbit Island before dark, I became so faint for the want of food that I had to get some tepee walrus from the natives, and I ate it with a keen appetite. It did not taste as badly as I anticipated, so I ate a quantity, including some pieces of hide, about three quarters of an inch thick, which was cut into small pieces and looked like cheese. After eating several pieces I thought I would bite off the outside rind, which, on closer examination, I noticed to be the short stiff hair of the animal which I had been eating. Presently I began to feel warm all over my body, despite my frozen clothing—a condition attributable partly to the peculiar qualities of frozen food, and partly perhaps to the rasping in my interior, produced by the stiff walrus hair that I had eaten. It was now nearly dark, but we could see that the ice-floes were coming together, and crunching up a pudge of soft ice between them. At last the men started out over this pudge, stepping quickly from one piece of moving ice to another, until at last we reached firm footing again, though only by the exercise of considerable agility and looking sharply to where you went. It was a great relief to be again upon the shore; but we were still a considerable distance from the ships, and the Inuits proposed to lie down on the snow until daylight, as they could not see and did not know the route. I was afraid to stop moving, and proposed to keep walking in the direction of the harbor. All who came ashore, therefore, started with us; but the road at last became so difficult that I felt it necessary to rest quite often, wearied as I already was by previous hardships.

The route chosen by our guide was to follow the shore ice around until the harbor was reached. This was a very circuitous and dangerous road, as in the darkness one would frequently pitch headlong over a steep precipice upon the snow beneath. My trousers were so stiff that I could not bend my knee or lift my foot high enough to clear ordinary impediments, and I fell very often. It was fortunate for me that I never fell upon the shore ice beneath the cliff, for in many places it was very deep, and I could not see where I trod. When I commenced falling I never knew where I would alight, though I usually brought up in some friendly snow-drift. At last all the Inuits grew so impatient to reach the ships that they left Henry and me to find our way as best we could, and pushed on as rapidly as their better vision and greater familiarity with the country would permit. In half an hour from the time they left us they had reached the harbor; but with their accustomed indifference to the comfort of others they failed to say that two "kodlunars" (white men) were still out upon the island—one of them too weak and frozen to keep up with them. As soon as the officers learned the fact from them, Captain Barry despatched "Domino," one of the natives with his ship, to find us and bring us to the vessel. We saw a lantern which he carried, and, coming down from the cliff upon the smooth ice, were overjoyed to find ourselves in the harbor and but a few hundred yards from the ships. We shouted at the top of our voices, and "Domino" ran at once to us. I never was so glad to see any one in my life, for I felt that the terrible ordeal through which I had passed was at an end. We were soon in the warm cabin of the 'Eothen', where my frozen garments were removed and warm, dry "kodlunar" clothing substituted. Were it not for the previous training we had undergone in igloo life, I could not have survived the hardships of that day. As it was, I felt very little inconvenience, except from a severe cold, which always follows a change such as moving from an igloo into the heated air on shipboard. My appetite was enormous, and it seemed as if I could not eat enough of the generous fare of our hosts. I soon regained my usual robust health, and gained flesh at the rate of a pound a day for three weeks.

In the harbor, besides the 'Eothen', and the 'Abbie Bradford', the latter commanded by Captain Fisher, we found the 'Abbott Lawrence', Captain Mozier, and the 'Isabella', Captain Garvin, all except the 'Eothen' being from New Bedford. The ships were all comfortably housed with boards, and so banked up with snow that ordinary coal fires made them uncomfortably warm. It was painful to see, however, that scurvy had broken out in the fleet, and each vessel has had an average of half a dozen cases during our stay with them. They had more than the usual amount of fresh meat at this season, and it was difficult to account for the unusually large percentage of scurvy, unless

Captain Fisher's theory were the correct one. He attributed it to the unusual severity of the fall and early winter-season, which, he said, was unprecedented in his experience of over fourteen years in these waters. The ships were driven into winter quarters nearly a month previous to the usual time by a succession of gales and heavy weather, which occasioned the loss of one vessel of the fleet—the brig 'A. J. Ross' of New Bedford, Captain Sinclair, which went ashore near Cape Kendall, on the eastern coast of Rowe's Welcome during the latter part of August. Though scurvy had been so prevalent it had not been so severe as usual, and as yet the graveyard on "Deadmen's Island," on the outer harbor, had received no accession from the crews. The successful treatment of the disease seems to be to compel the patient to eat abundantly of raw walrus or seal meat, and to take moderate exercise, at first under shelter and then in the open air.

The Ships in Winter Quarters

The officers of the vessels treated us with the most unbounded generosity, and readily placed at our disposal whatever they could spare that we required. The wreck of the 'A. J. Ross' had thrown the care of another crew upon them, and yet they could find plenty to add to the comfort of those who have another season in this climate and a long and severe journey before them. Captain Sinclair, though himself so great a sufferer by the loss of a vessel in which nearly his whole means were invested, had been a large contributor toward the search party. They expected to be frozen in here till about the 1st of June, when they could saw a channel through the ice to the clear water beyond Deadmen's Island. Marble Island has been the winter quarters of whaling vessels for many years, though not altogether a safe harbor. In the winter of 1872 two vessels were wrecked here, the 'Ansel Gibbs' and the 'Oray Taft'. The hulk of the latter still lay upon the shore of the inner harbor, but the 'Ansel Gibbs' broke up outside and had long since gone to pieces. The graves of a number of their crews are in the graveyard by the sea. Upon the bald face of a rock near the outside harbor is a list of names written in red paint nearly a century ago; but whether a visitor's list or a gigantic tombstone to record those who perished here long ago by shipwreck is unknown. Upon the north-east end of the island, partly hidden by moss, is a quantity of soft coal, which was probably left here by one of the early Arctic explorers.

The loss of so many vessels in these waters is chiefly attributable to the imperfections in the admiralty charts. The coast line is altogether wrong, and Marble Island is laid down several degrees west of its actual position. Lieutenant Schwatka and Henry Klutschak made careful surveys from Cape Fullerton to the island, and made a chart which has already proved useful to the whalers.

But our more immediate business was with Captain Potter. I asked him if he remembered Captain Barry's getting a Franklin spoon while with him on the 'Glacier', and he said he had never heard anything about it until he read in the newspapers that

Barry had sent one to Sir John Franklin's niece, Miss Craycroft, which surprised him very much. He further said that he (Potter) had received three spoons at that time, one of which mysteriously disappeared shortly afterward. The published description of Barry's spoon corresponded exactly with the one he had lost, even to its being broken off near the bowl and mended with copper, as was the one he had received from Sinuksook's wife. Captain Potter further said, that to one who had lived with the Esquimaux, and acquired the pigeon English they use in communicating with the whalers in Hudson's Bay, and contrasted it with the language they use in conversation with each other, the assertion of Captain Barry, that he overheard them talking about books and understood them, was supremely ridiculous. There is probably no white man in the Arctic, or who ever visited it, that would understand them under such circumstances unless it be one or two in Cumberland, who have lived with them for fifteen or twenty years.

In this crucible of fact the famous spoon melted. So far as Captain Barry and his clews were concerned, we had come on a fool's errand.

CHAPTER III

OUR DOGS

There being no cairn, as a matter of course there was no guide to conduct us to it; but instead of returning to New York from Camp Daly, as he would have been justified in doing, Lieutenant Schwatka determined to make the summer search in King William Land, in order to find the records, if possible; or, at any rate to so conduct the search as to make it final and conclusive of the Franklin expedition. Lieutenant Schwatka was much impressed with the statements made by Nutargeark, especially as this native's intelligence and veracity were tested by his pointing out correctly upon the map the location of cairns which he had seen, including one at Cape Herschel, built by Dease and Simpson in 1839, and the spot where McClintock saw a boat with skeletons. Both Hall and McClintock account for the fact of so few bodies being found, by the presumption that Captain Crozier and his men followed the shore ice down, and, dying there, fell through into the water when the ice melted during the summer. Nutargeark, however, said that there were plenty of bodies lying upon the ground on King William Land, which would be invisible in winter from being covered with snow. To verify these statements was the purpose of our journey.

The first thing necessary was to get dogs enough for our teams. To that end I made a visit to the land of the Kinnepatoos, which is about seventy miles west and north from Marble Island. I found them in igloos, upon a large lake on the western shore of Hudson Bay, and was the first white man who had been there. Many of this tribe had never seen a white man before, but all were exceedingly friendly. I found that they had but few available dogs, but succeeded in securing from them several fine animals by the exchange of ammunition, tobacco, and matches, which are the staples of trade with these people. I found their igloos to be much larger and better built than those of the northern natives. The entrance would usually be by a narrow passage-way, excavated from a snow-drift, six to eight feet below the surface, and perhaps twenty-five or thirty feet long. They had no fires for heating the igloos, and, consequently, there was a clammy, vault-like atmosphere indoors that was anything but pleasant. They use oil only for light, and, even in the depth of winter, cook what little food they do not eat raw with moss. As I approached the village I was walking ahead of my guides, who were with the sled. It was getting late, and we were endeavoring to trace the direction by following the tracks on the snow which covered the lake; but a high wind, which was blowing from the north, had nearly obliterated all signs and rendered the task a difficult one. Presently, however, I heard the barking of dogs and the voices of a number of children, who soon appeared approaching over a hill on the right bank of the lake, beyond which the village was built. I hastened toward them, and was shortly conducted into an igloo where all the men were seated, tailor fashion, around bones which showed that justice had been done to a hearty repast of frozen deer meat. They extended a rude but cordial welcome, and hospitably inquired if I was hungry; but as I had recently eaten a quantity of frozen salmon I declined further food. I had long ago learned to relish fish and meat which they call "topee," and which civilized people denominate "rotten". When frozen it does not taste any worse than some kinds of cheese smell, and is a strong and wholesome diet unless eaten in great quantities. It fortifies the system against cold, and, shortly after eating, causes a healthy glow of warmth to pervade the body, even in the coldest weather. I can now eat almost anything an Esquimau can, and almost as much. Though the weather during the four days of my journey out was intensely cold—the thermometer ranging from thirty to sixty degrees below zero most of the time, with a strong wind blowing—I did not suffer with the cold, except that my nose and cheeks would occasionally freeze. In fact, if I had no nose I believe I could stand the cold nearly as well as the natives. Even they are constantly freezing their noses and cheeks, and there seems to be no way of avoiding this very disagreeable contingency.

I was with the Kinnepatoos a week, during which I lived upon frozen meat and fish, and enjoyed myself studying their habits and customs. Every night they met in one large igloo, twenty-five feet in diameter at the base, and twelve feet high, where the men would play upon the ki-lowty while the women sung in unison. The ki-lowty is a drum, made by stretching a thin deerskin over a huge wooden hoop, with a short handle on one side. In playing, the man grasps the handle with his left hand, and constantly turns it, while he strikes it upon the wooden side, alternately, with a wooden drumstick shaped like a potato-masher. With each blow he bends his knees, and though there are various degrees of skill in playing, I have never yet learned to be critical. I can only see a difference in style. Some are dramatic, some classical, some furious and others buffo. The song is a monotonous, drawling wail, with which the drumming has no sort of connection, for it increases and diminishes in rapidity according to the pleasure or strength of the player. I am sure a concert, such as I witnessed nightly, would cause a sensation in New York, though I do not believe it would prove a lasting attraction to cultivated audiences. I frequently got very weary of it, and often slept during the performance without giving offence to my hosts by my lack of appreciation. One night the entertainment was varied by a dramatic performance that was exceedingly interesting. There were three players, who walked about the arena and conversed, occasionally passing off the stage, not by the right and left, but stooping down and darting in and out of the door of the igloo, an entrance two feet high and about the same width. As nearly as I could understand, while outside in the dark the players saw some supernatural horror, which on entering they would endeavor to explain to the audience; but words failing to convey all they felt, they resorted to pantomime, until at last one, who was more affected than the others, came in and expired in the arms of his comrades. I was intensely interested during this novel performance, and imagined I recognized considerable histrionic ability on the part of the players.

Esquimau Playing the Ki-Lowty

During the daytime those men who were not out hunting engaged in playing a game somewhat allied to gambling, which they call "nu-glew-tar." A small piece of bone is suspended from the roof by a line made of walrus hide, and a heavy weight dangles below it to keep it from swinging. The bone is pierced with four small holes, and the players, as many as choose to engage, stand around, armed with sharp sticks, with which they jab at the bone, endeavoring to pierce one of the holes. Some one starts the game by offering a prize, which is won by him who pierces the bone and holds it with his stick. The winner in turn offers something for the others to try for. It is perfectly fair, because unless one wins it costs him nothing. They are very fond of this game, and play almost incessantly. Another similar game is played by placing a prize in a bowl made out of a musk-ox skull, the players standing in a circle around the bowl, which is then set twirling rapidly. The one toward whom the handle points when the bowl stops moving is the winner, and replaces the prize with another. This game, like nu-glew-tar, has no end, and the players only stop when they get hungry and adjourn to eat. The men all dine together in one igloo, no women being allowed to be present, and generally demolish the whole of a carcass of reindeer at a meal. This may be called their dinner, but when they have plenty of food on hand they eat nearly all the time. In the morning, before getting out of bed, they eat; and at night, after getting into bed, or "sin-nek-pig," as they call it, they eat. A few whiffs from a pipe are always in order, and especially so after eating. The pipe is passed from mouth to mouth, without regard to any foolish civilized notions of cleanliness. Eating frozen fish or meat always makes one cold at first, but presently warm. So always, after eating the mid day repast, the men pull their hoods over their heads, draw their arms out of their sleeves and cross them over their warm, naked breasts, and wait patiently and in silence for the heated term to ensue; but during the silent period they resemble a group of mummies, and are about as cheerful. When they begin to feel warm their spirits rise, and they are soon like a parcel of good-natured children. When their stomachs are full they are contented and happy. The principal diet of the Kinnepatoos is deer meat, as that of the Iwilliehs is walrus and seal.

I left the Kinnepatoo village, returning to Marble Island in two days' journey, though it took me four days to go. I returned by a shorter route, and travelled after the sun had gone down, the moon affording sufficient light to see our way. On my return I discovered another large lake between the one on which the Esquimau village was located and the salt-water ice. This smaller lake is probably twelve miles long and from two to four miles wide. The larger one is about forty-five miles long and fourteen wide at the widest point. It is known among the natives as "The Big Lake," and with the approval of Lieutenant Schwatka I named it Brevoort Lake, after Mr. James Carson Brevoort, of Brooklyn, N. Y., whose deep interest in Arctic research was felt by this as well as other expeditions. The other lake I named after General Hiram Duryea, of Glen Cove, a warm personal friend and comrade in arms, who was also a contributor toward the expedition. On my way back to Marble Island, instead of following the shore ice along to the narrow place where the pack is choked between Rabbit and Marble islands, I struck off in nearly a direct line for our destination, crossing most of the distance over the thin new ice. The advantage in this route was that, besides being much shorter, the ice was free from snow, and the dogs could run at nearly full speed. To be sure it was open to the objection of being dangerous; but moving as rapidly as we did there was scarcely time for the sled to break through, though the water oozed up along the track of the sled as we sped swiftly over the surface of smooth thin ice. It was pretty venturesome, perhaps, and I might be excused if I was nervous, for twice before I had broken through on a sled and bathed in the waters of Hudson's Bay. But I was anxious to reach the ships and finish what work I had to do, so as to get back to Depot Island in time to have all the dogs well fed before starting upon our long journey.

I should here say that the dogs of Hudson's Bay and contiguous territory do not resemble those usually pictured in the illustrated editions of Arctic works, which are the Greenland dogs. From what I gather by reading of the performances of the dogs in Greenland and North-eastern Asia, and comparing them with our experience in Hudson's Bay, I should judge the animals from the latter country to be immeasurably the superior in endurance and pluck, though perhaps inferior in speed for one or two days' travel. When food is plentiful the dogs are fed every other day while travelling; but if living in camp once in ten or twelve days is considered enough, and often twenty days will intervene between meals. Not but that they pick up a trifle now and then, and by a raid on an igloo will secure meat enough to last for several days. Their mode of life forces upon them the character of thieves, and all their waking moments are devoted to the one object of making a raid. Whether it be on the meat in the igloo or the storehouse, or the bag of blubber for the lamps, or the seal-skin clothing, it is all the same. They know from experience that the severest penalty will be enforced as a punishment for their offence but to them the pleasure of theft and the exquisite bliss of greasing their stomachs with a slice of blubber outweighs every other consideration.

Too often have they felt the cruel snow-stick across their defenceless heads, and the sting of the long-lashed whip cutting a morsel of flesh at each blow, to doubt the quality of their reception, and the howl of pain as they start upon the grand rush is in anticipation of the end. A raid can sometimes be brought to an end with a good stout club that will knock a dog senseless at each blow; but there is nothing like the ip-er-ow-ter, the Esquimau dog whip, to bring them to their senses. The ip-er-ow-ter has a handle made of wood, bone, or reindeer horn, about twelve or eighteen inches long, and a lash from eighteen to thirty feet in length. The lash is of seal-skin or oak-jook, that part of the thong near the handle being plaited or doubled to stiffen it, or give a spring that adds materially to its usefulness.

The men acquire considerable dexterity in the use of this whip, the lash of which is thrown forward or back with a quick turn of the wrist. That portion of the lash near the handle strikes the ground first, and then the long seal-skin thong unwinds, gaining rapidity and strength as the end is reached, and this strikes with such force as to make the snow fly, and with a report like a pistol. It is not a handy implement, for it requires time to get in position to swing the long lash. First it is thrown back, and then forward—this time for execution; and it is no unusual thing to see a dog with an eye gone or a piece of ear missing—a witness to the power of the ip-er-ow-ter in the practised hand of the Esquimau dog driver. Even the boys are quite skilful in the use of the whip, and dog driving is taught them almost from infancy. The driver sits on the front part of the sled or runs alongside, the long lash of the whip trailing behind him on the snow, so that when occasion occurs calling for the administering of punishment it is already in the proper position for delivering the blow.

The first effect of the whip is to retard the sled. The dog that is struck invariably draws back, and then usually pitches upon his neighbor, and for a while there is a row that threatens the sled with stoppage. The driver usually takes advantage of this occasion to administer a general chastisement, each dog receiving a share of the punishment, whether guilty of insubordination or not. The Esquimau theory is, that if not deserving of the whip this time he would be before long, and so might as well receive it now as any time.

The dogs are attached to the sled by harness made of either reindeer or seal-skin. One loop passes around the neck, while each leg is lifted through a loop, all three loops joining over the back and fastened to a long seal-skin line. These lines are of different lengths, so as to allow the dogs to pull to greater advantage than if all the traces were of the same length, causing the dogs to spread out like a fan. At every few miles the traces have to be unloosened and extricated from the most abominable tangle that it is possible to conceive. This comes from a habit the dogs have of constantly running under and over the other traces to avoid the whip, or in some cases merely from a spirit of pure deviltry.

The leader of the team is a dog selected for his intelligence, and is one known as setting an example of constant industry under all circumstances. You will always see the leader of a team of dogs working as if the load was being drawn by him alone. He goes along, his head bent over and tugging in his harness, his mouth open and tongue lolling out, while his ears are ever ready to hear the word of command from the driver. To go to the left, the command is given, "Ah'-root," and to the right, "Why-ah'-wah-ha." Then he sometimes, to encourage or urge to greater exertion, says, "Ah-wah-hagh-oo-ar." To stop the team he says "Woah," as one says when driving horses. It is the noisiest method of travel yet invented, for the driver is constantly talking to his team, calling each by name, and usually following the word with a blow of the whip, so that the next time that dog is spoken to, he will understand that it means "hurry up." The conversation with a dog team is incessant, and the work of the driver is not confined to his team alone. He has to constantly keep watch over the front of the sled, to turn it to the right or left in order to avoid hummocks or stones that would upset the load or tear the ice from the bottom of the runners.

Inuits are fond of riding on the sled while travelling, and as long as there is a spot that would hold one they will pile up there. But should there be no place for them, they will run alongside without apparent discomfort for almost any length of time or distance. This is equally true of the children of both sexes, and when any are compelled to walk, for lack of dogs or of room on the sled, it is the women and girls who have to give way to the men and boys. With a light sled, and from nine to fifteen good strong dogs, the Esquimaux of North Hudson's Bay will sometimes make a journey of from eighty to one hundred miles during the long days of spring. A light sled has reference to one with nothing on it except the skins for the beds, a lamp and small quantity of oil, with not more than one or two days' rations of food. The same number of dogs will drag a sled, with about fifteen hundred pounds of load, at the rate of three or four miles an hour over the smooth salt-water ice and snow. When travelling with light sleds all the party ride, except when necessary to run for the purpose of getting warm. In travelling, and especially when starting from a halt, some one runs ahead of the team so as to get them to pull together. When the sleds are heavily loaded the start is effected in the same way, and the driver, gathering the reins in his hands, pulls back with all his might until he sees every dog straining against his collar, when he lets go his hold and all spring forward together.

It often happens that there are not a sufficient number of dogs, or that they are poor and unable to travel with sufficient rapidity, and then the people have to put on harness and help. First the women and children engage in this labor, and, lastly, the men. And the drivers will sit on the sled and smoke, with the utmost composure, while their wives and daughters are tugging in the harness. The women do not mind this treatment, for they are accustomed to it and look upon it as the proper thing. In the summer the Esquimaux use their dogs while travelling as pack animals, and a stranger would be astonished to see what loads these dogs will carry. I have seen a fine large dog that would carry two saddles of reindeer meat, or the entire fore-quarters of two reindeer. His back would be bent low beneath the burden he bore, but still he would struggle along, panting the while and regarding his master with a look of the deepest affection whenever he came near him yet ever ready to fight any other dog that got in his way.

These, then, were the faithful comrades of our march. Before the day appointed by Lieutenant Schwatka they were ready. We were all eager to start. The projected journey was one which more than one expedition had undertaken without success since Sir Leopold McClintock's memorable sledge journey, which accomplished so much, and left so much to be desired. We were determined to bring it to a successful issue. Our igloo life at Camp Daly during the previous winter had inured us to the climate, so that, though we often found the cold intensely disagreeable, we were free from the evil consequences that have assailed many expeditions and make Arctic travel so dangerous, though few have been exposed to such low temperature as was our party, especially during the return trip in the winter of 1879-80. Previous sledge journeys had taught us how to clothe ourselves and otherwise provide against the cold, and we had already become acquainted with Inuit fare, so that when the emergency arrived when we were compelled to subsist entirely upon such food, we did not regard it with that repugnance that those would who had not become accustomed to it. In other words, we had become thoroughly acclimated during the eight months we had already lived in the country.

CHAPTER IV

IN THE SLEDGES

It was eleven o'clock on the morning of the 1st of April when the three heavily laden sledges moved out from Camp Daly on to the shore ice of Hudson's Bay, and commenced the long march toward King William Land. Lieutenant Schwatka's preliminary sledge journey in the direction of Wager River, during midwinter, had determined him upon taking that route, though across land entirely unknown either to previous explorers or to any natives with whom we had come in contact. Whether we would find practicable watercourses, such as rivers and lakes, or whether mountain ranges would oppose their granite walls to farther progress, was yet to be ascertained. Its recommendation was that it was the most direct course, and whatever obstacles it might present would, when overcome, always leave us that much nearer our goal. As we reached the smooth salt-water ice, we turned to take a last look at Camp Daly, which had been so long our home—a comfortless dwelling-place indeed, but for all that a home—and I never expect to lose a feeling of affection for its barren rocks and forbidding scenery. Its snow-clad hills were almost hidden behind the hummocks that everywhere bound the shore and make it a difficult undertaking to get on or off the ice at low tide. The loaded sledges were making but slow progress as they wound through the rough ice, but greatly enlivened the landscape, which at other times is dreary and monotonous in the extreme. The drivers, by voice and whip, were urging on their teams; while the dogs made the wilderness ring with howls of pain or impatience. The men were bending their shoulders to the task, as the women and children walked ahead and coaxed the dogs to greater exertion. It was not difficult, as we looked upon this picture, to realize that we were at least under way, and the work for which we had renounced the comforts of civilization for so long a period had at last begun, and our spirits rose with the prospect of action.

It was not Lieutenant Schwatka's intention to make a long march this day, but to break loose from camp and get well straightened out on our course. Our direction was due east until we reached Winchester Inlet, where we turned north-north-west and took up our line of march upon the frozen waters of the newly-named Connery River. The sun was setting when we halted about ten miles from Camp Daly and built two igloos, one of which was occupied by Toolooah's family and the four white men, the other by the remainder of the party. After the first night, however, there were always three igloos, Joe and Ishmark, his father-in-law, building a separate one for themselves and their families. There was at first some dissatisfaction manifested by the Inuits of the party at the determination of our commander to move always with the entire outfit, whenever practicable, and never to make portages or, in other words, transport a portion of the loads ahead before moving on with the remainder, unless absolutely forced so to do, and experience demonstrated the wisdom of his decision. Inuits always prefer to move by portages when they have heavy loads and plenty of food on the sledges, and such had been the custom on all the previous sledge journeys made by "Esquimau Joe" in company with white men. He particularly was anxious to travel in that way, but Lieutenant Schwatka was resolute, and many days and many dogs were saved to us thereby.

Camp Daly in Winter

The party was composed of four white men, Lieutenant Frederick Schwatka, United States Army, commander; W. H. Gilder, second in command; Henry W. Klutschak, and Frank Melms, with thirteen Inuits, as follows: "Esquimau Joe," interpreter; Neepshark, his wife; Toolooah, dog driver and hunter; Toolooahelek, his wife, and one child; Equeesik (Natchillik Inuit), dog driver and hunter; Kutcheenuark, his wife, and one child; Ishmark, Karleko, his wife, Koomana, their son, aged about thirteen, and Mit-colelee and Owanork, Equeesik's brothers, aged respectively about twenty and thirteen. The sleds were drawn by forty-two dogs, accumulated by hard work, persistent effort, and overpowering liberality with regard to guns, ammunition, and other articles of trade. The loads aggregated about five thousand pounds on the day of starting; but a large part of this consisting of walrus meat, both for dogs and people they were materially lightened from day to day. Our provisions besides the walrus meat comprised—

Hard bread 500 Lbs.

Pork 200 Lbs.

Compressed corned-beef 200 Lbs.

Corn starch 80 Lbs.

Oleomargarine 40 Lbs.

Cheese 40 Lbs.

Coffee 40 Lbs.

Tea 5 Lbs.

Molasses 20 Lbs.

This, it will be seen, is only about one month's rations of civilized food for seventeen people, and was, in fact, nearly exhausted by the time we reached King William Land. Our main dependence was, therefore, the game of the country through which we were travelling; a contingency upon which we had calculated and were willing to rely, having full faith in the superior quality of the arms and ammunition with which we had been so liberally equipped by American manufacturers. It is well for us that our faith was well founded, for there can scarcely be a doubt that it was this that made our expedition possible. In all other respects we were probably in a much worse condition than any previous expedition; but the quality of our arms put us at once upon a footing to derive all the benefit possible from the game of the country, a benefit of which we availed ourselves, as the unparalleled score of 522 reindeer, besides musk oxen, polar bears and seals will show. This is what was killed by our party from the time we left Camp Daly until our return. The quality of our provisions was excellent, and it was only deficient in quantity. The Inuit shared our food with us as long as it lasted, and, indeed, that was one of the inducements to accompany us on the journey. Some of the compressed corned-beef, corn starch, and cheese was reserved for the use of detached search parties on King William Land, as being the most condensed form of nutriment among our stores, and even that was shared with the Inuits who accompanied us during the search. Late in the afternoon of the second day's march we left Connery River, after crossing, with much difficulty, three rapids where the ice was piled up from fifteen to twenty feet high. The Connery was abandoned here on account of its direct westerly bearing and we moved across land to the Lorillard River, which we reached about noon of the 4th. This gave us several days good travelling in a northerly direction, when we again took the land, and moved somewhat to the eastward in order to avoid the Hazard Hills, which Lieutenant Schwatka discovered in his preliminary sledge journey. He found that range exceedingly precipitous, and so devoid of snow upon its summit as to materially impede our progress were we compelled to force a passage that way.

We witnessed a most peculiar and interesting spectacle on the 8th, in what appeared to be a frozen waterfall, about twenty-five feet in height, where a branch seemed to flow into the Lorillard from the west. At a distance it looked like a mountain torrent which had been arrested in its progress by some mighty hand and transformed into stone. Its ripples of crystals gleamed in the sunlight, and sparkled as if studded with myriads of gems. After enjoying its varied beauties for some time, I climbed to the top of the bank to make a closer inspection of it. Tracing its course for a short distance from the shore, I found a shallow brook which had frozen in a level place at the top of the hill, forcing the water to the right and left until it spread in a thin sheet over the face of the rock for a space of about fifty feet in breadth. Successive layers of ice were thus formed, and this novel and beautiful effect produced. The first few days of our journey were excessively fatiguing. The sleds were heavy, and we often had to put on our harness and help the dogs over a ridge or through a deep drift. We had not yet become hardened, and consequently experienced much difficulty from blistered feet and chafing; but as we got rid of our superfluous flesh these petty troubles became less annoying, and we did not so easily become fatigued from walking.

During the afternoon of the 12th we came suddenly upon a

herd of reindeer, and the hunters killed three of them. The sleds then moved on and we went into camp in the vicinity of the carcasses, in order to get them in and cut up before dark. Soon we saw another smaller herd running over the hills pursued by five wolves, which we could hear howling at intervals during the evening until we went to sleep. That night they came into camp close to the igloos, and Toolooah, who always sleeps with one eye and one ear open, heard the dogs giving a peculiar low bark, with which they announce the presence of wolves. We had a box of Coston night signals close at hand in the igloo, and, knowing that a light frightens them away, made a small hole in the igloo and thrust out a "distress" signal with the most brilliant result. Toolooah was already dressed and outside the igloo as the light started, and said the wolves stopped and looked at it for a second and then fled in dismay, each change of color in the signal light seeming to lend additional wings to their flying feet. We saw them prowling around during the next day's march, but they kept at a respectful distance. During our entire trip the Coston signals served us a good purpose in keeping the wolves from our doors, though I don't remember that the prospectus mentioned this application as one of the advantages of keeping the signals on hand.

On the 14th of April the thermometer rose above the freezing-point in the middle of the day for the first time, and as we remained in camp while the hunters went ahead to pick out a better road, we gladly embraced the opportunity to dry our stockings. It is one of the greatest discomforts of Arctic travel that the exercise of walking wets one's fur stockings with perspiration. At night they freeze, and it is anything but an agreeable sensation to put bare feet into stockings filled with ice, which is a daily experience in winter travelling. But it is astonishing how soon one gets accustomed to that sort of thing, and how little he minds it after a while. The warmth of the feet soon thaws the ice, and then a wet stocking is nearly as warm as a dry one, except in the wind. During the next day we were passing through a high rolling country, but with plenty of snow and not bad sledging. We found the descent of the hills always greater than the ascent, and presumed that we were approaching the bed of Wager River, as our route crossed the lower branch of that river, as mapped, well down toward the fork. The slope of these hills was usually so steep that we had to take the dogs off the sledges and let them run down upon the lakes by gravity. This was an exciting but not very dangerous method of travelling. So rapid would be the descent, that we had all we could do to hold on to the sleds trying to retard their progress. Some would be taking steps ten feet long, while others, with their feet planted straight out before them, were ploughing up the snow and scattering it in every direction. The dogs followed behind the sleds, running and barking, some of them, entangled in their harness, rolling over and dragged along by their swifter comrades. We were gratified to see plenty of reindeer nearly every day, as it relieved our anxiety concerning our commissariat. The ice upon the fresh-water lakes where we encamped averaged about six and a half feet. An occasional salmon is caught through the water hole by one of the women, who usually drop a line in after the hole is made.

The sun for the last three days had been insufferably hot, and my forehead and face were blistered painfully. It was altogether a new experience to have my nose blistered on one side by the sun, and on the other by a frost-bite. During my first winter in this country my nose was particularly tender. I could scarcely go out of doors without having it nipped. There is no pain in a frost-bite, but the cold upon my nose would cause me much suffering when first exposed to it, without exciting the least sympathy in my companions; but just as it would begin to feel comfortable once more, some one would run up and tell me, "Tling-yack quark" (Nose frozen), at the same time pressing a warm hand against it to thaw it out. The person who has the frozen nose is almost invariably surprised when informed of the fact.

Down-Hill with the Sledges

During winter travel people always have each other's noses and cheeks in charge, and one readily acquires the habit of occasionally taking hold of his nose, especially when it feels comfortable, to see if it is frozen. The frost-bite is at once detected by a white, wax-like patch, with edges sharply defined against the ruddy color of the healthy flesh. When you touch it, it feels cold and hard, and as if you had hold of somebody else's nose. It thaws readily, and without further inconvenience, under the pressure of a warm finger, unless it has been frozen for a long time. During the second winter, though exposed to an intensity of cold that is seldom encountered, it was seldom that I had a frozen nose or cheek. No serious frost bites occurred to any of our party, and I noticed that the Inuits suffered from the cold quite as much as the white men. The skin invariably comes off the frozen part within a few days, even when only slightly nipped.

The consequence was that my nose was constantly peeling, and at all times as tender as an infant's. Now that the freezing days were about over, it began to peel from sunburn. I don't know how many layers of skin were thus removed, but more than I could account for, unless a man's nose is like an onion.

The sun was now having a very perceptible effect upon the snow, even when the black rocks began to peep up through the surface, and great patches of moss could be seen completely bare. The great bugbear of sledge travelling is stony ground, or a hidden rock beneath a thin layer of snow that cuts through and sweeps the ice from the runners before the sled can be stopped. When the ice is gone from the runners all comfort has gone with it. The sled that the dogs would drag without apparent difficulty suddenly seems to weigh tons. All hands in harness and pulling like slaves cannot accomplish more than two miles an hour. The ice is put upon the runners the first thing in the morning when coming out of the igloo. The sled is turned upside down, and the water, after being held in the mouth a little while to warm it, is squirted over the runners and freezes almost immediately in a temperature below zero. In this way successive layers are applied until a clean, smooth surface is acquired, upon which the sled slips over the snow with comparative case. Now, the ice was usually all off the sleds by noon, and progress was slow and laborious.

We got an observation on the 21st at noon, which showed us our latitude to be 65 deg. 45 min. north, agreeing closely with Lieutenant Schwatka's dead reckoning. This, according to the chart, would put us on the north bank of Wager River; but as yet we had seen no signs of it, nor did we subsequently see anything that looked like such river. This can be accounted for by the presumption that the survey was made during the early summer, when the lakes are full, and some of the valleys connecting them may have contained water enough to float a boat.

Hunting Musk-Oxen

Before winter these might dry up and leave only a series of disconnected lakes. Fresh musk-ox tracks were seen on the 27th, and on the 29th we lay over to hunt some that Equeesik had seen after coming into camp on the 28th. After a chase of about three miles we succeeded in killing four, which completed our musk-ox score, as we saw no more either in going to or coming from King William Land. May 3d, we found water at a depth of eight feet, and on the 6th had to dig through eight and a half feet. This was the thickest ice we saw of one winter's formation. About noon of the 7th we ran into a herd of fourteen reindeer, lying down upon a hillside, and in less than three-quarters of an hour ten of them lay dead upon the field, and I believe those who got away carried some lead with them. Lieutenant Schwatka, who remained with the sleds, said that when the firing began it sounded for a while like a sharp battle, so rapidly and incessantly were the shots delivered. It clearly illustrates the advantage of breech-loaders and magazine guns when game is plentiful and much is required.

The next day a storm kept us in camp, but on the 9th we pulled out again and found the sledging in a most wretched condition. The country was very hilly and the snow entirely gone in many places, so that it occasioned much halting and considerable trouble to pick out a route by which the sled could move at all. About noon, however, we were rejoiced by reaching the head of a small river or creek by a perilous flying switch down a very long and steep hill. One of the sleds was overthrown, but fortunately it sustained no material damage, and was soon righted and landed on the ice below. One more flying run and we were safe upon the river. We had to congratulate ourselves upon the good fortune by which we discovered this river, for the land was getting more rugged all the time, and we began to fear that the snow, which was disappearing very rapidly, would soon be in such a condition that we could not travel at all, and we be left so near and get beyond reach of our destination. The range of hills from which we descended to the river was from eight hundred to a thousand feet high and their peaks entirely denuded of snow.

Lieutenant Schwatka decided to keep to the river under all circumstances, though at present it was impossible to tell whether it was the Castor and Pollux or a branch of Back's River. It proved to be the latter, and quite an important branch, which we followed for upward of ninety miles, leaving it only when it turned due south and at a right angle to our course. The entire length is 110 or 120 miles. It empties into Cockburn Bay, on the eastern shore of Back's River. Lieutenant Schwatka named it Hayes River, in honor of the President. On the 11th of May we killed seven reindeer, and on the 13th nine. The country seems to be filled with game, and nearly every day we saw two or three large herds. Our dogs get well fed, and are really in finer condition than when we left Camp Daly.

The Great Bend in Hayes River

We had the misfortune to lose one of our best dogs, Toekelegeto, Toolooah's leader, on the night of the 13th, who choked to death with a piece of bone in his throat. He had eaten a piece of the shoulder-blade of the reindeer, which is thin and breaks into fine splinters. The Inuits usually hide this bone in the snow, as they say such accidents are frequent, especially when the dogs eat rapidly, as they always do when there is a number together. The northern shore of the river is here bounded by high hills—in fact, almost a mountain range, and as I walked along the crest on the 14th, the sleds moving along the river at my feet looked like toys. Inland I could see the rocky hills piled together, barren and forbidding, and I could not help feeling grateful that we had found so good a road out of this country, for it would have been next to impossible to have crossed these ridges with our heavy sledges. About noon we came upon a freshly cut block of snow turned up on end, an unmistakable indication that natives had been there within two or three days, and a little farther on fresh footprints in the snow led us to a cache of musk-ox meat, and near by a deserted igloo.

81

The Sources of the Hayes River

Equeesik knew by these signs that we were in the Ooqueesik-Sillik country, and as the natives never go far from Back's River, or the Ooqueesik-Sillik, as is the Esquimau name, this was joyful news and we were all excitement at the prospect of speedily meeting the natives. We followed the tracks upon the ice, and could see that they had used dogs to drag a musk-ox skin for a sled. This is a usual mode of travel with these people, who have very little wood with which to make sledges. Their supply consists entirely of drift-wood, with the exception of the material they obtained from the small boats of the 'Erebus' and 'Terror', two of which were found on Adelaide Peninsula and two on King William Land.

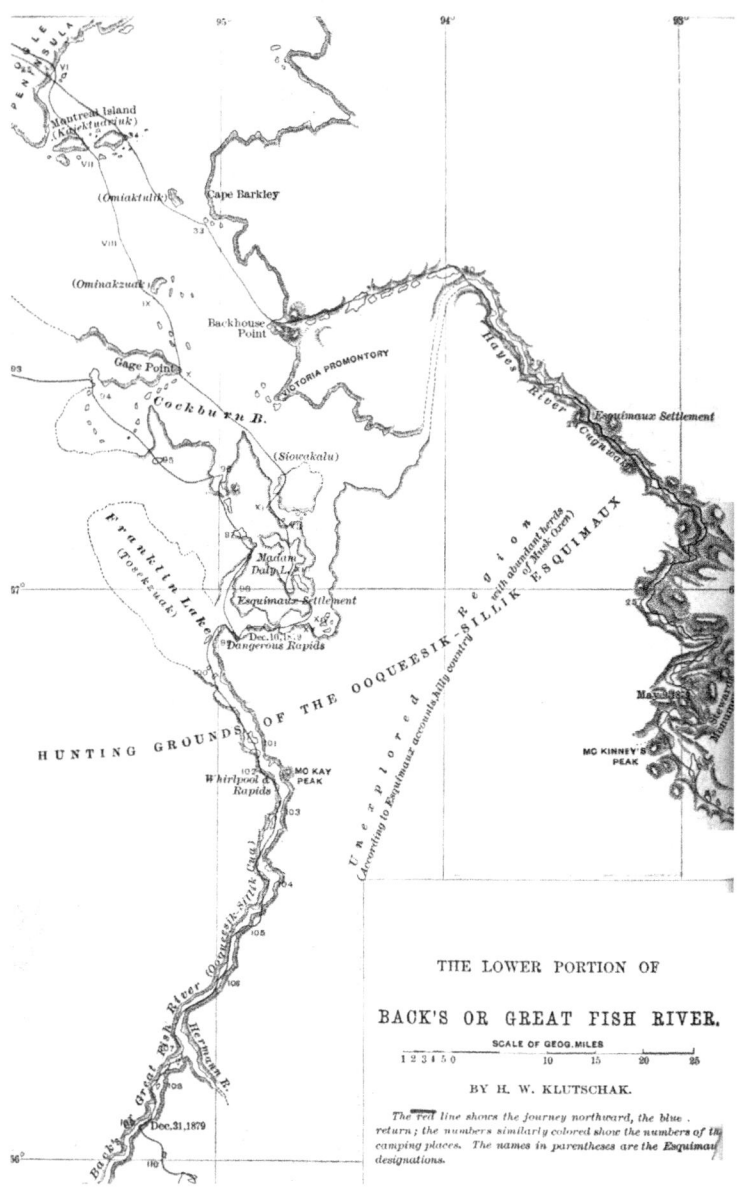

The Lower Portion of Back's or Great Fish River

CHAPTER V

NATIVE WITNESSES

We left camp at half-past seven in the morning of the 15th, a sharp wind blowing in our faces. We had not gone far when the dogs began to prick up their ears, and finally started off on a brisk run, barking and manifesting great excitement. The Inuits at once attributed this unwonted energy on the part of the dogs to the fact that there were people not far distant, and, sure enough, we soon saw several igloos about three-quarters of a mile ahead, with poles sticking in the snow around them— an evidence that they were inhabited. The sleds were now halted, and preparations made to open communication with the strangers. The Inuits of our party, especially Ishnark and Joe, were very much frightened, and said the people we were about to meet were as warlike as the Netchilliks, and always wanted to fight when they met strangers. They were somewhat reassured when their attention was called to the immense advantage we had over them with our breech-loaders and magazine guns against their bows and spears. In accordance with the custom of the country, the Inuits armed themselves with snow-knives and spears, while the white men carried their rifles or revolvers. All the men and boys then advanced toward the igloos, but not a soul was to be seen. Two or three dogs ran out and barked and then ran to where the sleds were halted, the women and children cowering down behind them. When within about three hundred yards of the camp our party halted, while Equeesik and Ishnark went a few paces further and began shouting something, which I afterward learned was Equeesik's

84

name, with which they were acquainted, and announcing the fact that there were white men with our party. Presently one man crawled timidly out of the doorway of an igloo and asked a question, which must have been satisfactorily answered, for others soon followed and arranged themselves alongside of him; then all of them shouted an invitation to advance, whereupon we approached, and conversation between the Inuits became general. We were objects of great curiosity to the strangers, most of whom now saw white men for the first time. It seems that when they first saw us they thought we were Netchilliks, and were in consequence very much frightened, so that while some of our people were dreading an encounter, these poor creatures were shaking in their shoes and afraid to come out of their igloos. They all carried knives in their hands, but as weapons they might as well have carried nothing. Most of them were bits of hoop-iron or copper, worked down to a blade, and fastened upon long handles of reindeer horn.

There were in the party nine men, nearly all belonging to the immediate family of an old man, who acted as spokesman. He said he was an Ookjoolik, but he and others had been driven from their country by their more numerous and warlike neighbors the Netchilliks. His family comprised nearly all that was left of the tribe which formerly occupied the western coast of Adelaide Peninsula and King William Land. We concluded to encamp with them, and get what information we could from them concerning our mate and the Franklin ships. We were fortunate in finding the old man, an interesting and important witness. "Esquimau Joe," Ishnark, and Equeesik acted as interpreters, and through them we learned that these people were in great distress for food. The musk-ox we saw cached was all the meat they had in hand, or had had for a long time. An old man of their tribe had starved to death about a month before our arrival. We gave them some reindeer meat, of which we fortunately had plenty on the sleds, and told them where they would find the carcass of a reindeer that one of our party had killed the day before and left on the field because the sleds were too far off to wait for it. Their clothing was in a dilapidated condition, though originally well made, and instead of reindeer gloves and shoes, they wore articles made of musk-ox skin, which had a most extraordinary effect.

Meeting with the Ookjooliks

The hair of the musk-ox is several inches long, and it looked as if they had an old-fashioned muff on each hand. They were very good natured and friendly, however, and helped to build our igloos and make them comfortable. We obtained from them a few trifling relics of the 'Erebus' and 'Terror', in exchange for knives and needles, which made them happy. It seemed strange to me that they should be hungry in a country swarming with reindeer, but our people explained to me that in winter it is almost impossible to get near enough to reindeer; to kill them with arrows, which are their only weapons. In summer they kill a few reindeer from their kyacks, or skin canoes, while crossing the big lakes on their migrations. The Netchilliks also kill a few reindeer in this way. In the summer and fall these people catch great quantities of salmon and cow-e-sil-lik, a species of fish peculiar to this country, and in the neighboring hills kill a few musk-oxen. Their main dependence, however, is upon fish from Back's and Harris's rivers.

From Ikinnelikpatolok, the old Ookjoolik, we learned at the interview that he had only once seen white men alive. That was when he was a little boy. He is now about sixty-five or seventy. He was fishing on Back's River when they came along in a boat and shook hands with him. There were ten men. The leader was called "Tos-ard-e-roak," which Joe says, from the sound, he thinks means Lieutenant Back. The next white man he saw was dead in a bunk of a big ship which was frozen in the ice near an island about five miles due west of Grant Point, on Adelaide Peninsula. They had to walk out about three miles on smooth ice to reach the ship. He said that his son, who was present, a man about thirty-five years old, was then about like a child he pointed out—probably seven or eight years old. About this time he saw the tracks of white men on the main-land. When he first saw them there were four, and afterward only three. This was when the spring snows were falling. When his people saw the ship so long without any one around, they used to go on board and steal pieces of wood and iron. They did not know how to get inside by the doors, and cut a hole in the side of the ship, on a level with the ice, so that when the ice broke up during the following summer the ship filled and sunk. No tracks were seen in the salt-water ice or on the ship, which also was covered with snow, but they saw scrapings and sweepings alongside, which seemed to have been brushed off by people who had been living on board. They found some red cans of fresh meat, with plenty of what looked like tallow mixed with it. A great many had been opened, and four were still unopened. They saw no bread. They found plenty of knives, forks, spoons, pans, cups, and plates on board, and afterward found a few such things on shore after the vessel had gone down. They also saw books on board, and left them there. They only took knives, forks, spoons, and pans; the other things they had no use for. He never saw or heard of the white men's cairn on Adelaide Peninsula.

Peowat, son-in-law of the previous witness, a man about forty, said that when about fourteen or fifteen years old he saw two boats come down Back's River. One had eight men in it, and the other he did not notice how many. He afterward saw a stone monument on Montreal Island, which, when he opened it, was found to contain a pocket-knife, a pair of scissors, and some fish-hooks, which he took away. He saw no papers anywhere about it.

We remained in this camp two days and a half, and before we left engaged a young man named Narleyow to accompany us as guide and seal hunter. His wife, Innokpizookzook, and their child, a little girl about three years old, also went with us. Our new hunter was given a gun and ammunition, and placed in the care of Equeesik to instruct in the use of fire-arms. I noticed that these people have slightly fairer complexions than the natives of Hudson's Bay, and the women are somewhat more elaborately tattooed, despite which they are quite comely. The children are all remarkably pretty, but the men have a ghastly look from wearing wooden goggles to guard against snow blindness, which makes the skin around the eyes, where protected by the goggles, several shades lighter than the rest of their face.

We reached Back's River in four more marches, two of which were on the Hayes River, and two on land, crossing from the great bend to avoid the detour that otherwise we would be compelled to make. We were compelled to remain in camp one day, while on the land, on account of a severe storm. The day we reached Back's River was also one of the most disagreeable days we marched, and it was a joyful sight to us, after nearly two months' travelling over an entirely unknown country, to find ourselves within easy reach of our destination. It seemed as if nothing now could prevent the accomplishment of our desire. As long as we were dependent upon the snow the prospect was growing more and more dubious; but with the salt-water ice beneath us, we felt assured of reaching our destination in due season. We remained one day at Montreal Island, to look for the remains of the cairn spoken of by Peowat, but every trace of it had been removed, as he said.

The Netchillik Ambassadress.

The day we left Montreal Island two seals were killed, which were the first since leaving Hudson's Bay. We found the distance from the north-east end of the island much less than mapped, and went into camp well up the coast, after killing three reindeer. We again took the land, crossing the Oyle Point and Richardson Point peninsulas, which we found much wider than mapped. In an inlet west of Richardson Point, or "Nu-oo-tar-ro," as it is known by the natives, we ran into the first of the Netchillik encampments, on the last day of May. The ceremony of opening communication was similar to that with the Ooquee-sik-silliks a few days before, with the exception that instead of remaining in their igloos the men were drawn up in line of battle in front of them, and sent out an old woman to find out who we were and what we wanted. If our designs had been hostile, and we had killed the old woman, their fighting strength would not have been reduced, and it would only have been one less old woman to care for. They carried their bows in their hands, with arrows fixed to the strings; but when the old woman shouted back that we were white men, they laid aside their arms and received us in a friendly manner, striking their breasts and saying, "Many-tu-me," though Joe afterward told me that one of the men wanted a fight anyhow. They have a custom of killing the first stranger who comes among them after a death in the tribe, and as we filled that requirement, it seems he wanted to carry out the custom. At Equeesik's suggestion a gun had been discharged in the air as we approached, and it is probable that the knowledge that we were better armed than they had some effect in securing peace. They acted in quite a friendly manner after we came among them, and Lieutenant Schwatka and I visited all their igloos, leaving needles, thimbles, spoons, knives, and fish-hooks with them in exchange for a few unimportant Franklin relics. The next day we interviewed an old man named Seeuteetuar, who had seen a number of skeletons near the water line in an inlet about three or four miles west from the present camp. He had also seen books and papers scattered around among the rocks along the shore and back from the beach. There were also knives, forks and spoons, dishes and cans. There was no sled there, but there was a boat, which was afterward broken up and taken away by the natives, with which to manufacture wooden implements. He was shown a watch, and said he saw several like it lying around, which were also taken and broken up by the children. Some were silver and some gold. He said the bones were still there, unless carried off by foxes and wolves. He had never seen or heard of a cairn erected by white men along the coast on this side of Simpson Strait, and had never heard of any other traces of white men here. It was a long time since he had been there, but he could show us the spot.

Toolooah, another Netchillik, about forty-five years old, had also been at the boat place, but after nearly everything had been removed. He had, however, seen traces of white men in the Ookjoolik country, on the western coast of Adelaide Peninsula, and as late as last summer had picked up pieces of bottles, iron, wood and tin cans on an island off Grant Point. Ookjoolik natives had pointed out this island as a place near which a ship had been sunk many years ago. A map was shown to him, and he pointed to a spot about eight miles due west of Grant Point as the place where the ship went down. Ooping, an Ookjoolik Inuit, who lived near the mouth of a big inlet that extends nearly across Adelaide Peninsula, from the head of Wilmot Bay, was the last Esquimau who had gone over the west coast of King William Land. This was two years ago. He had seen traces of white men near Cape Jane Franklin and along the coast of Cape Felix. This inlet, spoken of by Toolooah, seemed of sufficient importance to deserve surveying, and Lieutenant Schwatka decided to include it in the search of the Ookjoolik country.

The sun exerted sufficient power during the middle of the day to bring our igloo down; but we had finished our interviewing and were ready to visit the cove where the boat and skeletons had been found. One light sled, with plenty of dogs, took us over, with Seeuteetuar and Toolooah as guides, and our Toolooah as driver. We found the place about three miles from camp, and, though the ground was nearly all covered with snow, and nothing whatever distinguished it from the coast on either side, we could not but be impressed by the mournful interest with which the sad fate of the lost explorers invested it. To our minds there seemed little doubt but that this was the farthest point in the direction of Hudson's Bay that any of them had reached. The party was a small one, and had, probably, been sifted down to the few hardiest men, whose anticipation of rescue from the horrible death that awaited them had not faltered under all their terrible sufferings while they had the continent in view. It probably seemed that if they could only reach the mainland they would be comparatively safe. But even the bravest hearts must have sunk—and that there were many brave hearts among them cannot be doubted, when the awful desolation of this country forced itself upon them. No more powerful picture of utter abandonment could possibly be devised than this. The land low and barren, so low, indeed, as to be scarcely distinguished from the sea, as both lay covered with their mantle of snow. Neither tree nor sprout, and scarcely a hill visible—nothing whatever to relieve the crushing monotony of the scene—no living thing to be seen anywhere, though the eye had uninterrupted range over so vast a territory. Even a wolf prowling around would have been a relief in the utter loneliness that oppressed them. All this presented itself to our minds as we looked around but saw no traces of the lost ones. Had we known at this time what we learned a few days later, the place would have had an additional interest as the spot where the records of the expedition, which had been brought thus far with infinite toil and care, had been irrecoverably lost. We marked the spot carefully, for a thorough search when the snow was off the ground, and returned to camp. Our guides informed us that the boat was found upside down on the beach, and all the skeletons beneath it. They did not remember the exact number, but thought there were about five or more.

The Council with the Netchilliks

That night Equeesik learned from two natives who came in late that his sister was with another portion of the tribe near Richardson Point, and went there with his sled, returning the next day but one with several families, including an old woman whom we found to be another important and interesting witness. She was one of a party who met some of the survivors of the ill-fated ships on Washington Bay. Since then she had seen no white man until now. Her name was Ahlangyah, a Netchillik, about fifty-five years of age. She had a fine intelligent face, and a quantity of jet black hair, slightly tinged with gray, that had probably never been annoyed by any efforts at arrangement, and hung down over her shoulders or straggled over her face without reserve or molestation. I succeeded during the interview in getting a very characteristic portrait of her, the authenticity of which was subsequently attested when I had forgotten her name and her friends at once identified her by the portrait. It is but fair to state that we have reason to put great faith in the statements of these people, as truthfulness seems to be an inherent quality with them. They never attempted to deceive us in regard to relics, though perhaps it would seem easy and profitable. In many instances what appeared to us to be interesting relics they told us came from the natives of Repulse Bay and elsewhere.

Ahlangyah pointed out the eastern coast of Washington Bay as the spot where she, in company with her husband, and two other men with their wives, had seen ten white men dragging a sledge with a boat on it many years ago. There was another Inuit with them who did not go near the white men. The sledge was on the ice, and a wide crack separated them from the white men at the interview. The women went on shore, and the men awaited the white people at the crack on the ice. Five of the white men put up a tent on the shore, and five remained with the boat on the ice. The Inuits put up a tent not far from the white men, and they stayed together here five days. During this time the Inuits killed a number of seals on the ice and gave them to the white men. They gave her husband a chopping-knife. He was the one who had the most intercourse with the white crew. The knife is now lost, or broken and worn out. She has not seen it for a long time. At the end of five days they all started for Adelaide Peninsula, fearing that the ice, which was very rotten, might not let them across. They started at night, because then, the sun being low, the ice would be a little frozen. The white men followed, dragging their heavy sledge and boat, and could not cross the rotten ice as fast as the Inuits, who halted and waited for them at Gladman's Point. The Inuits could not cross to the mainland, the ice was too rotten, and they remained in King William Land all summer. They never saw the white men again, though they waited at Gladman's Point fishing in the neighboring lakes, going back and forth between the shore and lakes nearly all summer, and then went to the eastern shore near Matty Island.

Some of the white men were very thin, and their mouths were dry and hard and black. They had no fur clothing on. When asked if she remembered by what names the white men were called, she said one of them was called "Agloocar," and another

"Toolooah." The latter seemed to be the chief, and it was he who gave the chopping-knife to her husband. (Agloocar and Toolooah are both common Esquimau names, and it is probable the names she heard the white men call resembled these in sound, and thus impressed themselves upon her mind.) Another one was called "Dok-took" (Doctor). "Toolooah" was a little older than the others, and had a large black beard, mixed with gray. He was bigger than any of the others—"a big, broad man." "Agloocar" was smaller, and had a brown beard about four or five inches below his chin (motioning with her hand). "Dok-took" was a short man, with a big stomach and red beard, about the same length as "Agloocar's." All three wore spectacles, not snow goggles, but, as the interpreters said, all the same seko (ice).

The following spring, when there was little snow on the ground, she saw a tent standing on the shore at the head of Terror Bay. There were dead bodies in the tent, and outside were some covered over with sand. There was no flesh on them—nothing but the bones and clothes. There were a great many; she had forgotten how many. Indeed, Inuits have little idea of numbers beyond "ten." She saw nothing to indicate any of the party she met before. The bones had the chords or sinews still attached to them. One of the bodies had the flesh on, but this one's stomach was gone. There were one or two graves outside. They did not open the graves at this time; saw a great many things lying around. There were knives, forks, spoons, watches, many books, clothing, blankets, and such things. The books were not taken notice of. This was the same party of Esquimaux who had met the white men the year before, and they were the first who saw the tent and graves. They had been in King William Land ever since they saw the white men until they found the tent place.

CHAPTER VI

THE MIDNIGHT SUN

Such was the statement of Ahlangyah the Netchillik. When she had finished it we gave her some needles, spoons, a tin pan, and other articles that well repaid her for the trouble she had taken to reach us. Here was a woman who had actually seen the poor, starving explorers, and her story was replete with interest for us. Every word she uttered seemed fraught with the dread tragedy, and she appeared to share our interest, for her face was full of expression. At times it was saddened with the recital of the piteous condition of the white men, and tears filled her eyes as she recalled the sad scene at the tent place where so many had perished, and their bodies become food for wild beasts. It would seem, from what she related to-day, that the party which perished in the inlet we visited yesterday, was part of the same that Ahlangyah met on King William Land. She and her friends could not get across Simpson Strait, while the white men kept on over the rotten ice, probably at last compelled to take to their boat, and then, at the mercy of the wind and ice, after losing others of their number near Pfeffer River and Todd Islands, had drifted into the inlet where the dead bodies were found with the boat. How long it took them to reach this place will probably never be known, but there is little doubt that they were in a desperate condition. In fact, as we subsequently learned from other witnesses, there were almost unmistakable evidences of their being compelled to resort to cannibalism, until at last they absolutely starved to death at this point—at least all but one, whose remains were found, during the summer after our visit

96

here, about five miles further inland.

We secured one valuable relic here, in the sled seen by Sir Leopold McClintock, in Erebus Bay, which at that time had upon it a boat, with several skeletons inside. Since the sled came into the hands of the Inuits it has been cut down several times. It was originally seven feet longer than at present, the runners about two inches higher and twice as far apart. But even in its present state it is an exceedingly interesting memento. We have carefully preserved it in the condition in which it has been in constant use by the Esquimaux for many years. We met other portions of this tribe at intervals of from six to ten miles along this coast, until we reached Seaforth Point, where we crossed to King William Land, and left them behind until our return in the following September.

Meanwhile we were pushing steadily onward. We were beginning to get used to the phenomena of the Arctic, not the least among which is the "midnight sun." It is difficult for one who has not witnessed it himself to understand the meaning of this portent. The idea of the long Arctic night seems to be much more generally comprehended. Nearly all writers upon the subject, whether those who have themselves experienced its effects, or those whose knowledge is derived from study, dwell with great force on the terribly depressing effect upon the physical organization of natives of the median zones caused by the long Arctic night whenever brought within its influence. Though much less has been written or said concerning the interminable day, its effects are almost as deleterious upon the stranger as the prolonged night. Indeed, to the sojourner in high latitudes the day is much more appreciable, for at no point yet visited by man is the darkness the total darkness of night throughout the entire day, while the "midnight sun" makes the night like noon-day. Even when the sun passes below the horizon at its upper culmination, the daylight is as intense as at noon in lower latitudes when the sun's disk is obscured by thin clouds. The long twilight in the north, where the sun's apparent path around the earth varies so little in altitude at its upper and lower culminations, takes some of the edge off of the prolonged night at the highest latitude ever attained by the Arctic explorer; but there is nothing to relieve the "long, long, weary day" of its full power upon the system.

In this latitude the sun goes down at night, and we retire to our couches and sleep. In the morning the sun returns, and we arise to the pursuit of our various daily avocations. But there, in the spring, the sun never sets. There is no morning and no night. It is one continuous day for months. At first it seems very difficult to understand this strange thing in nature. One never knows when to sleep. The world seems to be entirely wrong, and man grows nervous and restless. Sleep is driven from his weary eyelids, his appetite fails, and all the disagreeable results of protracted vigils are apparent. But gradually he becomes used to this state of affairs, devises means to darken his tent, and once more enjoys his hour of rest. In fact, he learns how to take advantage of the new arrangement, and when travelling pursues his journey at night, or when the sun is lowest, because then he finds the frost that hardens the snow a great assistance in sledging.

The sun's rays then, falling more obliquely, are less powerful, and he avoids somewhat the evils that beset his pathway at noontime. He is not so much exposed to sunburn or to snow-blindness. It may sound strangely to speak of sunburn in the frigid zone, but perhaps nowhere on the earth is the traveller more annoyed by that great ill. The heat of ordinary exercise compels him to throw back the hood of his fur coat, that the cool evenings and mornings preclude his discarding, and not only his entire face becomes blistered, but especially—if he is fashionable enough to wear his hair thin upon the top of his head—his entire scalp is affected about as severely as if a bucket of scalding water had been poured over his head. This is not an exaggeration. At a later period than that of which I am writing, Lieutenant Schwatka's entire party, while upon a sledge journey from Marble Island to Camp Daly, were so severely burned that not only their faces but their entire heads were swollen to nearly twice their natural size. And a fine-looking party they were. Some had their faces so swollen that their eyes were completely closed upon awakening from sleep. When one could see the others he could not refrain from laughing, so ludicrous was the spectacle. All dignity was lost. Even the august commander of the party was a laughing-stock, and though he knew why they laughed at each other, he could not understand why he should excite such mirth until he saw his face in a mirror. Then, when he tried to smile, his lips were so thoroughly swollen that the effect was entirely lost, and it was impossible to tell whether his expression denoted amusement, anger, or pain. The torture resulting from these burns was so severe that it was almost impossible to sleep. The fur bedding, which also served the purpose of a pillow, irritated the burns like applying a mustard-plaster to a blister. Then it was that the night was turned into day for the rest of the journey, and during the heat of the day the party were comparatively comfortable in the shelter of their tent. Straw-hats would have been the proper style of head-dress, but they had been omitted from the outfit, as was also another very important source of comfort, mosquito nettings. It is in the summer, however, that the necessity for the latter luxury is encountered.

While the sun's rays pour down with all their force upon the devoted head of the traveller the reflection from the snow is almost as intense and still more disagreeable, for there is no possible escape from it. Not satisfied with producing its share of sunburn, it acts upon the eyes in a manner that produces that terrible scourge of the Arctic spring—snow-blindness. It is a curious fact that persons who are near-sighted are generally exempt from the evils of snow-blindness, while it appears to be more malignant with those who are far-sighted in direct ratio to the superior quality of their vision. Lieutenant Schwatka and his companion, the present writer, are both near-sighted, and during the two seasons that they were exposed to the disease neither were at any time affected by snow-blindness; while the other members of the party, and especially the natives, who have most powerful visual organs, were almost constantly martyrs to the disease whenever exposed to its attacks.

It seems the only method of guarding against it is to wear what we called snow-goggles all the time one is out of doors. The natives use those of home manufacture—that is, a piece of wood with a notch to fit over the bridge of the nose, and a narrow, horizontal slit opposite each eye. This rude spectacle, called by them igearktoo, is made to fit close to the eyes, and is held in place by strings passing behind and over the top of the head. It serves to shelter the eyes from the direct and reflected rays of the sun, but also interrupts the vision so much that they habitually push it up on top of their heads, and run a risk which almost invariably results to their disadvantage, yet their goggles are so unsatisfactory that no amount of adverse experience is sufficient to serve as a warning to them. The civilized visitors among them wear goggles of various patterns and degrees of excellence. Some are made of differently colored glass, from the various shades of smoked glass to blue and green of varying degrees of opacity; some are of glass surrounded with wire gauze; others of wire gauze without the glass, and some are merely a strip of bunting hanging from the peak of the cap. Of all the various kinds the general experience seems to be in favor of the wire gauze without glass. They interfere very little with the vision, and yet furnish a perfect protection for the eyes. Glass of any pattern or shade subjects the wearer to constant annoyance by fogging from the breath, which congeals very rapidly upon the surface of the glass, and apparently always at the most inconvenient time, as when the hunter is stalking a deer by crawling a long distance upon his hands and knees, and just as he raises his rifle for a shot his goggles are like pieces of ground glass. The native spectacles give such a limited field of vision that it is impossible to use them in hunting; but the wire-gauze seems to be free from all these objections. A well-supplied expedition is provided with every kind of snow-goggles, as they are absolutely essential to the well being of the party. The superiority of the wire-gauze pattern seemed to have been appreciated by the Franklin expedition, for many of them were subsequently found at the various burial-places and at other points where relics were obtained. It is also said that painting around the eyes upon the upper and lower lids with burned cork or some dark pigment is a protection against snow-blindness; but it is doubtful if this method has been sufficiently tested to admit of its being relied upon. The symptoms of snow-blindness are inflammation of the inner coating of the lids, accompanied by intense pain and impairment of the vision, so as to disable the sufferer from the performance of his duties. A wash of diluted tincture of opium is probably the best remedy, and gives almost immediate relief. The patient should remain within doors for two or three days, by which time he will usually be sufficiently cured to resume his out-door labors.

It might be supposed that in the utter barrenness of the Arctic landscape, flowers never grew there. This would be a great mistake. The dweller in that desolate region, after passing a long, weary winter, with nothing for the eye to rest upon but the vast expanse of snow and ice, is in a condition to appreciate, beyond the ability of an inhabitant of warmer climes, the little flowerets that peep up almost through the snow when the spring sunlight begins to exercise its power upon the white mantle of the earth. In little patches here and there, where the dark-colored moss absorbs the warm rays of the sun, and the snow is melted from its surface, the most delicate flowers spring up at once to gladden the eye of the weary traveller. It needs not the technical skill of the botanist to admire these lovely tokens of approaching summer. Thoughts of home, in a warmer and more hospitable climate, fill his heart with joy and longing, as meadows filled with daisies and buttercups spread out before him, while he stands upon the crest of a granite hill that knows no footstep other than the tread of the stately musk-ox or the antlered reindeer, as they pass in single file upon their frequent journeys, and whose caverns echo to no sound save the howling of the wolves or the discordant cawing of the raven. He is a boy again, and involuntarily plucks the feathery dandelion, and seeks the time of day by blowing the puffy fringe from its stem, or tests the faith of the fair one, who is dearer to him than ever in this hour of separation, by picking the leaves from the yellow-hearted daisy. Tiny little violets, set in a background of black or dark green moss, adorn the hill-sides, and many flowers unknown to warmer zones come bravely forth to flourish for a few weeks only, and wither in the August winds. Very few of the flowers, so refreshing and charming to the eye, have any perfume. Nearly all smell of the dank moss that forms their bed.

As soon as the snow leaves the ground, the hill-sides in many localities are covered with the vine that bears a small black berry (called by the natives parwong,) in appearance, though not in flavor, like the huckleberry. It has a pungent spicy tartness that is very acceptable after a long diet of meat alone, and the natives, when they find these vines, stop every other pursuit for the blissful moments of cramming their stomachs with the fruit. This is kept up, if the crop only lasts long enough until they have made themselves thoroughly sick by their hoggishness. But the craving for some sort of vegetable diet is irresistible, and with true Inuit improvidence they indulge it, careless of consequences. Fortunate for them is it that their summer, is a short one, and the parwong not abundant, or cholera might be added to the other dangers of Arctic residence. But the days of the buttercup and the daisy, and of the butterfly and the mosquito are few. With the winter comes the all-pervading snow, and the keen, bracing north-west wind, the rosy cheek and the frozen nose; but with it also comes rugged health and a steady diet of walrus meat.

CHAPTER VII

RELICS

From this point onward our march was attended with the most profitable results. On the evening of the 4th of June we met a young man, named Adlekok, who, during the previous summer, had found a new cairn erected by white men near Pfeffer River, which had never been seen by any other Inuits. Near by were three graves and a tent place in which he found a pair of wire-gauze snow-goggles, which we bought from him. This information seemed of sufficient importance to be followed up immediately before any other natives should find and rob the cairn. Consequently the next day Lieutenant Schwatka and I took a light sled, with Toolooah to drive and Adlekok as guide, and visited the spot. We took a day's rations with us, to use in case we did not get back that night, and started with a head wind and storm that confined our view to the immediate vicinity of the sledge. Our guide, however, took us through this trackless waste of smooth ice, a distance of over twenty-five miles, without deviation from the direct line, with no landmarks or sun to steer by; but on he went with the unerring instinct of a dog, until we struck the land at the western banks of Pfeffer River. Arrived at the cairn we found it as he said, "a white man's cairn" unmistakably, but before proceeding to take it down we examined it carefully and found scratched on a clay stone with the point of a sharp instrument,

MAY
H   XII
1869

and on the opposite side,

ETERNAL HONOR TO THE DISCOVERERS
OF THE NORTH WE-

and knew it to be the cairn erected by our countryman, Captain Hall, over the bones of two of Franklin's men which he speaks of having found here. A portion of the inscription was lost by the breaking off of a piece of the stone on which it was written. We did not take down the monument, but after making a hasty sketch, returned to camp, having travelled over fifty miles in ten hours.

At this camp we found another interesting relic, in a pine board that seems to have been part of the head of a bunk or other permanent fixture, and has the initials "L. F." in brass tacks upon it. This was picked up on the west coast of Adelaide Peninsula, near where the ship went down that drifted through Victoria Strait, and may serve to identify that vessel, thus proving a most interesting and valuable historic relic. At the next camp, which was our last stopping-place on the mainland, we met an old woman named Tooktoocheer, widow of Pooyetah, who was among the first to visit the boat place we saw a few days ago. We were somewhat disappointed in her as a witness, for she was so old that her memory was at fault, and she would wander about to different places and relate circumstances without explanation. Her son, who was present at the interview, was a lad of about twelve years when he visited the boat place with his parents, and retained a vivid recollection of the place. His testimony, therefore, proved to be what we had hoped of his mother's. All the time he was talking the old woman sat nodding approval as the circumstances he was relating were recalled to her memory. His name is Ogzeuckjeuwock, and he is an aruketko, or medicine-man, in his tribe. The recollection of the boat place was somewhat impressed upon his mind by the explosion of a can of powder with which he and another lad were playing after the articles were found there. The effects of the explosion came near proving fatal at the time, and when I met him during the fall on King William Land, he told me he had never entirely recovered from the shock.

I give the interview with Tooktoocheer and her son as I recorded it in my note-book at the time, so that each reader may draw his own conclusions. Some of the statements will undoubtedly appear strange, but in the main they are perfectly intelligible and exceedingly interesting. Tooktoocheer said she was from Okbillegeok (Pelly Bay of the charts), a portion of the Netchillik country. She is the widow of Pooyetah, spoken of by Sir John Ross and Captain Hall. She appeared to be about seventy years old, and was an object of high esteem by her people, as was evinced in the care that was bestowed upon her comfort. She said she had never seen any of Franklin's men alive, but saw six skeletons on the main-land and an adjacent island—four on the main-land and two on the island. This she pointed out on the southern coast near ninety-five degrees west longitude. There were no graves at either place. Her husband was with her at the time, and seven other Inuits. This was when she was at the boat place west of Richardson Point. In fact, she seemed to have the two places somewhat mixed up in her mind, and Ogzeuckjeuwock took up the thread of the narrative here. In answer to a question which we asked his mother, he said he saw books at the boat place in a tin case, about two feet long and a foot square, which was fastened, and they broke it open. The case was full. Written and printed books were shown him, and he said they were like the printed ones. Among the books he found what was probably the needle of a compass or other magnetic instrument, because he said when it touched any iron it stuck fast. The boat was right side up, and the tin case in the boat. Outside the boat he saw a number of skulls. He forgot how many, but said there were more than four. He also saw bones from legs and arms that appeared to have been sawed off. Inside the boat was a box filled with bones; the box was about the same size as the one with the books in it.

He said the appearance of the bones led the Inuits to the opinion that the white men bad been eating each other. What little flesh was still on the bones was very fresh; one body had all the flesh on. The hair was light; it looked like a long body. He saw a number of wire snow-goggles, and alongside the body with flesh on it was a pair of gold spectacles. (He picked out the kind of metal from several that were shown him.) He saw more than one or two pairs of such spectacles, but forgot how many. When asked how long the bodies appeared to have been dead when he saw them, he said they had probably died during the winter previous to the summer he saw them. In the boat he saw canvas and four sticks (a tent or sail), saw a number of watches, open-faced; a few were gold, but most were silver. They are all lost now. They were given to the children to play with, and have been broken up and lost. One body—the one with flesh on—had a gold chain fastened to gold ear-rings, and a gold hunting-case watch with engine-turned engraving attached to the chain, and hanging down about the waist. He said when he pulled the chain it pulled the head up by the ears. This body also had a gold ring on the ring finger of the right hand. It was taken off, and has since been lost by the children in the same way that the other things were lost. His reason for thinking that they had been eating each other was because the bones were cut with a knife or saw. They found one big saw and one small one in the boat; also a large red tin case of smoking tobacco and some pipes. There was no cairn there. The bones are now covered up with sand and sea-weed, as they were lying just at high-water mark. Some of the books were taken home for the children to play with, and finally torn and lost, and others lay around among the rocks until carried away by the wind and lost or buried beneath the sand.

His statement in reference to one of the deceased wearing a watch by a chain attached to his ears appears strange, but I give the statement as he made it. The chain may in some way have become attached to the ears, or, ridiculous as the story sounds, there may have been some eccentric person in the party who wore his watch in that way, and if such should prove to be the case, this would certainly identify him beyond doubt. While the old woman sat in our igloo giving her statement, or trying to recollect the circumstances, I succeeded in getting a good portrait sketch of her, which attracted considerable interest among the natives, and Ogzeuckjeuwock, who toward the latter part of the interview had begun to exhibit symptoms of impatience, turned quickly around as soon as he had finished, and asked to have his portrait taken also, in which I accommodated him, much to his gratification.

In reviewing the testimony of the foregoing witnesses it appears confirmatory of the opinion that the skeletons found at this place were the remains of some of the party who were seen by Ahlangyah and her friends on Washington Bay. She said that "Toolooah," "Agloocar," and "Doktook" wore spectacles, and spectacles were found at the boat place. Gold watches being found, there is also an evidence that there were officers in the party. It is probable that the five men who had a tent on shore near the Inuit "tupics" were all officers. It is also a very natural deduction that the books that were found in a sealed or locked tin case, which had to be broken open by the natives, were the more important records of the expedition, and in charge of the chief surviving officers, as it is not probable that men who were reduced to the extremity that these were, and having to drag everything by hand, would burden themselves with general reading matter. The boat, judging from the relics that we found, was a very heavy one, and copper bottomed; for most of the kettles that we saw in use among the Netchilliks were made of sheet copper that they said came from this and the other boats in Erebus Bay. But the boat was an absolute necessity and could not be abandoned. There is no doubt, however, that everything superfluous had been dropped from time to time, until nothing remained that could possibly be dispensed with, and such books as they had, besides the Nautical Almanac and Ephemeris, if indeed under the circumstances they would even carry them, were probably the most important records of the expedition.

During the year and a half that the 'Erebus' and 'Terror' were frozen fast in the Victoria Strait, the officers had probably surveyed the adjacent shores very carefully, and had undoubtedly made observations that were highly important. Especially would this be the case with their magnetical observations, as they were right upon the magnetic pole. We saw some tall and very conspicuous cairns near Cape Felix, which had no records in them, and were apparently erected as points of observation from the ships. As their terrible experience commenced after abandoning the vessels, it is probable that their time previous to that was occupied in a manner creditable to themselves and exceedingly valuable to all interested in scientific work. The records of these observations were in all probability contained in the tin box which Ogzeuckjeuwock speaks of as having been found and lost beyond recovery. An old Netchillik, named Ockarnawole, stated that five years ago he and his son, who was also present in the igloo, made an excursion along the north-western coast of King William Land. Between Victory Point and Cape Felix they found some things in a small cask near the salt water. In a monument that he did not take down, he found between the stones five jack-knives and a pair of scissors, also a small flat piece of tin, now lost; saw no graves at this place, but found what, from his description of the way the handle was put on, was either an adze or a pickaxe. A little north of this place found a tent place and three tin cups. About Victory Point found a grave, with a skeleton, clothes, and a jack-knife with one blade broken. Saw no books. In a little bay on the north side of Collinson Inlet saw a quantity of clothes. There was plenty of snow on the ground at the time they were there.

Snow-Huts on Cape Herschel

Viewing this statement in the light of our subsequent search upon this ground, I am inclined to believe that the grave they found was not at Victory Point, but was Irving's grave, about three miles below there. We saw no evidence of any grave at Victory Point, though we made a particularly extended search around that entire section of the country. The little bay spoken of is also probably the little bay where Lieutenant Irving's grave was discovered. There is a little bay on the north side of Collinson Inlet, but Lieutenant Schwatka and I visited it several times without finding any traces of clothing or any other evidences of white men having been there; and from what we saw at other places it seems almost impossible that there could have been much there as late as five years ago without some indications remaining. The vicinity of places where boats had been destroyed, or camps where clothing was found, were invariably indicated by pieces of cloth among the rocks, at greater or less intervals, for a long distance—sometimes as far as one or two miles on either side, and it would be almost impossible to escape seeing the principal point when led to it by such gradually cumulative evidence.

From this camp we went in two marches to Cape Herschel, where we left the heaviest of our baggage, with Joe and the other Inuits, taking only the white men of the party, with Toolooah and his family, and Owanork, Equeesik's youngest brother, to assist in the management of the sled, and started for Cape Felix on the 17th. We left instructions with Joe to remain at Cape Herschel as long as they could find enough to eat there; but if there was more game further down the coast, or on the mainland, to go there, and leave stones to indicate their route, so Toolooah would know where to look for them when we returned from Cape Felix. We took a course but little west of north, and at night encamped at the head of Washington Bay. Here we left the salt-water ice and started across land, keeping the same direction, with the intention of striking Collinson Inlet near its head. Our surprise can then be imagined when, after two days' travelling, we came out on Erebus Bay, which we thought was far to the west. This discrepancy was afterward accounted for when we found, by a comparison with the position of points between Cape Jane Franklin and Cape Felix, established by Sir James Ross, and confirmed by the officers of the 'Erebus' and 'Terror', that Cape Herschel is really about eighteen or twenty miles further west than mapped on the Admiralty charts.

The travelling across land was exceedingly heavy and tedious, owing to the softening condition of the snow, and to the lakes being covered with water to the depth of about six or eight inches. In the morning the slight crust on the snow, formed during the night, would break through at nearly every step; while during the rest of the day it was simply wading through slush or water. We found the salt-water ice also in a bad condition for travelling. It was very old ice, and as hummocky as it is possible for ice to be. We usually kept near the coast, where we found pretty good sledging; but one day we took to the hummocks, to avoid a great detour that following the shore ice would have entailed upon us, and did it to our sorrow. The fall snows and winter winds had piled up around and among the hummocks, filling in the interstices, so that, were the snow frozen, the sledging would not have been so very difficult; but the sun had already poured his rays upon it, day and night, for so long a time that the snow was soft, and nearly every step would break through.

Sometimes we would sink to our waists, and then our legs would be dangling in slush and water without finding bottom. The sled would often sink so that the dogs could not pull it out, light as was the load, and when we would gather round to help them, we could only get an occasional foothold, perhaps by kneeling in a hummock, or holding on with one hand while we pulled with the other. Even the dogs could not pull to any advantage. Some would be floundering in the slush and water, while others were scrambling over the broken ice, and yet under all these disadvantages we were able to make a march of ten miles, through the skill and experience of our Inuit dog driver. Without the assistance of dogs and natives, it is altogether probable that we would not have been able to accomplish more than two or three miles at the best; and I can well understand that Dr. Hayes had so much difficulty in crossing Smith Sound through the heavy hummocks in the spring of 1861. But at the same time I feel pretty well convinced that with plenty of good dogs and competent native drivers to manage the sledges, there is no ice in the Arctic that would prevent an average march of ten miles a day, with light loads, during the long days of spring. I would not even stipulate for such an exceptionally excellent guide and driver as our faithful Toolooah. Such as he are rare anywhere, and especially so among the Esquimaux. He is not only the best hunter in his tribe, but the best dog driver, and the most energetic man I have seen among all the tribes with whom I have come in contact. He is more like a capable white man, in that respect, than an Esquimau, and there is a legend in his tribe that he was never known to be tired. It is certain that to him, more than to all the other natives with us, combined, is due the success of our enterprise.

When the weather was unpropitious for hunting, and we would be without food, it was nothing more than the usual Inuit custom to say, "Ma-muk-poo-now" ("No good"), and sit down to wait for the weather to improve. But under such circumstances I have known our brave-hearted Toolooah rise equal to the emergency and go out to hunt for game until he found it. The others would perhaps go out and look around for a short time, and if they saw no game would come in, while he would not get in until nearly midnight, if, as was seldom the case, he came in empty-handed. I remember one time when we were without food, and moving into a portion of the country which we knew to be but thinly stocked with game. The hunters all went out, though the weather was thick with snow, and the only probability of seeing reindeer was that they might stumble upon them unobserved by the accident of approaching them against the wind. The others came in about noon, discouraged, having seen no game. Toolooah, on the contrary, did not get in until about five hours later; then he came in for the dogs, to bring in three reindeer that he had killed a few miles north of the camp. He went out in a south-westerly direction, and started to make a circuit of the camp on a radius of about five miles. By this ingenious course he came upon the fresh tracks of three reindeer, and at once started in pursuit, determined to follow them until he came up to them. The days were short, and he had to move rapidly, so that he absolutely ran about twelve miles until he overtook and killed them. I merely mention this incident to show the kind of metal our Toolooah is made of; not as a sample of Inuit character, but as a remarkable contrast to it.

Our ten-mile march through Erebus Bay occupied fifteen hours, and we were all pretty well worn out when we reached the shore and encamped, still some distance below Franklin Point. We lay over the next day, for Toolooah, who had exerted himself even beyond his great powers of endurance, was still quite exhausted, and though he expressed his readiness to resume the journey, Lieutenant Schwatka did not think it sufficiently urgent to run the risk of breaking him down altogether; not only out of personal regard for the noble fellow, but, as he was our sole dependence, losing his services would have been a sad if not a fatal disaster to the entire party.

Crossing Erebus Bay

During the day I shot two of an apparently distinct species of snipe, to preserve their skins for the Smithsonian Institute collection. One of them was distinguished by a sweet, simple song, somewhat similar to the lark's, its silvery tones gushing forth as if in perfect ecstasy of enjoyment of sunshine and air; at the same time rising and poising itself upon its wings. It seemed almost inhuman to kill the sweet little songster, particularly as it was the only creature I saw in the Arctic that uttered a pleasant note. All other sounds were such as the scream of the hawk and the gull, the quack of the duck, the yell of the wolf, the "Ooff! ooff!" of the walrus, or the bark of the seal—all harsh and unmelodious, save the tones of this sweet little singer. Nothing but starvation or scientific research could justify the slaughter of one of these innocents. I believe I shut my eyes when I pulled the trigger of my gun, and I know my heart gave a regretful thump when I heard the thud of its poor, bleeding body upon the ground. When we started for Franklin Point the next day, Lieutenant Schwatka concluded to follow Toolooah's advice, and keep upon the smooth ice near the shore, even though it should increase the distance marched. Our experience of the hummocks of Victoria Strait was not one that we were anxious to repeat. We had a short stretch of similar work in crossing the mouth of an inlet just below Franklin Point, and we were glad enough when we got through. The thermometer registered thirty-seven degrees in the shade, and sixty degrees in the sun. There was scarcely any wind, and coats were a burden of which we had soon to relieve ourselves. The heat while walking was quite as exhausting as ninety-eight degrees in the shade at New York. We saw a number of seals on the ice opposite the mouth of the inlet, and Toolooah shot one which was an unusually big specimen. In fact, the average of those we saw in this part of the country is much larger than those at Hudson's Bay.

During the entire day and night small flocks of ducks were flying swiftly past the tent, and so unaccustomed are they to meeting human beings in that wilderness, that they would be almost directly on the tent before they saw it, which only caused them to deviate a little to the right or left, or put on a little more steam. Lieutenant Schwatka seated himself on a rock alongside the tent, with his double-barrelled breech-loading shot-gun in his hand, and in a short time stopped three—two drakes and a duck. The drakes are exceedingly pretty, especially about the head and neck. The head is of a pale olive-green hue, a fashionable color in silks a few years ago, and known by the extraordinary name of "Elephant's Breath." This gradually merges into a very pale, warm gray, the line of demarcation between it and the very dark brown, which constitutes the general color of the body, being very abrupt. The bill is of a vermilion red, and surmounted by a bright orange-colored crest, with a black border as positively marked as if of black tape. At this season we usually see the drakes flying together, and the ducks in separate bands, reminding one of the division of sexes in a country meeting-house. We often came upon an immense body of drakes sitting upon the edge of an ice-floe, looking very much like a regiment of hussars at a distance drawn up in line of battle. The duck is not so gaudy as her husband. She is quite contented in a full suit of mottled brown and olive gray, presenting a texture on the back somewhat similar to the canvas-back species of Chesapeake Bay. About half-past ten o'clock in the evening, Toolooah and I walked up to the crest of a ridge, north of camp, to see if there were any points still to the north of us in this meridian. We found the coast bearing off well toward the eastward, and then toward the north-east, and knew it to be the upper coast of Franklin Point. We also saw a reindeer, which Toolooah shot before returning to camp.

When we left Franklin Point, the four white men of the party kept upon the land near the coast, and left the sled in charge of the Inuits to follow along the shore ice. The snow was entirely off the ridges, and only lay in great patches of soft slush in the valleys and upon occasional marshes. We spread out on the land, so as to cover as much ground in our search as possible, moving along like a line of skirmishers, with instructions that in case we saw anything that we did not understand, or which required further investigation, to make signals to assemble. In this way, before reaching Collinson Inlet, we found the graves of two white men, near one of which was lying the upper part of a skull; while within the pile of stones we found the upper maxilla, with two teeth, and a piece of the cheekbone. No other human bones were found; but these were laid together for burial on our return, when we could give a more thorough search.

CHAPTER VIII

IRVING'S GRAVE

The next day we stayed at Cape Jane Franklin to make a preliminary search of the vicinity. Lieutenant Schwatka and I went up Collinson Inlet, but saw no traces of white men. Henry and Frank, who had been sent up the coast, were more fortunate. About a mile and a half above camp they came upon the camp made by Captain Crozier, with his entire command from the two ships, after abandoning the vessels. There were several cooking stoves, with their accompanying copper kettles, besides clothing, blankets, canvas, iron and brass implements, and an open grave, wherein was found a quantity of blue cloth, part of which seemed to have been a heavy overcoat, and a part probably wrapped around the body. There was also a large quantity of canvas in and around the grave, with coarse stitching through it and the cloth, as though the body had been incased as if for burial at sea. Several gilt buttons were found among the rotting cloth and mould in the bottom of the grave, and a lens, apparently the object-glass of a marine telescope. Upon one of the stones at the foot of the grave Henry found a medal, which was thickly covered with grime, and was so much the color of the clay stone on which it rested as to nearly escape detection. It proved to be a silver medal, two and a half inches in diameter, with a bass-relief portrait of George IV., surrounded by the words,

GEORGIUS IIII., D. G. BRITTANNIARUM REX, 1820.

on the obverse, and on the reverse a laurel wreath surrounded by

SECOND MATHEMATICAL PRIZE,
ROYAL NAVAL COLLEGE,

and inclosing

AWARDED TO JOHN IRVING.
MID- SUMMER, 1830.

This at once identified the grave as that of Lieutenant John Irving, third officer of the 'Terror'. Under the head was found a figured silk pocket-handkerchief, neatly folded, the colors and pattern in a remarkable state of preservation. The skull and a few other bones only were found in and near by the grave. They were carefully gathered together, with a few pieces of the cloth and the other articles, to be brought away for interment where they may hereafter rest undisturbed. A re-burial on King William Land would be only until the grave was again found by the natives, when it would certainly be again torn open and despoiled.

The day after this discovery was made by the men we moved camp to the vicinity of the grave, and spent two days in searching for other matters of interest; but there was still some snow on the ground, and little ponds in the vicinity of the articles were partly frozen, so that an exhaustive search was impossible. Upon our return from Cape Felix, on the 11th of July, we found the snow entirely gone, and the ponds near the shore nearly all dry; we therefore had little difficulty in completing the search at that time. Among the various articles found was a brush with the name "H. Wilks" cut in the side, a two-gallon stone jug stamped "R. Wheatley, wine and spirit merchant, Greenhithe, Kent," several tin cans, a pickle bottle, and a canvas pulling strap, a sledge harness marked with a stencil plate "T 11," showing it to have belonged to the 'Terror'. We also found a stocking, rudely made of a piece of blanket, showing that they were in need of good stockings, which are so essential to the comfort of the Arctic traveller. For this purpose nothing is so good as the fur of the reindeer, but next to that well-made woollen stockings are the best. It was heart-rending to see this mute testimony to their destitution.

At our second visit Toolooah's wife found in a pile of stones, where had formerly stood the cairn seen by Lieutenant Hobson, a piece of paper which had weathered the storms of more than twenty Arctic winters. It was with much difficulty that I could open it without tearing it, while all stood around in anxious expectancy, confident that it was an additional record from Captain Crozier, as it was in a tattered and weather-beaten condition.

It, however, proved to be a copy of the Crozier record found by Lieutenant Hobson, of McClintock's expedition, and was in the handwriting of Sir Leopold McClintock. The document was written with a lead pencil on note-paper, and was partially illegible from exposure. It was literally as follows:—

MAY 7, 1859,
Lat. 69 deg. 38 min., long. 98 deg. 41 min. W.

This cairn was found yesterday by a party from Lady Franklin's discovery yacht 'Fox', now wintering in Bellot Strait * * * * * * * * a notice of which the following is * * * removed:—

28ᵀᴴ MAY, 1847.

H. M. ships 'Erebus' and 'Terror' wintered in the ice in lat. 70 deg. 05 min. N., long. 98 deg. 23 min. W., having wintered at Beechy Island, in lat. 74 deg. 43 min. 28 sec. N., long. 91 deg. 39 min. 15 sec. W., after having ascended Wellington Channel to lat. 77 deg., and returned by the west side of Cornwallis Island.

Sir John Franklin commanding the expedition. All well. A

party of two officers and six men left the ships on Monday, the 24th May.

GRAHAM GORE.

CHARLES F. DES V * * *.

* * * * * into a * * * * * printed form, which was a request in six languages, that if picked up it might be forwarded to the British Admiralty.

Round the margin of this paper was:—

THE 25TH APRIL, 1848.

H. M. ships 'Terror' and 'Erebus', were deserted on the 22d April * * opens to the N. N. Wd. of this, having been beset since 12th Sept., 1846. The officers and crews, consisting of 105 souls, under the command of Captain F. M. Crozier, landed here in lat. 69 deg. 37 min. 42 sec. N., long. 98 deg. 41 min. W.

This paper was found by Lieutenant Irving, under the cairn supposed to have been built by Sir James Ross in 1831, four miles to the northward, where it had been deposited by the late Commander Gore in June, 1847. Sir James Ross' pillar has not, however, been found * * the paper has been transferred * * * this position which * * * * * * * * * * * * * * * * was erected.

Sir John Franklin died on the 7th of June, 1847, and the total loss by deaths in the expedition has been * * officers and fifteen men.

F. M. CROZIER, *Captain and Senior Officer.*

JAMES FITZ JAMES, *Captain H. M. S. 'Erebus'.*

And start to-morrow for Back's Fish River.

At this cairn, which we reached * * noon yesterday; the last cairn appear to have made a selection of gear for travelling—leaving all that was superfluous strewn about its vicinity. I re-

119

mained at this spot until nearly noon of to-day, searching for relics, etc. No other papers * * been found.

It is my intention to follow the land to the S. W., in quest of the wreck of a ship said by the Esquimaux to be on the beach. Three other cairns have been found between this and Cape Felix *   *   *   they   contain   no   infor *   *   *   *   * *   *   *   *   *   *   *   *   *   *   *   *   * * * * about it.

WILLIAM R. HOBSON,
Lieut. in charge of party.

This paper is a copy of a record left here by Captain Crozier when retreating with the crews of the 'Erebus' and 'Terror' to the Great Fish River—the information of its discovery by Lieut. W. R. Hobson is intended for me. As the natives appear to have pulled down a cairn erected here in 1831, I purpose burying a record at ten feet true north from the centre of this cairn, and at one foot below the surface.

F. L. McCLINTOCK, *Capt. R. N.*
* * * * * * * * * * *

The asterisks in the foregoing copy indicate illegible words, the paper being much torn and soiled by exposure.

We at once set about digging for the record that Captain McClintock proposed to bury ten feet true north from the centre of the cairn, and a foot below the surface; but though we dug a deep trench four feet wide from the centre of the cairn, due north, for a distance of twenty feet, nothing was found, and the inference is that Captain McClintock either failed to deposit the record, or that changes in the surface of the ground have brought it to light, and it has either been stolen by natives or washed into the sea. Some of the articles found were strewn along the beach for a long distance on either side of the pile of clothing and heavy implements, and were covered up with snow when we first visited the spot. There was a large quantity of cask hoops near by, but no wood. Even the handles of the shovels and pickaxes had been sawed off, probably by the natives who first found the place.

This was evidently the spot where the crews landed when they abandoned the ships, and, as Lieutenant Hobson says, it appears as if they had selected only what was necessary for their sledge journey. It would further appear that when the party reached the southern coast of King William Land after a tedious and wasting journey, and found themselves fast fading away without being able to reach the main-land, a small party was sent back to the ships for provisions. The testimony of the Ookjoolik, who saw the ship that sank off Grant Point, showed that there were some stores on board even then, though only a small quantity. It is probable that Lieutenant Irving was the officer in charge of this return party, and that he died after reaching the camp. It is also probable that these people, who, according to the Ookjoolik testimony, drifted with the ship to the island of Grant Point, were also of this party, and, with the sailors' instinct, preferred to stick to the ship to returning to the already famishing party which they left with scarcely any better prospects on the south coast. The appearance of the boat place on Erebus Bay seems to indicate that it floated ashore after the ice broke up, and had previously been abandoned by those who were able to walk. That skeletons were found in the boat by those who saw it before it was destroyed, and near by by our party, would seem to indicate that the whole party were in a desperate condition at the time, otherwise the helpless ones would not have been abandoned.

Such a state of affairs could scarcely have occurred on their southern trip, and is a strong indication of a return party. Lieutenant Irving's death had not occurred when they first left the vicinity of Cape Jane Franklin, or it would have been mentioned in Captain Crozier's record, which was written the day before they started for Back's River. That the boat on Erebus

Bay drifted in, is evident from its being found just at high-water mark, where the debris are still visible. At the time the party returned under Lieutenant Irving the sleds could not have been dragged along that line, as the snow would have been off the ground just then, and probably was gone when the large party got so far on their way south, as the testimony of the natives who met them in Washington Bay shows that they moved exceedingly slow by. That there were men on the ship that drifted down Victoria Strait is additional reason for believing that they returned, for Captain Crozier in his record accounts for all the survivors being with him. It is possible that those who went out to the ship were caught there by the ice breaking up, and could not rejoin their companions on the shore, if indeed there were any there, which is doubtful, for we saw no skeletons at the camping place except Lieutenant Irving's. The ice broke up in Erebus Bay and Victoria Strait the year we were there on the 24th of July, and it is probable that it was as late in the season when the return party reached the camp near Lieutenant Irving's grave.

We left Irving Bay on the 30th of June, caching all our heavy stuff in order to lighten the sled as much as possible, and reached Cape Felix on the 3d of July, having lain over one day on the north side of Wall Bay. We saw no traces of the Franklin expedition until we arrived at our place of encampment, near Cape Felix. The walking, however, was developing new tortures for us every day. We were either wading through the hill-side torrents or lakes, which, frozen on the bottom, made the footing exceedingly treacherous, or else with seal skin boots, rendered soft by constant wetting, painfully plodding over sharp clay stones, set firmly in the ground, with the edges pointing up, or lying flat and slipping as we stepped upon them and sliding the unwary foot into a crevice that would seemingly wrench it from the body. These are some of the features of a walk on King William Land, and yet we moved about ten miles a day, and made as thorough a search as was possible. All rocky places that looked anything like opened graves or torn-down cairns—in fact, all places where stones of any kind seemed to have been gathered together by human hands—were examined, and by spreading out at such intervals as the nature of the ground indicated, covered the greatest amount of territory. Lieutenant Schwatka carried his double-barrelled shotgun and killed a great many ducks and geese, and I, with my Sharp's rifle, got an occasional reindeer. We were now on a meat diet exclusively, and, as most of it was eaten almost as soon as killed, we all suffered more or less from diarrhoea. Nor did we have any other food until nine months later, when we reached the ship 'George and Mary', at Marble Island, except a few pounds of corn starch, which we had left at Cape Herschel when we started for Cape Felix on the 17th of June. In due course of time, however, we got used to the diet, and experienced no greater inconvenience from it than did our native companions.

Where we encamped, which was about three miles south of Cape Felix, was what appeared to be a torn-down cairn, and a quantity of canvas and coarse red woollen stuff, pieces of blue cloth, broken bottles, and other similar stuff, showing that there had been a permanent camping place here from the vessels, while a piece of an ornamented china tea-cup, and cans of preserved potatoes showed that it was in charge of an officer.

Our flag waved from the highest point of King William Land throughout the day following, which we were altogether too patriotic to forget was Independence Day. After firing a national salute from our rifles and shotguns our day's work was resumed. Henry and Frank were sent to explore the two points further along the coast, while Lieutenant Schwatka and I searched the vicinity of the camp and about a mile inland. It was a dismal, foggy day, but we derived great comfort from occasional glimpses of our country's flag through the lifting fog, the only inspiriting sight in this desolate wilderness—a region that fully illustrates "the abomination of desolation" spoken of by Jeremiah the prophet.

The next day Lieutenant Schwatka went further inland, Frank and Henry down the coast, and I took Toolooah, with the sled, and went around the point toward Cape Sidney, keeping well out on the ice, to see if any cairn might have been erected to attract attention from that direction. On the way we stopped and took down a cairn that I had seen on the day of our arrival. We found nothing in it, though, the earth beneath it being soft, we dug far down in the hope of finding something to account for its existence, as Toolooah believed, though he was not certain, that it was a white man's cairn. I did not go as far as Cape Sidney, which had been my intention, as a thick fog, which came up as we left the cairn, rendered the trip useless for the purpose intended, as we could only get occasional glimpses of the shore, and could not see inland at all.

Lieutenant Schwatka found a well-built cairn or pillar seven feet high, on a high hill about two miles back from the coast, and took it down very carefully without meeting with any record or mark whatever. It was on a very prominent hill, from which could plainly be seen the trend of the coast on both the eastern and western shores, and would most certainly have attracted the attention of any vessels following in the route of the 'Erebus' and 'Terror', though hidden by intervening hills from those walking along the coast. The next day Frank, Toolooah, and I went with Lieutenant Schwatka to take another look in the vicinity of the cairn, and to see if, with a spy-glass, we could discover any other cairn looking from that hill, but without success. It seemed unfortunate that probably the only cairn left standing on King William Land, built by the hands of white men, should have had no record left in it, as there it might have been well preserved. When satisfied that no document had been left there, the inference was that it had been erected in the pursuit of the scientific work of the expedition, or that it had been used in alignment with some other object to watch the drift of the ships. Before leaving we rebuilt the cairn, and deposited in it a record of the work of the Franklin search party to date.

CHAPTER IX

ARCTIC COSTUMES

We left Cape Felix on the 7th of July, reluctantly satisfied that Sir John Franklin had not been buried in that vicinity. The minuteness of our search will appear in the number of exploded percussion caps, shot, and other small articles that were found in various places. The Inuits who were with us evinced a most remarkable interest in our labors, and with their eagle eyes were ever finding things that would have escaped our attention. Everything they did not fully understand they brought to us, and though many of such things were of no account they were not discouraged. Since Toolooah had found the inscription scratched on a clay stone on the monument erected by Captain Hall over the remains near Pfeffer River, he had always been watchful, and often, while away from camp hunting, he has come upon a stone near a demolished cairn, or on some conspicuous place which had marks on that he thought might be writing. These he invariably brought into camp, though often compelled to carry them a long distance, in addition to a load of meat. We always praised his efforts in that line, and were pleased to notice that he did not get discouraged by repeated failures to discover something of interest.

He is as untiring in his efforts to aid us in our search as in securing food, and there is always a degree of intelligence displayed in whatever he undertakes that is wholly foreign to the Inuit character. Even the stones that he brought into camp bore marks that were most astonishingly like writing. You could almost read them. If we had not been so straitened for

125

transportation we would have brought some of these remarkable specimens home.

As far as we had now progressed scarcely anything had given us more trouble than the question of clothing. In countries where tailors and dressmakers are abundant, clothing is a matter of very little labor to the masses—in fact, it simply resolves itself into a question of pecuniary resources. The dwellers in civilized cities can, therefore, scarcely appreciate the toil which all must share to secure the necessary garments to protect those who live in the highest latitudes.

In the fur of the reindeer nature has provided the best possible protection from the cold, with the least amount of weight to the wearer. It might be possible to cover one's self with a sufficient quantity of woollen clothing to guard against the severest weather in the north, but it would require a man of immense muscular power to sustain the load. Two suits of reindeer clothing, weighing in all about five pounds, are quite ample for any season, and are only worn in the coldest weather. At other times one suit is all that is necessary. The inner coat is made of the skin of the reindeer killed in the early summer, when the hair is short and as soft as velvet, and is worn with the hairy side next to the bare skin. It is at first difficult for one to persuade himself that he will be warmer without his woollen undershirts than with them; but he is not long in acquiring the knowledge of this fact from experience. The trousers are made of the same material, as are also the stockings that complete his inner attire, or, so to speak, his suit of underclothing. This inner suit—with the addition of a pair of seal or reindeer skin slippers, with the hair outside, and a pair of seal-skin boots from which the hair has been removed, with soles of walrus or okejook skin, and drawing-strings which fasten them just below the knee—comprises his spring, summer, and fall costume. The boots have also an additional string passing through loops on the side, over the instep and behind the heel, which makes them fit comfortably to the ankle.

In winter seal-skin is entirely discarded by the native Esquimaux as too cold, and boots of reindeer skin, called mit-co-lee-lee', from the leg of the animal, are substituted, and snow-shoes of the same sort of skin, with the hair inside, and a false sole of skin from the face of the buck, with the hair outside, complete the covering of his feet. This hairy sole not only deadens the sound of his footsteps upon the hard snow, but makes his feet much warmer, as it has the same effect as if he were walking upon a carpet of furs instead of upon the naked snow. In cold or windy weather, when out of doors, the native puts on another coat, called a koo'-lee-tar, which is made of skin with heavier fur, from the animal killed in the fall.

The winter skins, with the heaviest and longest fur, are seldom used for clothing if a sufficient supply of the fall and summer skins has been secured. They are principally used for making what might be called the mattress of the bed. Sometimes, however, in the severest weather, a coat made of the heavy skin is worn when the hunter has to sit by a seal's blow-hole for hours at a time, without the least motion, waiting for the animal to come up and blow. In cold weather, when out of doors, he also wears an outside pair of trousers, called see'-ler-par, which are worn with the hair outside (all trousers are called kok'-e-lee, the outside see'-ler-par, and the inside ones e'-loo-par). The inside coat is called an ar-tee'-gee, and is made like a sack, with a tail attached, and a hood which can be pulled up over the head at pleasure. The kok'-e-lee are both made with a drawing-string at the waist, and only reach a short distance below the knee. They are very wide there, so that when the wearer sits down his bare knee is exposed. This is not as disagreeable to the wearer, even in that climate, as one would naturally suppose, but is really more unpleasant for the spectator, for he not only sees the bare knee but the film of dirt that incases it. The coats are very loose also, and expose the bare skin of the stomach when the wearer reaches his hands above his head.

The coats of the women differ from those of the men only

in having a short tail in front, and a much longer one behind. They also have a loose bag on each shoulder, and the hood is much longer than the men wear. The women's outside coats are always made of the short hair, the same as are their ar-tee'-gee. Their trousers reach further below the knee, fit closer to the leg, and are worn with the hairy side out. Women never wear but the one pair in any weather. Their stockings and boots are made with a sort of wing extension at the ankle, and, coming up over the bottom of the trousers, have a long strip, by which they are fastened to the belt that also sustains their trousers at the waist.

To secure the necessary amount of skins for his family taxes the skill of the best hunter, for they must be secured in the summer and fall. Each adult requires six skins for his outfit, besides the number for the bedding. Take, then, an average family of a hunter, two wives and three children, and he must have for the adults eighteen skins, eleven for the children, three for his blanket—one blanket is enough for the entire family to sleep under—and about five for the mattress—a total of thirty-seven skins. This is more than many of them can secure during the short season of good fur; but others may kill many more, now that they are supplied with fire-arms, and those who have a surplus will always supply the actual needs of the more unfortunate; but often much suffering occurs before their wants are met.

When a hunter kills a reindeer, the first thing he does is to skin it; then he eats some of the warm, quivering flesh. This is a very important part of his task. He cuts it open and removes the entrails, and, making a sack of the reticulated stomach, fills it with the blood that is found in the cavity of the body. He then regales himself with some of the spinach-like contents of the paunch, and, by way of filling in the time and the little crinkles in his stomach, cuts off and eats such little portions of fat as are exposed in the process of butchering. He then looks around for a stony place and deposits the carcass conveniently near it, together with the entrails and the bag of blood. Before cutting the body open it is turned back up, and the strip of muscles along each side of the backbone is removed, together with the sinew that covers it. Over this also lies the layer of tallow (tood-noo) when the animal is fat, as is usually the case in the summer and fall. The head is then severed from the body and placed on top of the rest of the meat, so that when the entire mass is covered with about a ton weight of large stones it is considered secure from the ravages of foxes and wolves. Not so, however, from the wolverine and bear—they can open any newly made cache; but after the snows have fallen, and the stones and meat are frozen in one compact mass, it requires the ingenuity of man to remove it. This is done by loosening as large a stone as possible with the foot, and with this stone as a battering-ram another and larger one is loosened, which in turn serves as the battering-ram to loosen the others. Often it is found necessary to use a narrow, wedge-like stone as a lever, or to force the other stones apart. The cache is always made more conspicuous by leaving the antlers to protrude above the stones.

After his meat has been secured and he has refreshed himself with a pipe, the hunter makes a bundle of the skin and the meat attached to the sinew and tallow, and wends his way to his tupic, where his wife or wives await him. His favorite wife takes the meat (oo-le-oo-she-nee) and strips the sinew (oo-le-oo-tic) from it by holding the meat in her teeth while she cuts the sinew from it with her knife, which is shaped like a currier's knife. She then chews off the meat that still adheres to the sinew until it is perfectly clean, and hangs it up to dry, when it is separated into its fibres and becomes thread (ever-loo). In the meantime the other wife, with her teeth, cleans the fleshy side of the skin of the meat and fat that may still adhere to it, and if the sun is still shining stretches the skin upon the ground to dry, holding it in place by small stones placed around the edge. At night the skins are brought into the tent to keep them away from the dogs, and they are again put out in the sun every day until thoroughly dried. They should be dried as soon after killing as possible, in order that they may be in the best condition to preserve the fur.

According to the old traditions and customs—the Mosaic law of the Esquimaux, so to speak—no work of any kind, except the drying of them, can be done upon new skins until the ice has formed sufficiently thickly upon the salt water to permit the hunter to seek the seal at his agloo or blow-hole. Until that time they are put carefully away in the tent, and have to be carried from point to point in their nomadic mode of life, or cached away where they will be presumably secure from the ravages of dogs and wild animals. When the season for making the new clothing arrives, that is, when the winter styles come out, then the work begins. The skins are dressed by the men, because it is hard work and beyond the power of most women, if they are required to be nicely dressed. Only one skin is prepared at a time. There is generally an old man at the head of each family of sons, or sons-in-law, or young men whom he has brought up and taught to hunt. The entire stock of the family is then spread out upon the ground some fine day, without regard to individual claims as having secured them, and are apportioned out by the patriarch—these for this son's outfit, these for his wife and children, those for the other hunter and his family, and these extra fine ones for the patriarch's own use and for his wives.

The clothing for the men must be made first, for they are the lords, and then they need them first as they must go out hunting, and should be made as comfortable as possible. The two skins that are to become his inside coat, and the one for his inner trousers—his dress suit, as it were—are selected, and the women dampen the fleshy side with water that is warmed in their mouths and squirted on the skin, to be spread evenly over the surface with their hands. They are then folded over, with the damp side in, and put aside where they will not freeze until the next day. After arising in the morning, and a breakfast of raw meat, followed by a pipe, he removes his coat, and, with nothing on from his waist up but the usual dirt, he sits upon his bed, and with a bone scraper, called a suk-koo, goes over every particle of the skin upon the fleshy side, breaking it thoroughly and stretching it. Then comes the woman's first part of the work. It is not considered best to dry the skin over a lamp, because it has a tendency to harden it somewhat. It should be dried gradually, and by the heat of the body, so the woman wraps it around the upper part of her body, next to her skin, and sits at work until it is thoroughly dried. One who has never had the experience of exhausting his caloric for the purpose of drying a wet blanket can have but a vague idea of the exquisite torture of sitting in a temperature far below zero with no covering upon his shoulders but a damp reindeer skin. It may not be unhealthy, and perhaps a physician of the water-cure practice might recommend it for certain ailments, but it would never become popular as a pleasurable pastime. At night the other two skins are put in the bed, one beneath and the other over the sleepers, and by morning are dry. But it seems almost a miracle that the occupants escape a severe attack of inflammatory rheumatism. In the morning the man again peels for work, and with a suk-koo of stone, that has a sharp edge, scrapes off every particle of the fleshy membrane until the skin becomes soft and pliant, and assumes a delicate cream-like color.

Only the skins of the does are used for clothing or the sleeping blanket. Buck skins, which are much less pliable compose the underlayers of the bed, and these are not scraped, but merely stretched on a frame while drying. The skin of a young buck is, however, sometimes used for making the trousers, and is nearly as fine in texture as the skin of the doe. The skins are now nearly ready for cutting out and sewing, but first have to be chewed, which is also women's work.

A man can scrape two skins in a day, and some of the women—many of them are, indeed, very skillful with their crude, home-made needles—can make a coat in two days, and a pair of trousers in one day. Some of the young men, whose wives are good tailors, affect considerable ornamentation upon the inside coat; but this is usually seen in the trimming that surrounds the lower edge and the border of the hood. Successive narrow strips of white and black fur, with very short hair, compose this trimming, and the lower edge is finished with fringe made of thin skin, which is quite ornamental in effect. It also aids in keeping out the wind, and is, therefore, useful as well. The outside coat is sometimes surrounded with a border of white fur, with the fringe attached of longer hair than that upon the inner coat. Some of the belles, and indeed some of the women whose beauty is a thing of the past, wear a breastplate of beadwork, which is further decorated with a fringe of reindeer teeth that has a most ghastly effect—they look so much like human teeth. The style of costume differs but little among the various tribes of North America; but in any part of the country the labor of producing the clothing is the same, and if a man would dress well he must work hard—he cannot order his suit from a confiding tailor. It has its advantages and disadvantages. He has no tailor's bills to avoid the payment of, but he must depend upon himself and a loving and skilful wife.

CHAPTER X

OVER MELTING SNOWS

We were now on the march from Cape Felix. Lieutenant Schwatka had kept about a mile east of Frank and Henry, who walked along the coast, and I about a mile and a half east of Lieutenant Schwatka. When about a mile and a half above our old camp at Wall Bay, he found a cairn very similar in construction to the one he found inland from Cape Felix. The top had been taken down, but in the first course of stones, covered and protected by those thrown from the top, he found a piece of paper with a carefully drawn hand upon it, the index finger pointing at the time in a southerly direction. The bottom part of the paper, on which rested the stone that held it in place, had completely rotted off, so that if there had ever been any writing upon it, that, too, had disappeared. He called Frank to his assistance, and they spent several hours in carefully examining the vicinity, without discovering anything else. It would seem, however, that whatever memorandum or guide it was intended for was only temporary, and was probably put there by some surveying or hunting party from the ships.

We encamped on a point below Cape Maria Louisa, after our next march, and after erecting the tent Owanork found a cache on the flats containing a wooden canteen, barrel-shaped, marked on one side

NO. 3,

and on the other,

G. B.,

under the Queen's broad arrow. There were also the staves of another canteen, a small keg, a tin powder can, several red cans marked

GOLDNER'S PATENT,

a narrow-bladed axe, several broken porter and wine bottles stamped

BRISTOL GLASS-WORKS.

and a few barrel staves. The cache was one evidently made by Netchillik Inuits, who had found the things along the coast. In fact, one of those we had interviewed mentioned having cached just such articles somewhere along the coast, and had afterward forgotten the place. This is worthy of consideration, as indicating that our search was sufficiently comprehensive to have discovered anything that had been cached away by the crews of the ships between Cape Felix and Collinson Inlet within five or six miles of the coast.

The following day Lieutenant Schwatka and I took Toolooah with us inland, and sent Frank and Henry down the coast toward Victory Point. From the top of a high hill, about six miles south-east from camp, we had an uninterrupted view for many miles in every direction, and swept the entire field with a spy-glass—but saw nothing like a cache or cairn. It was all a barren waste, with many ponds and lakes, some still covered with ice, and others, being more shallow, were entirely clear, as was the case with most of those near the coast. A few patches of snow could be seen here and there on the hill-sides. We had to cross one deep snowbank before reaching the crest of the hill, and upon our descent came upon a depression in the snow, which Toolooah recognized as a bear's igloo. A few patches of white wool near the entrance confirmed his opinion. I crawled in as far as I could, to see in what sort of a house the polar bear hibernated, and found it very much in size and shape like those of the Inuits. The only difference, as far as I could see, was that this was dug out of a snowbank, instead of being built upon the surface and afterward buried by the drift.

The country over which we travelled this day was like all the rest we had seen in King William Land—broken and jagged clay stone, with intervening marshes. Little patches of brown and green moss, covered with delicate purple flowerets, peep up occasionally from among the piles of dry stones, though there is apparently no vestige of earth or mould to sustain their delicate lives. These flowers appear as soon as the snow melts from off the moss, and are most welcome to the eye of the traveller in this desolate country. How glad we will be to see the grass and trees of the temperate zone once more, after living so long in this void! To-day, for the first, time I saw a few delicate little daisies, and the sight of them carried me in imagination to the woods and fields of New Jersey. I forgot the salt marshes and red "Jersey mud;" but even the marshes there would look like flower-gardens after the clay-stone deserts of King William Land.

We left Irving Bay on the 13th of July, after erecting a monument over the grave of Lieutenant Irving, and marking a stone to indicate the object of the cairn. We also buried a copy of the McClintock-Crozier record, together with the record of our work to date, ten feet north of the cairn, marking the fact on the tombstone. On our way back to Franklin Point we buried the skull found on our way up, but found no further bones until we reached Point Le Vesconte. We saw tenting places, both of white men and natives, at different points along the coast, and one cairn that had been torn down and contained nothing. We found an empty grave on a hill where we encamped, about four miles below this point, and a skull about a quarter of a mile distant from it, evidently having been dragged there by wild beasts.

135

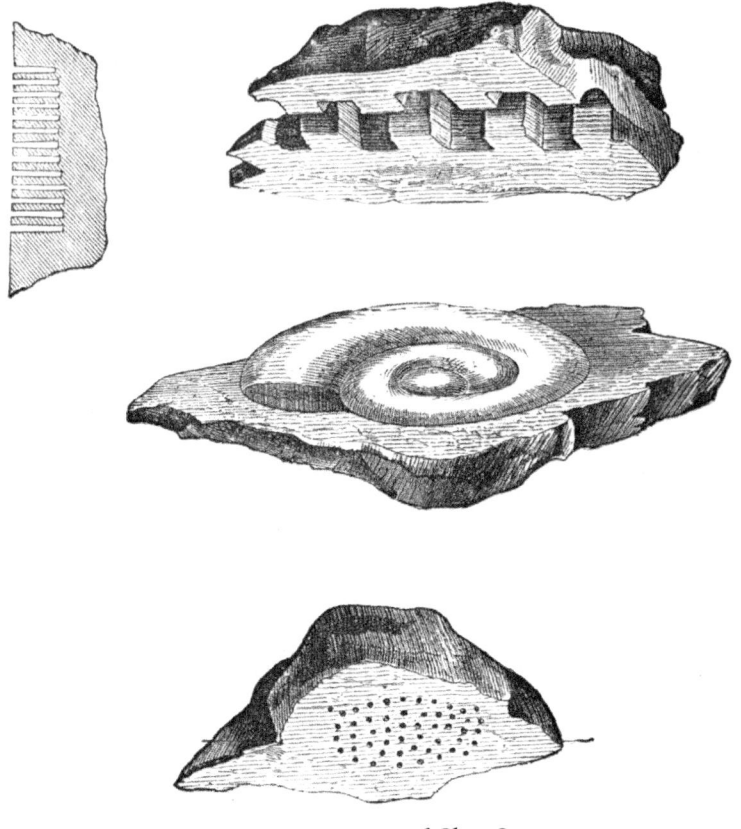

Curious Formation of Clay-Stone.

The only things found in the tomb were a large brass buckle and a percussion cap. Near by were traces of native tenting places. In fact, wherever we found graves we always found evidences that natives had encamped in the vicinity, like vultures.

From this camp we marched, to our first camping place on Erebus Bay, and from there had the most dismal day's work of the entire journey. In order to pass Erebus Bay on the land, we had to go a long distance inland to find a place where we could ford a wide and deep river that empties into it. Throughout the entire length of the river, on both sides, we had to wade through deep marshes, and at last crossed it through a swift current, the water reaching to our waists. A dense fog obscured the sun and hid the bay from view. It was impossible to ascertain our direction, and we were compelled to follow all the windings of the river and coast until the fog lifted. In the meantime we had no idea where the sled was, and as Toolooah had been told that we would make our usual ten miles' march, he might have gone that far before looking for us, and we have still a tedious tramp before us after reaching the bay. At last we heard the dogs, and finally saw the sled, still at a great distance on the ice. The gale that had been blowing all day long, and driving the damp, cold mist into our faces, making it intensely cold and disagreeable, had subsided, and we signalled Toolooah to join us.

Clay-Stone Mounds.

It was a joyful sight to see the sled once more alongside the shore, for, few as were the comforts it contained, it was our only home, and it meant the shelter and rest of our sleeping bags. We ate our dinner a little after midnight, and soon forgot our troubles in sleep. While Henry was cooking the last of our meat, he had occasion to leave the fire a few moments, when the dogs, seeing an opportunity for a raid, broke from their fastenings and poured down upon the culinary department like an army of devouring fiends. We were all in bed at the time except Henry; but Toolooah, well knowing the state of our larder, slipped out under the end of the tent, stark naked, from his sleeping bag, and poured such a shower of stones upon the dogs as to send them away howling. Fortunately they got nothing but some blubber, of which we have a good supply, and which is chiefly used to hasten the fire.

The next day the fog and gale recommenced with great fury; but as we were entirely without food, Toolooah went hunting, and came in about half-past nine in the evening with parts of three reindeer that he had succeeded in killing; so we had a good warm meal about midnight, and turned in out of the bitter cold. Though not in exactly the position to be epicurean in our tastes, we could not fail to remark with great satisfaction that the reindeer were getting fat, and the quality of the meat improving thereby. A little later in the season they were exceedingly fat, the tallow, or tud-noo, as the Inuits call it, lying in great flakes, from half an inch to two and a half inches thick, along the back and over the rump. This tallow has a most delicious flavor, and is eaten with the meat, either cooked or raw. The intestines are also incased in lace-work of tallow, which constitutes a palatable dish. Indeed there is no part of any animal used for food but what is eaten by the Esquimaux, and which we have partaken of with great relish. The ribs of fat reindeer are also an especial delicacy. A dish made of the contents of the paunch, mixed with seal oil, looks like ice-cream, and is the Esquimau substitute for that confection. It has none of the flavor, however, of ice-cream, but, as Lieutenant Schwatka says, may be more likened to "locust sawdust and wild honey." The first time I partook of this dainty

I had unfortunately seen it in course of preparation, which somewhat marred the relish with which I might otherwise have eaten it. The confectioner was a toothless old hag, who mixed the ingredients in a wooden dish dirtier than anything I ever saw before, and filled with reindeer hairs, which, however, were not conspicuous when well mingled with the half-churned grass and moss. She extracted the oil from the blubber by crunching it between her old gums, and spat it into the dish, stirring it with her fingers until the entire mass became white, and of about the consistency of cottage cheese. I ate some, merely to say I had eaten it, and not to offend my entertainers, but I cannot say I enjoyed it.

We left camp at a quarter past one o'clock the following day, our starting having to conform somewhat to the state of the tide, as at high tide we cannot reach the ice. The sledging was simply awful, and poor Toolooah was having a hard time of it and without a murmur or discontented look. I expected he would urge us to abridge our search, as there seemed to be imminent danger of the ice breaking up. But he constantly told us to go on and search as much as we thought necessary, and leave the sledging to him; he would do the best he could. It was a pleasure to see him do it so cheerfully. There is something reassuring even in the tone in which he addresses the dogs. Many a time we have started to go through a place that seemed absolutely impassable until I heard that cheery cry, "Why-ah-woo-ha-hu-ah!" and saw him bend his own shoulder to the task. It seemed all right then. Even the dogs were more hopeful, and pulled with renewed energy.

We found the coast on the south side of Erebus Bay cut into long, narrow points, separated by deep inlets, that made the work of searching much greater. All along the shore at the bottom of the inlets, we found pieces of navy blue cloth, which seemed to have been washed up by high tides. Quantities of driftwood also were seen; but we already had as much on the sled as, in the present condition of the ice, we could carry. At the bottom of one of the deepest inlets or bays, the men found the wreck of a ship's boat strewn along the beach, together with pieces of cloth, iron, canvas, and human bones. We gathered together portions of four skeletons, a number of buttons, some fish lines, copper and iron bolts and rivets, the drag rope of a sled, some sheet-lead, some shot, bullets, and wire cartridges, pieces of clothing, broken medicine bottles, the charger of a powder-flask, an iron lantern, and a quantity of miscellaneous articles that would naturally form part of the outfit of such an expedition. The bones were prepared for burial, and the relics gathered together in a pile, from which to select a few to take away with us. The prow and stern-post of the boat were in good condition, and a few clinkered boards still hung together, which measured twenty-eight feet and six inches to where they were broken off at each end, showing it to have been a very large boat.

We spent several hours here, gathering together the various articles, in a thick fog and strong north-west wind that came down across the heavy ice-fields of Victoria Strait and Melville Sound, and was intensely cold. We then went to the next point south of us at eleven o'clock, and for four long weary hours walked up and down waiting for the sled to come up, while new ice was rapidly forming in the margin of the salt water as the tide went down. When Toolooah at last arrived, we found he had been compelled to abandon the stoves and firewood as it was impossible to handle so heavy a sled during the present wretched condition of the ice. It was after four o'clock when we got to bed, our blankets and sleeping bags all wet, as it was impossible to keep them out of the water that everywhere covers the ice.

The next day we remained in camp to bury the remains found at the boat place, and during the evening I went hunting with Toolooah, who killed two fine bucks. We got back to camp, tired and sleepy, at half-past two in the morning The sky was clear and the sunset supreme. It was nothing unusual for one from the temperate zone to see a magnificent sunset, but to see a grand combination of sunset and sunrise in one continuous representation was glorious beyond description. The next day Toolooah returned to the island off the mouth of the little bay, and brought on the things he had abandoned there; while we searched the vicinity with the hope of finding the second boat place, which the natives mentioned as being about a quarter of a mile from the one seen by McClintock. If this is the boat seen by him, it is certainly a long way from the position represented on the maps. We found no trace of a second boat place anywhere in the neighborhood, though we made an extensive search for it. We found a deep inlet entering near Point Little, too wide and deep to cross.

At a quarter past five the next morning, Lieutenant Schwatka and I started on our search along the coast, leaving the men to assist Toolooah in loading the sled and making a selection of what to abandon, if anything had to be left, and to follow later. We had not got more than a mile on our way when we heard a gun fired from camp, and, turning around, saw Frank running after us. We waited for him, and were surprised to hear that the tide, instead of falling, was actually rising, and that it would be impossible to load the sled. We therefore had to return to camp. In the meantime it commenced raining, and when we reached the tent we found the water nearly up to the door, though it was the hour for low tide. About two hours afterward Lieutenant Schwatka went outside the hut, and almost immediately called for his glasses, saying he thought the ice was breaking up. We all went out and saw the ice coming in from the Straits, and piling up in great masses. Already the sled was crowded high up in the air, and one of the stoves occupied a lofty position poised on the pinnacle of a hummock Toolooah at once got upon a loose cake of ice, and pulled himself out to the edge of the floe and brought the sled and stove down to where, when the ice came in closer, they could be pulled ashore, and were thus rescued from then imminent peril.

The Breaking up of the Ice.

It was now quite evident that our sledging was over for the season, and we were stuck here with all our heavy stuff. All day long we could hear the booming of the ice in the distance, as the great fields were torn asunder, and we felt thankful that Toolooah had not already got started when the break came, or he would have been in great danger. At any rate we might have lost our sled, together with the dogs and all our baggage, which would have been a sad affair for us. We determined to cross the land to Terror Bay, and from there send down to Gladman Point, or that vicinity, all that the dogs and men could carry, while Lieutenant Schwatka and I waited for their return, and in the meantime searched the coast back from Terror Bay to the inlet near Point Little.

Terror Bay was reached on the 3d of August, after a tedious journey across the narrow neck of land that separates it from Erebus Bay. Our camps were not far apart, as everything had to be carried upon our backs or upon the dogs. It was necessary to make two, and often three, trips between camps before everything was brought up, consequently only two of the Franklin stoves were brought along. The largest and heaviest of these Henry took in charge, and carried all the way overstrapped to his back like a knapsack. Toolooah brought the empty sled over, with all the dogs after removing the bone shoes from the runners.

The March Southward.

While at our first camp overland, Toolooah had returned to the coast with the dogs to bring up some firewood, and, not expecting to see any reindeer, had left his gun in camp. But near the coast he came upon a she-bear with her half-grown cub.

Nothing daunted, he drove the old bear off into the sea with stones, and killed the cub with a handleless snow-knife. Henry and Frank, with all the Inuits, left us on the 6th of August to reach the rest of our party, whom they expected to find somewhere east of Gladman point. Frank and Henry remained there and Toolooah returned with the dogs, and moved what we could to the same point.

Lieutenant Schwatka and I were then left alone to provide for ourselves until Toolooah's return, which was on the 1st of September. We kept half of the double tent, and one of the dogs to help us when we moved camp, and to carry our meat. Reindeer were plentiful, and we killed eight, which kept us well supplied with food. We could have killed many more had it been necessary. This was altogether the pleasantest part of our experience in the Arctic. During the time we were alone we searched the neighboring coast as far west as Cape Crozier, but found only one skeleton. The tent place spoken of by Ahlangyah and others—and which we confidently expected to find without much trouble, marked by quantities of human bones and clothing scattered far around, as at the company places at Irving Bay and Cape Felix, and the boat place on Erebus Bay—could not be found, though Lieutenant Schwatka passed over the spot that the natives spoke of as the site. This was a great disappointment to us, and seemed unaccountable until we subsequently learned from them that it was so close to the water that all traces of it had disappeared. When we again met the natives we saw one man who had been there not a great while ago, and said there was nothing to be seen where he previously saw many skeletons and other indications of the white men's hospital tent.

In the division of labor at our lonely camps the searching devolved chiefly upon Lieutenant Schwatka and the cooking and hunting upon me, though he also killed several reindeer, and I occasionally assisted in the searching. Our diet was exclusively reindeer meat, eaten either raw or cooked, and, as the animals were very fat, there was nothing to complain of in that respect.

The quantity that we ate was simply astonishing; in fact, we found it easier to adapt ourselves to that phase of Inuit life than any other.

Our greatest discomfort arose from the lack of sufficient shoes and stockings. It requires women always to keep you comfortable in that respect. Natives never go anywhere without their women. Our shoes were completely worn, beyond possibility of repair, and the hair was entirely worn off our stockings. The consequence was that walking was torture. I could generally manage to patch up my shoes so that I could start out hunting when necessary, well knowing they would last only for a short distance, but trusting to my ambition in the chase to keep me going, and the necessity of the case to get me back to the tent.

Most of the time we were confined to the tent by storms and fog, and only a few days were fit for the prosecution of our work. Unfortunately, the only thermometer we brought from Cape Herschel was lost, with other articles, from the sled in an ice crack near Wall Bay, while on our trip to Cape Felix, so we could keep no record of the temperature. I noticed, however, that there was scarcely a night when there was not a thin sheet of ice formed near the margin of the ponds. On the night of the 28th it froze to the depth of about three-quarters of an inch, and the next night about an inch and a half. It was sufficiently cold at any time, when the wind blew, to remind us that we were in the frigid zone. Our experience at this place was of interest in showing that white men can take care of themselves in this country, independently of the natives; but at the same time the presence and assistance of natives add much to the traveller's comfort.

Several days before Toolooah's return we were anxiously looking for him, as he was to bring in shoes and stockings, and the time was rapidly passing in which we could complete our search. We had already finished what was required toward the west, and as far east as was feasible from this camp. We had therefore made up our minds to move slowly eastward on the

1st of September, if he did not get back on the last day of August. A fierce gale, with snow, kept us in camp on that day; but the returning party, consisting of Toolooah's family with Equeesik, Mitcolelee and Frank, came in notwithstanding the storm, so great was their anxiety concerning our safety and comfort. It is needless to say that we were glad to see them, and when we heard Toolooah shout from the other side of the hill on which our tent was pitched, it seemed the pleasantest sound I ever heard. The Inuits had never known white men to live alone in their country as we had, and were afraid we were very hungry; but we relieved their anxiety in that respect by giving them a hearty meal of cooked meat.

We learned from them that the Inuits were all on the mainland, in the neighborhood of Thunder Cove, and that Joe had been, and still was, very sick with rheumatism. Henry remained there with them, and prosecuted the search of Starvation Cove, building a monument over the remains found there, and depositing a record that Lieutenant Schwatka had sent to him for that purpose. Before he got there, however, Joe and a party of Netchilliks had been searching the spot, and in a pile of stones found a small pewter medal, commemorative of the launch of the steamer 'Great Britain', in 1843, and among the seaweed some pieces of blanket and a skull. This was all that could be seen at this memorable spot.

CHAPTER XI

AMATEUR ESQUIMAUX

The prosecution of our search had been largely dependent upon our imitation of the life of the Esquimaux, and I should omit an important chapter in "Arcticology" if I did not leave on record the story of our exploits as amateur Esquimaux in subsisting upon the resources of the country through which our little exploring party passed, going and coming, in pursuit of its chief object. The seal was our beef and the walrus our mutton in this long journey.

Seal-hunting varies with the time of the year and the nature of the ice, for the seals are seldom killed except upon or through the ice. In the warm, still days of spring they come up through their blow-holes in the ice and enjoy a roll in the snow or a quiet nap in the sun. Then they are killed with comparative case. The hunter gets as close as possible upon the smooth ice without alarming his prey, the distance varying from four hundred to one hundred yards. He then lies down, or, more correctly speaking, reclines upon a small piece of bear-skin, which, as he moves, is dragged along and kept under him as protection against the cold and wet. His weight rests chiefly on his left hip, the knee bent and the leg drawn up beneath him upon the bear-skin mat. As long as the seal is looking toward him the hunter keeps perfectly still, or raising his head soon drops it upon his shoulder, uttering a noise similar to that produced by a seal blowing.

When the seal is satisfied, from a careful inspection, that no danger threatens, its head drops down upon the ice and it indulges in a few winks, but suddenly rises and gazes around if it hears the least noise or sees the least motion anywhere. The hunter takes advantage of the nap to hitch himself along by means of his right foot and left hand, preserving his recumbent position all the time, and if detected by the seal either stops suddenly and blows, or flops around like a seal enjoying a sun bath, as his experience suggests. In this way he can usually approach near enough to shoot his prey with a rifle, or strike it with a seal spear or oo-nar. Often, however, just as he is about to shoot or spear his game, it slips suddenly into the sea through its hole, upon the very verge of which it rests, seldom venturing further than a foot or two from its safe retreat. If they could only rest contented with a fair shot, the Inuits would probably secure more game than they now do, for the most of those I have seen them lose in this way went down after the hunter had approached within easy range—say twelve or fifteen yards. They are so anxious, however, to make a sure thing of it that they often try to get too near. I have frequently timed an Inuit as he started for a seal on the ice, and found it takes about an hour from the time he starts in pursuit until the shot is fired. It is amusing to watch the countenance of the seal through a spyglass. They have such an intelligent and human look that you can almost imagine what they are thinking. For instance, you will see one start up suddenly and look at the hunter, who by that time is perfectly still, with an intense scrutiny that seems to say, "I declare I was almost sure I saw that move that time, but I must have been mistaken." Then, with a drowsy look, almost a yawn, down goes his head, and the hunter begins to hitch himself along again very cautiously. Suddenly up goes the seal's head so quickly that the hunter hasn't time to subside as before, but begins to roll about, blow off steam, and lift its feet around like a seal flapping its tail, and at a little distance it is really difficult to tell which is the seal and which the man. Then you imagine a smile on the face of the seal, as though he was saying to himself, "I caught him that time. What a fool I was to be frightened, though. I thought it was a man, and it's only an ookjook."

When the hunter at last reaches the point at which he considers it safe to risk a shot, you hear the report of his gun and see him immediately spring to his feet and rush for his prey. If his bullet strikes the head or neck of the animal it rarely gets away, though sometimes even then it slips out of reach, so close do they keep to their holes. If it is hit anywhere else it almost invariably escapes the hunter, though it may not escape death. Often the hunter reaches the hole in time to seize his prey by the hind flipper just as it is passing down into the water. I remember standing and gazing mournfully down into a hole one day through which a seal that I had shot had just escaped, though his blood tinged the water and edges of the ice, and while I was lamenting my ill-luck I heard a splash behind me and turned in time to see the seal come up through another hole. He looked awfully sick, and didn't see me until I had him by the flipper, sprawling on his back, at a safe distance from the hole. This was quite good luck for me, for such an opportunity rarely occurs, though I have occasionally known Toolooah to recover a lost one in the same way.

When struck with a spear they seldom escape, for the line is fastened to the side of the spear-head, which detaches itself from the staff and holds in the flesh like a harpoon. Sometimes, however, the seal will slip away after the spear is thrown, and, instead of striking him, it strikes the ice where he had been lying. This is very aggravating after the cold and tedious labor of working up upon it has been accomplished; but the Esquimau bears his misfortune with equanimity. It is seldom that he says more than "ma-muk'-poo now" (no good), or "mar-me an'-ner" (which means "angry," or is an expression used when one is angry). He gathers up his weapons, sits down and lights his pipe, and after a recuperative smoke moves on in search of another opportunity to go through the same process.

Sometimes he is fortunate enough to find a seal absolutely

asleep upon the ice, and then he can walk right up alongside of him and put the rifle barrel to his ear before firing. In some parts of the Arctic, as at Iwillik (Repulse Bay), there is a species called "wandering seal," which in the spring are known to come upon the ice in great numbers, usually through a huge crack, and move quite a distance from the open water. This affords the natives a grand opportunity, and the entire village—men, women and children—repair to the spot, and by getting between the seals and the water, cut off their escape, so that they fall an easy prey to the clubs with which they are slaughtered by the men. In this way they sometimes kill as many as seventy-five or a hundred in a single day. But the haunts of the "wandering seal" are not found everywhere; they are favored localities. It is generally pretty hard work to kill a seal.

During the winter months the seals do not come out upon the ice, and are then hunted usually with dogs that are trained for the purpose. The hunter, equipped with his spear-shaft in his hand, and his line, with the barbed spear-head attached, thrown over his shoulder, starts out, leading his dog, whose harness is on and the trace wound several times around his neck, so that but a yard or two is left to trail along the snow. When they reach the wide stretch of smooth ice that usually lines the shore in these regions, the dog is allowed to work to windward, and when his sensitive nostrils are saluted with the scent of a seal he indicates the fact by the excited manner in which he endeavors to reach the spot from which the odor emanates. The hunter restrains the dog's ardor, but follows his guidance until the spot is found at which the seal's blow-hole is situated. Often it is entirely covered with snow, but sometimes a small hole about an inch in diameter is seen. The blow-hole is a spot to which the seal resorts to get an occasional puff of fresh air, and here the hunter awaits him in order to secure him for the larder. When first found, the hunter merely marks the spot for a future visit by building around it a wall of snow blocks to cut off the wind, and making a seat of similar material upon which to rest while waiting for the blow. This is the tedious proceeding in the life of an Esquimau, or at least would be for a civilized person so situated. Sometimes the seal comes up within half an hour or an hour, but often the hunter stands or sits by the hole all night long, and sometimes for a day or two. I have heard of instances in which they sat for two days and a half waiting for the seal to put in an appearance. In fact, Papa told me that he once sat for three days at one seal hole, and then it did not come up. During all this time the hunter must keep perfectly still—that is, he must not walk around or move his feet off the ice. He can move his body to keep up a circulation of the blood, or move his feet inside his stockings if they are sufficiently loose to allow of such motion, but no noise must occur which would alarm the game if in the vicinity of the hunter.

Some funny incidents occur at these prolonged sittings. I remember one experienced old seal-hunter who told me that when he was a young man he was once out all night watching a blow-hole and got very sleepy—so sleepy, indeed, that he could not keep his eyes open. After vainly endeavoring to arouse himself, he finally succumbed, and, falling asleep, tumbled over backward and wandered in the land of dreams. Suddenly awakening he saw what he supposed to be a man with hostile intentions standing and looking down upon him through the dim starlight. Every time he moved in the least, in order to get up, the strange man moved in a threatening sort of way, and he had to lie still again. At last, after getting thoroughly awakened, he discovered what he had taken for an enemy, and had caused him such alarm, was only his own leg sticking up in the air and resting against the snow-block seat from which he had tumbled when he fell asleep. Another hunter was overcome by sleep at a seal hole, and awakened by the consciousness of danger, saw a great white bear watching the hole, which in his sleepiness he had neglected. The hunter had fallen behind his snow seat in such a way as to be concealed from the bear, which had been attracted by the scent of the seal and arrived just at the moment when the young man awoke. To jump to his feet and fly from the vicinity of danger was, with the frightened Esquimau, the work of a minute, and so startled the bear that it also made off in the opposite direction as fast as feet would carry it.

When the seal comes up to breathe it stays about ten minutes, which gives the hunter plenty of time to get his spear and line ready. He then must take accurate aim and make a vigorous thrust through the little hole, withdrawing the spear quickly and holding the line tightly, so as to exhaust the game as much as possible before the line is all run out. The end is wound tightly around his right arm, and he sits down, bracing himself to resist the struggles of the animal to free itself. It usually makes three desperate efforts to escape, and then the hunter begins to haul in on his line, and, breaking away the snow around the hole, to admit of the passage of the body, lands his prey on the ice.

The next operation at this stage of the proceedings is to make a slit in the stomach of the sometimes still breathing animal, and to cut off some of the warm liver (ting'-yer), with a slice or two of blubber (oks-zook), wherewith the hunter regales himself with a hearty luncheon. Then the entrails are drawn out and passed through the fingers of the left hand to remove the contents, and are afterward braided and returned to the cavity of the stomach, and the slit drawn together and pinned with a little ivory pin (too-bit-tow'-yer) made for the purpose. The dog is allowed to lick the blood from the snow, but gets no more for his share unless an opportunity occurs to help himself when his master's back is turned. The trace is then attached to the nose of the dead seal, which is thus dragged into camp by the faithful dog, the hunter walking alongside urging the dog by his voice, and occasionally assisting him over a drift or amid hummocky ice.

The seal in the early spring builds a habitation in the snow over and around the hole through which it breathes, and here its young are born and live until old enough to venture into the water. This house is called an oglow, and is constructed very much like an Esquimau igloo in shape, though it is more irregular and has ramifications that extend to neighboring holes. These oglows are found with the assistance of dogs, as previously described, or by prodding with a seal spear the hillocks of snow that look like seals' houses. When a hunter finds an oglow during the season that the young seals are living in them, he immediately breaks in the roof with his heel in search of the little one, which usually remains very quiet even when the hunter looks down and pokes his head through the broken roof. The young seal is then easily killed with the spear and dragged out on the ice, and the hunter waits for the mother, which is never absent a long time from its baby. The young seal is generally cut open as soon as killed, and its little stomach examined for milk, which is esteemed a great luxury by the Esquimaux. When young, the seal is covered with long, white hair, very much like coarse wool. This skin was at one time very much used in making clothing, but lately has not been much in vogue among the natives, though occasionally coats and trousers of this material may still be seen. The whalers esteem it highly as an adjunct to woollen clothing, as being sufficiently warm for those who are living on shipboard, yet not so warm as reindeer clothing, which becomes oppressive in high temperature.

The older seals have short, smooth hair, of a yellowish-gray color, with large black spots on the back, which become smaller and less frequent on the sides, and disappear entirely before reaching the belly. The finest quality of seal-skin in the eastern North American waters, which are devoid of fur seal, is that of the kos-se-gear, or fresh-water seal, which is found at or near the mouths of nearly all rivers emptying into the sea. This species of seal is marked very much like the common seal (net-chuk), except that the spots are of a more positive and a glossier black, while the body color is whiter, making a more decided contrast. The hair is also of a much finer texture, and is as soft as the finest quality of velvet. These are only killed in the early summer, and their skins are extensively used for summer clothing by those Esquimaux who have not come much in contact with the whalers. When they have been in communication with the ships, they are usually, during the summer months, clad in cast-off clothing of the sailors—that is, the men are. And funny enough they look, with the curious methods they have of wearing civilized costumes. They always choose a shirt for the exterior garment, and wear it with the tail outside. The women seldom are seen with any civilized clothing, the only exception being, probably, a few of the natives of Cumberland Sound and Akkolead, near North Bay. The finest quality of kossegear skins I have seen were killed in Hudson's Strait. They are much superior in texture and color to those of the tributaries to Hudson's Bay. The next skin in quality is that of the ki-od-del-lik, or "jumping" seal, or, as it is sometimes called, "spotted" seal. This is very similar in color and texture to the fresh-water seal, except that the black in the back and sides is in great splotches that are odd, but very pretty in effect. Kioddelliks are seen in great numbers in Hudson's Bay and Strait, but are not often killed, as they generally keep pretty well out from shore. They are often seen by the whalers, playing like a school of porpoises, whose actions they simulate somewhat, except that they make a clean breach from the water every time they jump.

The nets-che-wuk, "bladder-nosed" seal, has a skin which is a grade or two superior to the netchuk, and is much larger. It, however, lacks the fineness and gloss of the kossegear and kioddellik.

The largest of the seal species is the ookjook. Its skin is thick and coarse, with coarse, short hair. It is not used in the manufacture of clothing, except for the soles of rum-nigs (boots). It is, however, employed to make walrus and seal lines, lashings for their sleds, and traces for dog harness. It is as much used for this purpose as is the skin of the walrus, which it much resembles. In making lines from ookjook or walrus skin, a piece is cut from the neck or body by making cross sections—that is, without slitting it down the belly, the piece for the line being removed from the body in a broad band. The blubber is then cut from the fleshy side, and the skin is soaked for a short time in hot water, after which the hair is readily removed with an ood-loo, the semicircular knife that is the one constant and only tool of the Esquimau woman. A line is then made by cutting this piece of skin into one continuous strip, half an inch wide, by following around and around the band. The line is then about twenty-five yards long, and while still green is stretched between two large rocks, where it is submitted to the greatest tension that the limited mechanical appliances of these savages can supply. While so situated the line is carefully trimmed with a sharp knife to remove all fatty particles, and to partially round off the sharp edges.

It is then allowed to remain until thoroughly dry, when it is taken from the stretcher and coiled up in the owner's tent until he has leisure to finish it and render it pliable. This is accomplished by the slow and tedious process of chewing. Traces and lines for the seal spears are usually made of seal skin, and in the same way as walrus and ookjook lines. They also require chewing before being sufficiently pliable for use. Indeed, all skins require to be chewed before they are made into clothing. The men chew their lines, but all other skins are chewed by the women and young girls. It is one circumstance that is early remarked by the visitor in the Arctic regions, that the middle-aged and old people have teeth that are worn down to mere stubs by the constant chewing of skins. A pair of ookjook soles, before being submitted to the chewing process, are nearly as thick and much stiffer than the sole-leather of civilized commerce, and it requires the leisure hours of two days to reduce them to the necessary pliability for use. It is not only the action of the grinders that brings them to the proper state, but the warm breath and saliva play an effectual part in the process. This is usually their visiting work. When they go to each other's tupics or igloos to make calls, instead of taking their knitting, the belles of the polar circle take their chewing. It does not add much to the charms of female society to see them sitting before you gnawing and sucking a pair of ookjook soles, or twisting an entire seal-skin into a roll, one end of which is thrust into a capacious mouth to undergo the masticating and lubricating process. But it does increase your respect for them to see with what cheerfulness these women apply themselves to their exceedingly disagreeable labor.

Seal-skins for making coats and trousers are dressed with the hair on, the fleshy membranes, or "mum'-me," being cut off with an oodloo before they are washed, stretched, and dried. One good warm spring day is sufficient to dry a seal-skin, which for this purpose is stretched over the ground or snow by means of long wooden pins, which keep it elevated two or three inches, thus allowing the air to circulate underneath it. Sometimes in the early spring, before the sun attains sufficient power, a few skins for immediate use are dried over the lamps in the igloos. This, however, is regarded as a slow and troublesome process, and the open air is preferred when available. A few seal-skins and walrus skins, from which the hair has been neatly removed, are left to hang in the wind and sun for several days, until they acquire a creamy whiteness, and are then used for trimming. The Kinnepatoos, who are the dandies of the Esquimau nation, tan nearly all their skins white. Their walrus and seal lines, and indeed their sled lashings and dog harness, are sometimes white, as well as the trimmings of their boots and gloves. Nearly all the varieties of seal are sometimes killed during the summer and fall, while swimming in the open water; but though often seen when the weather is calm, the Esquimaux seldom fire at them, because until the latter part of September they will sink to the bottom, though killed instantly by a shot through the head or neck.

At a later period a funny incident occurred. We were at Marble Island. The weather was calm, so that seal heads were sprinkled plentifully upon the surface of the water. This inspired Lieutenant Schwatka to try his skill. So, fetching his rifle from the cabin and wiping his eye-glasses, he shot at a large head about a hundred yards from the vessel. The seal made a desperate effort to get down in a hurry, but was evidently badly hurt, and showed a good deal of blood before it accomplished its descent. Presently it came up again, and a boat was lowered to pick it up, but it managed to escape capture, though it was evident that it would soon die. After breakfast the next morning, when we went on deck, the water was still quite smooth, and presently we were surprised to see what appeared to be a dead seal floating in on the tide. There was no doubt that this was the seal that Lieutenant Schwatka had killed the previous night, and again the boat was lowered to secure it. No precautions were deemed necessary to avoid making a noise, and when the boat came alongside one of the men threw down his oar, rolled up his sleeves, and stooped down to lift the carcass on board. His surprise may be imagined when, after passing his arms around it and proceeding to lift it, he felt it suddenly begin to struggle and slip from his hold and dive below the surface, while a loud shout went up from the spectators. It was not Lieutenant Schwatka's seal, but an entirely well one that was sound asleep when it felt the rude embrace of the sailor.

The seal is an exceedingly useful animal to the Esquimau, for it not only supplies him with food and clothing, but its blubber furnishes the fuel for cooking its flesh, lighting the igloo, and drying its skin before making into clothing. The skin also is made into dog harness and traces, whip lashes, boots and shoes, gun-covers, water-pails, bags for the storing of oil and blubber, and his boats are covered with it. Seal-skin bags, inflated and fastened to walrus lines, are used in hunting walrus and whales, and finally, the summer dwelling of the Esquimau is a tent made of seal-skin. A single tent, or tupic, as it is called by them, is composed of from five to ten skins, which are split—that is, the mumme is split off and dried separately from the skin. The rear portion of the tent is made of the skins with the hairy side out, while the front is made of the transparent mumme, which admits the light almost as freely as if made of ground glass. The skin portion is impervious to water, but the mumme admits the rain about as readily as it does the sunlight. This is no objection, in the mind of the Esquimau, for it is something he is thoroughly accustomed to. In the summer his tent is wet with rain, and in the winter, whenever the air in the igloo is raised to an endurable temperature, the roof melts and is constantly dripping ice-water down his back or upon his blankets.

CHAPTER XII

WALRUS DIET

The staple food of the Esquimaux of North Hudson's Bay and Melville Peninsula is "ivick" (walrus). The season for killing the walrus lasts nearly all the year—that is, all the time when the natives are not inland hunting reindeer, in order to secure sufficient skins to make their winter clothing and sleeping blankets. The Kinnepatoos, who inhabit the shore of Hudson's Bay in the vicinity of Chesterfield Inlet and its tributaries, are the only tribe I know of who live almost exclusively upon the reindeer. Indeed, they only kill a sufficient number of walrus and seal to provide them with shoes and gloves for summer wear. The Netchillik and Ookjoolik tribes live mostly by sealing, and as they are not provided with fire-arms, find it almost impossible to kill reindeer when the snow is on the ground. The Ooquesiksillik people, who live on Back's Great Fish River and its tributary, Hayes River, live almost exclusively on fish. The Iwillik tribe, that inhabits the coast of Hudson's Bay from near the mouth of Chesterfield Inlet to Repulse Bay, the Igloolik, Amitigoke, Sekoselar, Akkolear, and, indeed, all the various tribes along the northern shore of Hudson's Strait, Fox Channel, and Southampton Island, rely chiefly upon walrus meat for their food. The walrus is one of the largest animals that inhabits these waters, and when one is killed it supplies a quantity of food. An average-sized walrus weighs about a thousand or twelve hundred pounds, and when it is remembered that every particle is eaten except the hardest bones, the reader will see that it is a valuable prize for the captors. The blood, blubber, intestines,

159

even the hide, the undigested contents of the stomach, and the softer bones, as well as the oesophagus and windpipe, are all eaten, raw or cooked. If my experience might be mentioned, I would say that all of these enumerated delicacies I have eaten and relished. Walruses are usually found resting upon the ice near the edge of the floe or the shore piece, unless there is much loose ice near it, in which case they will most always be found on the larger cakes of loose ice.

There they are hunted in boats, or when the wind is from such a direction as to keep the pack on to the floe they can be successfully hunted on foot. The method of hunting is precisely the same as that already described in reference to hunting seal, except that the spear is generally used in preference to the rifle to secure the walrus, and the rifle is preferred to the spear in seal-hunting. Usually there are two hunters who approach the walrus, one hiding behind the other, so that the two appear but as one. When the spear is thrown, both hold on to the line, which is wound around their arms so as to cause as much friction as possible, in order to exhaust the animal speedily. The spear-head is of walrus tusk, and is about three inches long and three-quarters of an inch thick, with an iron barb that is kept very sharp. The line is attached to the middle of the spear-head, the near end being slanted, so that when the line is tightened it lies cross-wise in the wound, like a harpoon, and it is almost impossible for it to draw out after once passing through the tough hide of the animal. When the line is nearly run out, the end of the spear-shaft is passed through a loop in the end of the line and held firmly by digging a little hole in the ice for the end of the spear to rest in, the foot resting upon the line and against the spear to steady it. This gives the hunter an immense advantage over his powerful game, and if he is fortunate enough to secure this hold, there is no escape for the walrus except that the line may cut on the edge of the sharp ice, or the thin ice break off, and hunter, line, and all be precipitated into the water—a not unusual experience in walrus hunting. Another cause of misfortune is for the line to become entangled around the arm of the hunter, so that he cannot cast it off, in which case he is most assuredly drawn into the sea, and in nine cases out of ten drowned, for his knife is seldom at hand for an emergency, and no amount of experience will ever induce an Inuit to provide against danger.

Sometimes the hunter is alone when he strikes a walrus, and in that case it requires considerable dexterity to secure the spear hold in the ice; or if he fails to get that he may sit down and brace his feet against a small hummock, when it comes to a sheer contest of muscle between the hunter and the walrus. In these contests victory generally perches upon the banner of the walrus, though the Inuit will never give up until the last extremity is reached. Often he is dragged to the very edge of the ice before he finds a protuberance against which to brace his feet, and often he is drawn down under the ice before he will relinquish his hold. He is very tenacious under such circumstances, for he knows that when he loses the walrus he loses his line and harpoon also.

Occasionally a dead walrus is found with a harpoon and line fastened to him, in which case the walrus and line belong to the finder. I remember a curious incident of this kind that occurred at Depot Island. Toolooah and Ebierbing (Esquimau Joe) were hunting together and Toolooah struck a fine young bull walrus, and got the spear hold against the ice for Joe to hold. It is a powerful hold, and a child could hold a whale in that way if the line did not break. But poor unfortunate Joe, for some unaccountable reason, raised the spear, and, of course, the line was drawn from under his foot, and both walrus and line were lost, notwithstanding Toolooah and Sebeucktolee (familiarly "Blacksmith") caught the running line and held until their hands were cut to the bone. They did not know at this time that another walrus had been killed a mile or two further along the edge of the floe. The loss of the line was also a sad misfortune. Joe felt so badly about it that he was ashamed to come in, and walked several miles farther along the ice with an Inuit companion, in the hope of killing a seal with his rifle; but Toolooah, who had taken no rifle, inasmuch as he had taken a spear and line instead, returned to camp and came into the igloo which he and I occupied in common, looking very much dejected in consequence of the loss of his walrus and line, the circumstances of which he explained to me, showing his terribly lacerated hands. The fact that another walrus had been killed was a relief to him, but did not dissipate his grief for the lost line, which was the last we had.

About half-past ten o'clock that night, while we were eating some boiled walrus meat and entrails (about the fifth meal since four o'clock on the afternoon, when the meat arrived), some one came to the entrance of the igloo and handed in Toolooah's walrus line, saying Joe and Blucher had found the walrus dead upon the ice near where it was struck, the animal having crawled out and died after the hunters had left. Now for the first time Toolooah's face brightened up, and he was so impatient to hear the circumstances of the recovery of the lost game that, late as it was, he went to Joe's igloo to inquire. He soon returned with an exceedingly woebegone expression, for which I failed to elicit an explanation until the morning, when I found out from Joe that, according to the laws and customs of the Inuits the walrus belonged to him because he found it.

"What interest has Toolooah in it?" said I.

"None," was Joe's reply. "All over here country same way. Man he strikee walrus; let he go again; somebody else findee; he walrus."

"Well, Joe, suppose the somebody else lets the walrus go, how is it then?"

"All same way."

"So Toolooah has no interest in that walrus he killed and that you let go again?"

"Yes, all same way here country. But I give 'm back he line last night. Line my, all same; I findee."

"That was certainly noble in you, Joe, I am sure."

"Oh, yes; Toolooah my friend."

And so, I noticed, always was the case whenever there was any doubt about a point; "custom here country" always managed to give Joe the best of it, and I came to the conclusion that he had become pretty thoroughly civilized during his residence in the United States.

Sometimes an inflated seal-skin, called an ah-wah-tah, is attached to the end of the line, that buoys it up and soon exhausts the wounded walrus. This is a very good plan, but is not considered advantageous when working in loose ice unless hunting from a boat, for the wounded animal is apt to get beyond the reach of the hunter. After the ice disappears walruses are then killed on the small islands, to which they resort to sleep, and are sometimes found in great numbers.

In the fall of 1878 I went with a party of Inuit hunters to a small rocky island opposite Daly Bay, where we found a herd of from seventy-five to a hundred, most of them asleep; but some were complaining and grunting, and punching their bed-fellows with their long tusks. Our approach was made cautiously up the slippery side of a wet rock until within range, when at the suggestion of my Inuit companions I fired at a fine young bull, being instructed to hit him just behind the ear. I did so, and sent a 320-grain slug from my Sharp's rifle through his skull. His head dropped to the ground and he never moved a muscle. At the same time another shot was fired by one of the Inuits; but the hunter's foot slipped at the same moment, and the bullet whistled harmlessly over the heads of the herd. A grand rush was then made by all the hunters, and the walruses were wriggling and sliding down the slimy rocks into the sea. One of the Inuits darted his harpoon into what he took to be a sleeping walrus, but it proved to be the one I had already killed. I followed into the midst of the herd and put a bullet through the head of another bull before they had all left the rock. Had Oxeomadiddlee not struck a dead walrus we might have had

163

three, for an ahwahtah was attached to his line, so that we could have regained it at any time with the boat. The walrus never appeared to me the dangerous animal I have known him to be represented. If wounded and brought to bay he will certainly turn upon his assailants, and many Inuits have been killed in these encounters, while others still bear scars received from the tusks of those which they were hunting. But as long as there appears to be a chance to escape by flight the walrus usually will seek safety in that way.

One of my companions in this hunt—Toogoolar, or Oxeomadiddlee, as he is usually called—is a famous walrus hunter, and his success is probably largely due to his immense physical strength. He is a perfect Esquimau Samson, and when he is on one end of a line, with his feet braced against a hummock, the walrus at the other end has no advantage. Indeed, the odds are in favor of Oxeomadiddlee. His singular name is self-imposed, and is an Inuit expression of greeting, or rather when one unexpectedly arrives, as the clown says, "Here we are again," and occurred in this way. Several years ago he was hunting walrus in the pack-ice, when the wind changed and blew the ice away from shore. This is a contingency to which the hunters are constantly liable, and is the greatest danger to which they are subjected in their pursuit. Many are thus carried away, sometimes out to sea, and are never heard from again; while others have been drifted a long distance from their homes before the drift again touched the shore-ice and allowed them to find their way back, if possible. Sometimes they starve to death before the ice again lands, though occasionally they are quite comfortable under such circumstances, as, for instance, were four who were carried off just before we started on our trip to King William Land a year ago last spring. Equeesik and his brother Owanork, who were to accompany us, and Nanook and Blucher were thus carried off from Depot Island, with one of our sleds and a dead walrus which they were cutting up at the time. They did not get back for four or five days, but suffered scarcely at all while away. They built an igloo on the largest cake they could reach, and of course had plenty to eat. They made a lamp of walrus hide, and burned the blubber to heat their house. When the ice touched the shore below Chesterfield Inlet they jumped on the sled and drove home. There is always more or less risk attending these adventures under all circumstances.

The time of which I was speaking that Toogoolar was carried away, he was gone a long time, until, indeed, his tribe had given up all hope of his returning. But one morning during a severe snow-storm he arrived in camp, and no one had noticed his approach until, crawling through the door of an igloo, he stood amid his friends and exclaimed, "Ox'-e-o-ma-did'-dle-e" (Good-morning. Here we are again). He had been carried from Repulse Bay to the vicinity of Whale Point, when an easterly wind drove the pack on shore and he escaped, but had to make his way on foot from there back home again. He had his walrus line and spear with him, and had killed a walrus while in the pack; but the piece that held his food was broken off and floated away from him, so that he was for many days without anything to eat. Inuits are somewhat accustomed to such experiences, and can be deprived of food for a long time without starving. When a walrus is killed it takes some time to cut it up and prepare it for removal to camp. There are usually several helpers in the vicinity of any one who carries a line and spear. Others walk along the edge of the pack until they find some one working up to a walrus, or a party engaged in cutting it up.

According to Inuit custom, all who arrive while the walrus is being cut up, no matter how many, are entitled to a share of it. The man who strikes it, however, has the first pick, which, if there are four of them, is one of the hind quarters; if there are only two or three, he has both hind flippers if he prefer them, and is always entitled to the head, which contains some of the choicest morsels either for cooking or eating raw. I know of nothing more palatable in that climate during winter and spring than raw frozen walrus head and tongue. It is not an inviting-looking dish, but is most enjoyable. The meat is hard, but not particularly tough—for walrus—and consists of alternate layers of lean and fat. It is eaten with the addition of more blubber, and is generally the occasion of a common feast for all the men in the camp. If there is any left the women can eat it if they want to, but the women never eat with the men, and if the tupic or igloo where the feast is being held is small, even the women that dwell there are banished until the feast is over. An ookjook, when killed, is divided up in the same way as a walrus, all the bystanders receiving a share. In making the division of the carcass the portions are kept in a bag made by lacing the edges of the skin that holds the share with a line made of a strip of the raw hide. In this bag are also deposited such portions of the entrails, liver, etc., as fall to the share of each. In hunting on foot the men usually take one or two dogs apiece to drag home their dividends. When encamped upon a hill, such as Depot Island, which commands a view of an extensive tract of ice, the natives seldom go walrus hunting unless they first see one on the ice, in which case one of the best hunters starts immediately with his weapons, and the "bummers" follow later with a sled and dogs. The arrival of a sled-load of walrus meat into a hungry camp is one of the most cheerful sights that it ever falls to the lot of a traveller to witness, and I have noticed that his interest is seldom diminished by the fact that his own is one of the hungry stomachs to be fed from this plenty. The women see the sled coming, while still at a great distance, and then the big stone lamps are lit, and snow put into the kettles to melt, so that no time need be wasted after the meat gets there. The cooking is seldom done in each dwelling separately; but he who has the largest kettle or the biggest heart, when his own meal is ready, goes to the door of his igloo or tupic and calls out, "O-yook, O-yook," which means warm food, and all the men and boys gather in, each with a knife in his hand, and without further ceremony they fall to and devour what is set before them. The largest part of an Inuit's food is, however, eaten raw.

These o-yooks are merely festal occasions, though they occur several times a day, and may happen at any hour of the day or night when the natives are assembled in villages and have plenty of food on hand. It is then that they recompense themselves for starvings in the past or in prospect.

CHAPTER XIII

THE RETURN

We reached our permanent camp on our return from King William Land on September 19th. It was about six miles southeast of Gladman Point, and at the foot of a high hill, which Toolooah remarked would make a good look-out tower for deer-hunting. All along this part of the coast, where Simpson Strait is narrowest, would soon swarm with reindeer waiting for the salt water to freeze, so they could continue their navigation southward. It is for this reason that we selected it as our permanent camp while we also awaited the freezing of the strait, so that we could cross with our heavy sleds. When Henry and Frank went down the coast they found reindeer everywhere else but at Gladman Point and that neighborhood, and were there for three days without food. In the meantime Toolooah crossed the strait in a kyack and found the natives. On his return he killed a reindeer on the main-land and relieved their distress. Long before we reached the spot the meadows and ponds were frozen, so that we could cross them with perfect impunity. In many places the ice was so clear that it required considerable moral courage to step upon it, it looked so exactly like still water.

Henry came up to see us the next day, his camp being about seven miles below. The Inuits crossed to the King William Land side on the 17th. It was a picturesque sight to see the whole of Joe's and Ishnark's families, with Henry and a number of dogs, upon a raft made by lashing together four kyacks. They had to choose a still day for the crossing, and keep very quiet while upon the raft.

Schwatka's Permanent Camp.

Lieutenant Schwatka paid a visit to the other camp on the 22d, and the day following Toolooah and I moved our camp about two miles farther east, to a large lake, where we at once set to work, the ice being already eight inches thick, to build an ice igloo of large slabs three feet by six, which standing on end and so placed as to support each other, formed the walls, which afterward were covered with the tent, and made a much warmer house than the tent alone, as it is a complete shelter against the wind.

Reindeer were now seen daily in immense herds. The day we moved camp we ran upon a herd of about fifty, and Toolooah killed seven before they could get away, following them up, running and dropping on his knee to fire. So rapid and effective was his delivery with his Winchester repeating carbine, that this unequalled achievement was accomplished in less than ten minutes; and, well knowing that it was to his splendid weapon that the credit largely belonged, this undemonstrative savage held up his rifle and kissed it while he was talking to me about the affair. On the 30th Toolooah killed twelve reindeer, Joe eight, and Equeesik and I each three, making a grand total of twenty-six by our party alone in one day.

Henry Klutschak's Camp.

We ate quantities of reindeer tallow with our meat, probably about half our daily food. Breakfast is eaten raw and frozen, but we generally have a warm meal in the evening. Fuel is hard to obtain, and consists entirely of a vine-like moss called ik-shoot-ik. Reindeer tallow is also used for a light. A small flat stone serves for a candlestick, on which a lump of tallow is placed, close to a piece of fibrous moss called mun-ne, which is used for a wick. The tallow melting runs down upon the stone and is immediately absorbed by the moss. This makes a very cheerful and pleasant light, but is most exasperating to a hungry man, as it smells exactly like frying meat. Eating such quantities of tallow is a great benefit in this climate, and we can easily see the effect of it in the comfort with which we meet the cold. The mean temperature for the month of September was 22.1 degrees Fahr., and the lowest 5 degrees, and yet though we wore only our woollen clothes, except a fur koo-li-tar, or overcoat, when away from home, the cold is not annoying. During October the mean temperature was -0 degree, and the lowest -38 degrees.

On the afternoon of the 27th of September a heavy snow-storm set in, and the next morning the snow was knee-deep on the level ice. The storm continued until during the night of the 29th. The snow was very deep, but the winter winds soon blew it around and packed it down so as to be almost solid. By the 14th of October the sledging was sufficiently good for Toolooah to go to Cape Herschel and Terror Bay for the sled and other articles that were left there during the summer for the want of transportation. As his little boy would suffer with the cold, Toolooah exchanged wives with Joe for the trip, a very usual and convenient custom among the Esquimaux.

The ice was sufficiently strong for the reindeer to commence crossing to the main-land about the 1st of October, and in a few days their numbers had very perceptibly diminished. After the 14th we saw none at all; they seemed to have entirely disappeared. The Inuits had been very busy making up fur clothing for the winter trip, and we had fixed upon the 1st of November as the day for starting, by which time everything would be ready. Toolooah got back on the 23d. He killed three bears the day he reached Terror Bay. All of them got into the water, and he had to go to the edge of the new ice, using a pole to stand upon while fishing them out. He killed one reindeer at Cape Herschel, which was all he saw while away.

Joe came up and built an igloo adjoining ours on the 3d of October. He wanted to get away from the vicinity of Ogzeuckjeuwock, the Netchillik Arn-ket-ko, or medicine-man, of whom he was apparently very much afraid. He alleged that the medicine-man was constantly advising his people to kill some of our party. Joe said that he had sak-ki-yon to that effect—that is, during one of his inspirations exhorted them to that end. There is no doubt but they would be very glad to kill us all, and get our guns and knives, but they were thoroughly afraid to undertake it. After Toolooah's return he and Joe gathered in the meat we had cached in the vicinity, preparatory to starting on the 1st of the next month. Lieutenant Schwatka decided that he and I would take Toolooah's sled, with Joe to assist, and go by the way of Smith and Grant Points, and through the big inlet spoken of by the natives as putting in from Wilmot Bay, and meet the other sleds which, in charge of Henry, would go by the way of Richardson Point and Back's River, meeting at the bend of the river above the Dangerous Rapids, where we would find the Ooqueesiksillik natives and take on board a supply of fish to last us until we reached the reindeer country once more. As the other sleds had the shorter route, they would start a day or two later and wait for us at the appointed rendezvous, unless they were getting short of food, in which case they would push on into the reindeer country. Narleyow, the Ooqueesiksillik guide, would accompany them. We started on the 1st, as proposed, but did not succeed in getting farther than the shore of the strait, about three miles from camp, owing to the heavy sleds and the dogs being so fat that they were lazy. We took Ishnark's sled to help us for the first day, as we had such a quantity of meat—one sled loaded entirely with it and the other with about half a load. We had to keep the extra sled the following day also, as we wanted to get well over the salt-water ice.

We had fondly hoped to be at the Dangerous Rapids by the 10th or 15th of November, but we only reached the native camp near the mouth of Kigmuktoo (Sherman Inlet) on the 12th, owing to our heavily loaded sled and the much bad weather, fogs, and wind that would blow the snow around so that we could not see our course. There was quite a large camp of Netchillik and Ookwolik Esquimaux on a big lake near the mouth of Sherman Inlet, the largest camp we had yet seen. The sled was pulling heavily and slowly across the lake, and I went ahead toward the igloos. All the men were standing outside awaiting our arrival, and among them were some Netchilliks we had met during the spring. As soon as they recognized me they set up a great shout of "Many-tu-me!" which is their salutation of welcome, and means smooth. They seemed very glad that we were coming among them again, and hurried me into a big, warm igloo, while most of the men ran out and helped the sled in. They built our igloo in short order, and during the time we were with them did everything in their power to contribute to our comfort. It seemed as if some one was on the roof of our igloo all the time patching up holes, and they changed the direction of the doorway every time the wind changed, and that kept them busy nearly all the time.

We found but few interesting relics among them. Only a piece of the boat found in Wilmot Bay after the big ship sunk, and part of the block branded either "10" or "O R," with part of the R obliterated. If the ship's blocks were branded with the name of the vessel to which they were attached, this would be important as establishing the identity of the ship that drifted down as the 'Terror'. As an instance of the perversity of fate, I mention that we found among them a piece of wax candle that they had preserved all these years, while every scrap of paper had perished. We saw here a Netchillik, named Issebluet, who with his family had nearly starved to death during the summer. He was separated from the rest of his tribe, as it is customary for them to scatter during the summer, and though not lacking in skill or energy, had simply been unfortunate and unable to procure food. He was still very thin and weak when we saw him, and when he went abroad had to take a couple of dogs, whose traces, tied around his waist, helped him along. Joe was very much frightened all the time we were here, for Netchillik Toolooah was here also—the man who it was said wanted to kill some of our party—and Joe said they intended to kill all our party except the women, and obtain possession of the baggage and the two women. He said their apparent kindness was only a blind, and the day we left them he made me prance around with my pistol in my belt while the sled was being loaded. Toolooah, though not so nervous as Joe, had his rifle handy and kept his eye upon it closely. I noticed that the men all stood around, but never offered to assist in loading the sled. Toolooah said they could not very well without exposing a fact that he had noticed— that they all had their knives in their sleeves. But if they had, they took good care not to use them. Two of them accompanied us a part of the way to show us the easiest route over the heavy hill we had to cross before reaching the salt-water ice, and kindly put their shoulders to the load whenever the sled pulled hard. I saw nothing in the conduct of any of them to complain of, but everything to praise. I noticed that most of the men in this camp had their hair cut close to their heads, the style that at home is profanely called "a Reilly cut." This I ascertained was not for personal adornment, but for convenience in hunting, where fine-tooth combs are unknown, but could be put to good use.

We met a sled with a few natives coming from Kigmuktoo to join the rest of the tribe on the lake, and with them was an aged crone named Toolooah, who had seen white men in Boothia Isthmus, when a young woman, and had also been with the party who found the boat and skeletons in Starvation Cove, near Richardson Point. She confirmed the testimony previously obtained in every essential particular. We gave her a few needles and a spoon, for which she was very grateful, especially to her namesake, our Toolooah, to whom she gave her walking-stick and two locks of her hair, which he severed with a snow-knife as she knelt beside the sled. This was a charm to protect him from evil until he got home. Besides this old woman there were three other women on the sled. One I noticed particularly, because she looked so much like the Goddess of Liberty. Her hood was over her head and hung with the same jaunty air as a liberty cap, and her artiger, cut loose in the throat, looked not unlike the classic toga. Though not quite so large as the statue on the dome of the Capitol at Washington, she was immense, and had arms like a gymnast. Modesty, either natural or assumed, and fear of the strange white men made her keep on the opposite side of the sled from us, though, as Lieutenant Schwatka remarked, she could have handled both of us if she wanted to.

We marched in a south-east direction in the inlet five days, during which we travelled upon it about forty-five miles, and when we left it could still see it running in a southerly direction for about ten or fifteen miles farther. It is bottle-shaped, not more than a mile wide at its mouth, and for a considerable distance, when it gradually widens out to five or six miles, and is about twenty miles wide at its head. Nearly every night we were able to find water in some lake on the land, but had to carry it from two to four miles into camp. This duty Lieutenant Schwatka and I took upon ourselves, while the Inuits were building and preparing the igloo.

The sun was so low now that we had either sunrise or sunset during the whole time it was above the horizon. At noon it was not more than four degrees high. We were gradually moving southward, or we would have been left with nothing but this light during the daytime. In fact, several days before we left Back's River, the sun only showed his diameter above the hills along the shore, where it lazily rolled for a few minutes and left us the long twilight in which to build our igloos, which were scarely ever finished before the utter darkness came upon us. Short days, together with our heavy sleds, and dogs not more than half fed, kept us back most provokingly. The snow on the land was soft, not having got thoroughly packed as yet, while the intense cold covered its surface with minute particles of ice that impeded the sled like so much sand. In many places the river and lakes were entirely denuded of snow, and the bare ice would take the ice from our runners as if we were moving over rocks. As long as the river ice was bare this made no difference; the sled would slip along merrily, the dogs on a run, but this seldom lasted for more than half a mile, when we would again run upon snow and have all the more laborious drag as a consequence. Our usual marches at this time were from five to ten miles, instead of from ten to twenty, as on our way north.

The most unpleasant feature of winter travelling is the waiting for an igloo to be built. To those at work even this time can be made to pass pleasantly, and there is plenty that even the white men of a party can do that would keep them busy, and consequently comfortable. When travelling overland the halt is made, if possible, on some lake where a water hole may be dug. This, through average ice—that is, about six or seven feet—will take about an hour and a half, though an expert native will do it in perhaps half that time. It is a blessing to get water at this time, and a great shout goes up from the well-digger, as the delicious fluid comes bubbling up through the narrow well, that is echoed by the igloo builders and spreads throughout the camp. Then the women repair with tin dippers and cups cut from musk-ox horn, and after refreshing themselves carry a drink to their husbands. One can drink enormously at this time, especially after working; but it will be well to keep up pretty violent exercise for some time afterward, as filling the stomach with such a quantity of ice-cold water will soon produce a shiver.

Another task that the white men can interest themselves in is the unloading of the sled and beating the snow and ice out of the fur bed-clothing. The Esquimaux do not use sleeping bags for themselves, but instead have a blanket which they spread over them, while under them are several skins, not only to keep the body away from the snow, but also to prevent the body from thawing the snow couch and thus making a hole that would soon wet the skins. While on the march the skins for the bed are usually spread over the top of the loaded sledge, and then the whole is securely lashed down with seal-skin thongs. It is the invariable custom to turn the fur-side of the skins up, because it is easy enough to beat the snow from the hair, while it might thaw and make the skin-side wet. You often, therefore, find that water has fallen upon the skin that makes your bed, and formed a great patch of ice, which has to be beaten off with a wooden club.

Until experience has taught you it makes you shudder to think that soon your naked body is to rest upon the place where now you see that patch of ice. But continued pounding will remove every vestige of it without disturbing the fur, if the weather is sufficiently cold. Therefore exposure is the best treatment for bedding, though it certainly gives the skins a degree of cold that can scarcely be appreciated until experienced. It is astonishing, however, how soon the bed becomes warm from the heat of the body. For, perhaps, from five to ten minutes you may lie there and shiver, when gradually a genial warmth begins to pervade the whole body, the shiver subsides, and you are as comfortable, as far as cold is concerned, in bed in an igloo in the Arctic, as you would be in a civilized mansion in the temperate zone.

The Esquimaux are not acquainted with the qualities of the magnetic needle, and, it is needless to say, do not travel by the compass. Like all savage tribes they have, however, methods for keeping their direction while making long voyages. These are usually made on the salt-water ice, and they follow the land; but when travelling over land, either in summer or winter, they can generally distinguish north from south, at least approximately. In summer the running vines point to the salt water, they say, which, in going around Hudson's Bay, would indicate the south. And then there are certain species of moss that are only found in the vicinity of salt water. In winter they notice the ridges of snow along the ice, or the land spots on the highlands, and can keep their course by them with surprising accuracy.

The Esquimaux, however, are not a people given to exploration. They are not curious concerning unknown territory. What they are chiefly interested in is, "what they shall eat and drink, and wherewithal they shall be clothed." Certain districts within their knowledge furnish the different kinds of game, and these they visit at the accustomed seasons. Occasionally they will visit neighboring tribes, and sometimes settle down in the new country, depending upon their skill in the chase for the support of their families. But this country, new to them, is well known to those whom they visit, and they have the benefit of competent guides until such time as they are sufficiently acquainted with the country themselves. Though they are constantly moving in summer and winter, their journeys are seldom extended. They will sometimes go from the mouth of Chesterfield Inlet to the Wager River or Repulse Bay, and occasionally to the tribes at the north part of Melville Peninsula, but generally spend one year at least at some intermediate point. The tribes they pass through on these journeys are so connected by marriage as to be almost like one large tribe, so that they are all the time in the land of their friends.

Twice since leaving the Inuit camp in Wilmot Bay the dogs had an interval of eight days between meals, and were in no condition for hard work. That they could live and do any work at all seemed marvellous. I am constrained to believe that the Esquimau dog will do more work, and with less food, than any other draught animal existing. On the night of the 20th Lieutenant Schwatka observed a meridian culmination of the moon, which showed in latitude 67 deg. 32 min. 42 sec. north, only three miles from our reckoning. It is a difficult task to make astronomical observations with a sextant in a temperature thirty-eight degrees below zero, or seventy below the freezing-point, as it was this night. It is not pleasant to sit still for any length of time in such weather. A thin skim of ice over the surface of the kerosene oil used for an artificial horizon has to be constantly removed by the warm breath of an assistant. The sextant glasses become obscure from the freezing upon them of the breath of the observer, and can only be cleaned with the warm fingers, which they blister in return for such kindness. These are some of the obstacles to determining one's position astronomically in an Arctic winter; while in summer, there being no night, one is dependent upon the sun alone.

The mean temperature for November was -23.3 degrees and

the lowest noted -49 degrees.

We ran upon a narrow strip of salt water, apparently an inlet from Cockburn Bay, on the 28th. We had to halt the next day for Toolooah to rest, as he was completely prostrated with the hard work of the last four days. We moved, however, on the 30th, Joe driving and Toolooah strolling along at his ease. We emerged upon Cockburn Bay soon after starting, and crossed to the southern shore by noontime, a distance of about nine miles, our rapid moving being entirely owing to the superiority of the sledging on salt-water ice.

We crossed the narrow neck of land between Cockburn Bay and the fresh-water portion of the river between the two great bends in three days' travel, and emerged about eight miles above the Dangerous Rapids on the 5th of December, where we had hoped to be by the 15th of November. Our igloos were made on the southern bank, and we were greatly surprised that we saw no sled tracks in crossing the river. We had supposed that they, with the shorter route and smooth salt-water ice nearly all the way, would have been ahead of us, and either waiting or forced to move into the reindeer country for food. Our first object, therefore, was to find the natives, who live here all the year round, as Narleyow, one of the tribe, who was with Henry, constantly assured us was the case. From these people we expected to get information concerning the other sleds, and also to get a large quantity of fish for food for man and beast. We found some fish caches near our camp, and some sled tracks and footprints about one mile and a half farther down the river, which Joe said led a long distance. The day after our arrival we appropriated one large cache to feed our starving dogs, and then started the next day for their camp to pay for the fish and buy more. But shortly after all the men started, one of the women ran out and called us back, saying that Inuits were coming to the igloo. We hastened back and found three young men of the Ooqueesiksillik tribe, who had found their cache robbed and traced the tracks to our igloo. Joe explained the case to them, and said we had knives to pay for the fish and to buy more, which they said would be gladly accepted, and they would tell their people to bring us more fish that night. We were astonished when they said they had neither seen nor heard of any others of our party.

That night, after the igloo was closed and we were eating our evening meal, we heard a sled drive up to the door and supposed our fish had arrived; but what was our joy when we recognized Koumania's voice driving the dogs, and then heard Henry at the door of our igloo. We then learned that they had reached the Dangerous Rapids only that afternoon, and while building the igloos the three young men we had seen in the morning returned and reported having seen us up the river. As soon as Henry heard this he had the load dumped from one of the sleds, and took Koumania to drive and an Ooqueesiksillik native as guide, and came at once to report. He said it had been very difficult to get his party of natives away from the camps that they met daily, and that they had moved by portages, which doubled the distance. He had bought dog food of the natives all along the route, and his dogs were, consequently, in good order. They would remain in camp where they were a day or two to feed up the dogs and get what fish they wanted for his two sleds, and then join us on the 10th.

About five miles inland from Starvation Cove the natives had found during the summer the skeleton of a white man which no one had ever seen before. On the way down, Henry visited the place and erected a monument over the remains. The pieces of clothing found indicated that deceased was a sailor, not an officer. The finding of this grave is worthy of notice, as showing that the natives were thoroughly aroused by our visit and its object. We had promised them liberal rewards for everything of importance found, and for valuable information—that is, anything new—and were always particular to keep our promises. The consequence was that they had greatly aided us by searching everywhere within reach of their camps or hunting grounds. In approaching the Dangerous Rapids from Cockburn Bay, Henry had found an island where on the Admiralty chart is marked a point of the mainland. In fact, there is a delta at the mouth of the river. Narleyow led them to a place in the branch of the river flowing to the westward of this island, where he said a rocky ridge froze to the bottom, making a pocket which held fish. They dug four holes within an area of ten feet, and in one day caught fifty-seven of the immense salmon for which this river is famous. He cooked one for us, which was the largest I ever saw. Joe measured the cross-section of one he saw in the native igloos below our camp that measured over one foot. I asked him how much over, but he couldn't tell, he said, as his pocket measure was "only a foot long".

View on Back's River.

The largest number of fish caught here are what the natives call "cow-e-sil-lik," and are peculiar to these waters. They are something like very large herring, and the flesh much coarser than salmon or trout. All the fish here are quite fat, the salmon especially. We bought several bags of salmon oil from the natives, which we used, so long as it lasted, as a substitute for reindeer tallow, which is all gone now. The weather is intensely cold -62 degrees Fahrenheit on the 10th, the day the remainder of our party rejoined us at this camp. There was scarcely any wind, and it did not seem so cold as at -10 degrees or -20 degrees, with the wind blowing in one's face, as it was the last few days of our travelling, with the thermometer at -46 degrees and -48 degrees. Yet we were so well fortified against the cold by the quantities of fat we had eaten that we did not mind it. The prospect was that now we were out of fat we would suffer a great deal with the intense cold that we might expect in going across land from Back's River to Hudson's Bay.

The rapids on Back's River are all marked by open water, and are recognizable at a long distance by the column of black smoke arising from them like steam from a boiling caldron. The ice in the vicinity is dangerous to travel upon, there often being thin places, where the moving water has nearly, but not quite, cut through, and not distinguishable from the surrounding ice, which may be four or five feet thick. The natives test it, before going upon it, with a knife or stick, and know from the sound whether or not it is safe to travel upon. In some of the many open water places that we found in our journey up the river we could walk boldly up to the very edge and lie down and quench our thirst from the rushing torrent, while in other places it was not safe to go within several hundred yards of the open water. On the 20th we passed open rapids about half a mile long, where we had to take the land. From the top of the hill it was a grand spectacle to look down upon the seething torrent and see the great cakes of ice broken off above and crushed to atoms as they passed through and under the ice below.

The Dangerous Rapids, Back's River.

We had hoped to have Narleyow go with us to Depot Island, as he had previously been up Back's River and knew a route overland by which in three days we could reach a river where some Kinnepatoos were encamped all the year round. Here we could refit with meat and clothing and follow the river, which flows into Chesterfield Inlet, and then keep upon the salt-water ice to Depot Island. But with true Inuit perverseness he decided at the last minute not to go. He, however, gave Toolooah minute directions for finding the place where to leave Back's River, which is nearly as far west as Lake McDougal, and the route overland, where we would find sledge tracks and footprints to guide us to the camp.

We found the travelling on Back's River much more tedious than we had anticipated, owing to the bare ice in the vicinity of the open-water rapids and the intense cold which kept the air filled with minute particles of ice from the freezing of the steam of the open water. These little particles of ice would fall upon the hard snow, which otherwise would have been good sledging, and remain separated from each other so that you could brush them up like sand, and were, in fact, nearly as hard as sand, so that it was almost impossible to drag the sledges along. The thermometer would frequently register -50 degrees and -60 degrees when we were moving with a strong wind blowing directly in our faces. Such travelling as this is simply terrible, and it is astonishing that we were able to do it without encountering any severe frost-bites. Indeed, we travelled one day with the thermometer -69 degrees, and, a gale blowing at this time, both white men and Inuits were more or less frost-bitten, but merely the little nippings of nose, cheeks, and wrists that one soon gets accustomed to in this country. As Lieutenant Schwatka says, it is like almost all other dangers that you hear and read about, they seem to dwindle when you meet them boldly face to face. A battle always seems more terrible to those in the rear than to those in the front lines.

It was a noticeable fact that our course up the river was considerably east of south, instead of west, as mapped upon the Admiralty chart. There could be no mistake in regard to this when we could daily see the sun rise and set on the right of our general line of travel. It was near the end of December before we reached the vicinity of Mount Meadowbank, though we had hoped to be far beyond it by that time. Storms had kept us in camp several days during the journey up the river, and our provisions were nearly all exhausted, so that we had to lie over to hunt for game. The hunters could find nothing near the river, and were obliged to go with a sled one day's march to the east, build an igloo, and hunt from there. It was terribly cold for them, sleeping in an igloo, without fire or blankets, merely a shelter from the wind, and forced, as they were, to sleep in their clothes. I have had such experience and know what it is. In such cases one suffers more from cold feet than anything else. They would be intensely cold with dry stockings, but one's stockings are always wet from perspiration after walking, and when compelled to wear them at night cause great suffering.

Equeesik killed four reindeer, and we had to wait for them

to be brought in. At this time this was all the food we had, and before more was obtained we were upon short rations. The dogs were beginning to feel the effect of hard work, cold weather, and low diet, and already we had lost two fine young dogs that died in consequence of privation. Before we had reached Depot Island we lost twenty-seven dogs, all but four of which died from the hardships incident to the journey. All hands were in harness whenever we marched, and the work was too hard to admit of feeling the cold as the greatest discomfort we had to encounter.

CHAPTER XIV

FAMINE

The last day we travelled on the river, December 28th, the thermometer had registered during the day -69 degrees in the morning, -64 degrees at noon, and -68 degrees at five o'clock in the evening; the lowest, 101 degrees below the freezing-point. Toolooah, Joe, and Ishnark went hunting the next day, but were unfortunate in not being able to secure any game, though they saw a small herd of reindeer. Toolooah reported the land sledging in good condition toward the south-east, much better than upon the river, and said there appeared to be plenty of game a day's march from the river in that direction. Lieutenant Schwatka, therefore, decided to abandon the river at once and strike directly for Depot Island, which had the advantage of being a straighter route than the one by the unsurveyed river proposed by Narleyow. With a guide that would have been feasible; but it would be running much risk to attempt to find our way by the longer route in a country whose game we knew nothing of, with a large party dependent upon the very difficult hunting for support.

It is a difficult matter to keep guns in working order in the intensely cold weather we were experiencing. At sixty and seventy degrees below zero everything freezes. Even the iron and wood are affected. Strong oak and hickory will break almost like icicles, and when guns were brought into the warmer temperature of an igloo to clean, they would gather moisture, which had to be removed from every portion of the lock and working parts before again meeting the cold, or they would be worthless as weapons. They must also be kept free from oil or any kind of grease, as all lubricants of that sort will harden and prevent the working of the lock. It is but fair to state in this connection that our fire-arms, in which all the best American manufacturers were represented, worked admirably under these trying circumstances, and I feel justified in saying that it was their superiority in rapid and accurate delivery, in the hands of good hunters, that carried us through this ordeal. It is a matter of great difficulty to get near enough to such wary game as the reindeer, in winter, when the sound of the hunter's footsteps, though the soles of his shoes are covered with fur, is carried on the wind and can be distinctly heard more than a mile away. I have frequently heard the crunching of the sled runners on the brittle snow—a ringing sound like striking bars of steel—a distance of over two miles. It was one advantage in travelling against a head wind, to counterbalance the discomfort, that it carried the sound of the sleds away from game we might be approaching. After the first day's march from Back's River we were never compelled to lie in camp for the purposes of hunting game, for when we did come upon a herd the breech-loaders and magazine-guns did their work so effectively that we could lay in a stock of meat for a day or two ahead.

We left Back's River behind on the last day of the year, and made about seven miles in a south-east direction, and encamped and stopped to hunt, the last halt we made for that purpose. The mean temperature for December was -50.4 degrees Fahrenheit, the lowest -69 degrees, and the highest -26 degrees. January 3d the thermometer reached the lowest point that we saw during our sojourn in this climate—in the morning -70 degrees, at noon -69 degrees, and at five o'clock in the afternoon the extraordinary mark of -71 degrees. Equeesik moved his igloo about ten miles ahead this day, but the other two igloos were compelled to wait for their hunters to come in. The day, notwithstanding the intensity of the cold, was very pleasant. There was scarcely a breath of wind, and our igloo door was open the entire day. In fact, it was a far pleasanter day to be out of doors than with 50 degrees warmer and the wind blowing. January proved a very stormy month; indeed, there were but eleven days in which we could travel, and we only accomplished ninety-one miles toward our destination during that time. One day, the 19th, we lay over to follow up some musk-ox tracks we had seen the day previous. The weather was fine, notwithstanding a pretty strong wind and a temperature of -65 degrees.

We followed the tracks about twenty-five miles, and only desisted when we found that wolves were ahead of us and had already frightened the game away. The country is filled with reindeer, and on every hill-side their breath can be seen rising like clouds of steam. A herd that was frightened by the dogs, which were following the musk-ox tracks, scampered off in every direction, and it looked as if a lot of locomotives had been let loose over the country, the smoke coming from their lungs in great puffs as they ran, and streaming along behind them. When the sledges are moving during a clear cold day, the position of any one of them is known to the team, though they may be widely separated. Sometimes, for the advantage of hunting to be obtained thereby, our igloos have been separated by a day's march of about ten miles, and at that distance the condensed breath of the dogs and people could be distinctly seen and the position of the igloos located.

January proved the coldest month of our experience, with a mean thermometer of -53.2 degrees, lowest -71 degrees, and the highest -23 degrees Fahrenheit. We experienced one storm of thirteen days' duration during the latter part of January and early part of February, and found but thirteen days during which we could travel in the latter month.

It was almost our daily experience now to lose one or more dogs. They got plenty of reindeer meat, but it was usually fed frozen, and has but little nourishment in it in that state for cold weather, when fat and warming food is required.

The March in Extreme Cold Weather.

A seal-skinful of blubber each week would have saved many of our dogs; but we had none to spare for them, as we were reduced to the point when we had to save it exclusively for lighting the igloos at night. We could not use it to warm our igloos or to cook with. Our meat had to be eaten cold—that is, frozen so solid that it had to be sawed, and then broken into convenient-sized lumps, which when first put into the mouth were like stones—or cooked with moss gathered from the hillsides and the snow beaten off with a stick. Meat will freeze in a temperature a little below the freezing-point, but it is then in a very different condition from the freezing it gets at from sixty to seventy degrees below zero. Then every piece of meat you put in your mouth has first to be breathed upon to thaw the surface, or it will stick to your tongue and sides of your mouth and lips like frosty iron, and with the same disagreeable results. The luxury of a cooked meal could only be indulged in on the days when we were lying over in camp, as to gather the moss and cook the meal would take from three to four hours.

The country began to swarm with wolves now, as well as with reindeer, and we would meet them daily. Often they would come close to the igloos, and one night Toolooah shot one of three that were eating the meat he had thrown out for food for our dogs.

They killed and ate four of Equeesik's dogs, and attacked him when he went out of the igloo to drive them off. He killed two of his assailants with his rifle, and two others by the most infernal traps ever devised. He set two keenly sharpened knife-blades in the ice and covered them with blood, which the wolves licked, at the same time slicing their tongues, the cold keeping them from feeling the wounds at the time, and their own warm blood tempting them to continue until their tongues were so scarified that death was inevitable. He also prepared some pills by rolling up long strips of whalebone, bound with sinew and hidden in meat, which freezing would hold together until it had passed into the animal's intestines, when the meat having thawed, and the sinew digested, the whalebone would open out and produce an agonizing death. If anything were bad enough treatment for wolves, these devices of Equeesik's might be so classed.

Toolooah was out hunting on the 23d of February, when a pack of about twenty wolves attacked him. He jumped upon a big rock, which was soon surrounded, and there he fought the savage beasts off with the butt of his gun until he got a sure shot, when he killed one, and while the others fought over and devoured the carcass, he made the best of the opportunity to get back into camp. It was a most fortunate escape, as he fully realized.

On the 25th we were detained in camp by a storm, which Toolooah took advantage of for hunting. He saw a reindeer not far from camp, and was soon astonished to see another Inuit following the same animal. The stranger, when he saw Toolooah, ran back to his igloo; but Toolooah let the reindeer go and followed the man, whom he found to be a Kinnepatoo acquaintance named Tsedluk. From him he learned that Depot Island was only two igloos, or three days off, with long marches and light sledges. We moved up to Tsedluk's igloo the following day, and bought some meat from him, as game was scarce beyond. Here we cached all our heavy stuff, and with light sleds and forced marches reached Depot Island on the 4th day of March, by way of Connery River, which we came upon on the 2d. The mean temperature for the past month had been -44.8 degrees, and the coldest recorded -69 degrees Fahrenheit.

We found open water at the rapids where Connery River empties into its estuary, and the ice four feet above water-line. It was with considerable difficulty that a safe passage was found for the sledges, but once on the salt-water ice we moved along rapidly. The prospect of reaching home the next day was very exhilarating, and the dogs seemed to catch the infection from their masters. The poor, jaded beasts coiled their tails over their backs and ran along barking until we halted for the night, within about twenty miles of our destination. We still knew nothing concerning Hudson's Bay since we left a year before, Tsedluk having seen no one since he came to the camp where we found him. The great question with us was, "Were any ships in the bay?" If there were, the prospect was that there would be some news from home and letters from our friends. We hoped that there were ships, and believed that they would be wintering at Depot Island, as it was the unanimous opinion of the officers of the fleet at Marble Island the previous year that Depot Island was a far preferable place to winter at, on account of the difficulty of getting fresh meat for the crews at the other harbor.

View on Connery River.

At any rate, we felt sure of finding our hard bread, pork, and molasses, together with some other provisions that Captain Barry said he could spare and leave with Armow, the native who had charge of our stuff at Depot Island, and the prospect of again eating some civilized food was most cheering. The natives exhibited an unwonted degree of activity, and we got under way at seven o'clock the next morning, moving off at the rate of three miles and a half an hour. We soon arrived in sight of Depot Island, and looked anxiously for sledge tracks, which we felt sure would be abundant here if the ships were near by. We saw no tracks for so long a time that we soon began to doubt that there were even any natives there.

About noon we were within four or five miles of the island, and saw some natives on the ice in the dim distance. Then all was excitement in our party, and it increased as the distance diminished. I never expected to feel so agitated as I did when I found myself running and shouting with the natives. Toolooah fired a signal-gun, then jumped on the sled and waved a deer-skin, which had been agreed between him and Armow as announcing our identity on our return.

At last the sleds drew near enough to recognize Armow, who was hastening up to us ahead of the others. When they halted he grasped Lieutenant Schwatka by the hand and shook it long and heartily, saying, "Ma-muk-poo am-a-suet suk-o" ("Plenty good to see"), and then he came to me, and I noticed, as he held my hand, the tears, warm from his dear old heart, were coursing down his cheeks. I was moved, as I scarcely anticipated, at the tenderness and earnest warmth of our reception. There were Eeglee-leock, Nanook, Seb-euck-to-lee, Shok-pe-nark, Con-we-chiergk (Toolooah's brother), Koo-pah, Eve-loo, and a host of boys, while Petulark, Ter-re-ah-ne-ak, and others came in later from the direction of Camp Daly.

From Armow we learned that there was only one ship in the bay, and that it was at Marble Island; and furthermore, that there were no provisions for us at Depot Island. This seemed utterly incomprehensible to us, as Captain Barry had about a thousand pounds of hard bread on board the 'Eothen' that belonged to us, besides some other provisions, and had promised to leave them with Armow, at Depot Island, for us, well knowing that we would need them there.

Armow said he had a piece of paper with some writing on, that he thought was from Captain Fisher; but we supposed it must be some explanation of this extraordinary circumstance. We therefore hastened with our Inuit friends to their igloos, which were on the ice about three miles from Depot Island, and found the note to be from Captain Fisher, giving some excuse for not leaving some things that he had expected to. The inevitable conclusion was then forced upon us that Barry had absolutely gone away with the food from us without a word of explanation, though he had landed at Depot Island and taken off the casks that held our bread when we came ashore. It is usually considered that those who encounter the perils of Arctic travel have enough to contend with from the very nature of the undertaking, and not only their own countrymen but all civilized nations have hastened to help them when opportunity afforded. Even the savages with whom they come in contact have pity for them.

Before resuming our march there was a painful scene at the sledges. Toolooah heard of the death of his mother, in whose charge he had left his little daughter when starting on the expedition, and a group of relatives and friends stooped around the sledge weeping, the women giving vent to their feelings in prolonged wails and moaning. This lasted for about ten minutes, during which I learned from the other natives that they had a very severe winter and much suffering for lack of food. Several deaths had occurred in the tribes since we left. A large portion was now at Wager River, but would be down in the spring or early in the summer. We afterward learned that they, too, had suffered for food. After shaking hands with other old friends at the camp we went into Armow's igloo and ate some frozen walrus meat and blubber that tasted delicious to us, the blubber especially, it having been so long since we had eaten fat food, though so much requiring it. They had but a short supply of meat on hand when we arrived, and the advent of twenty-two hungry travellers and nineteen starving dogs soon reduced their stores, so that, a storm at once setting in from the north-west, making it a useless task to hunt walrus, there was a famine in camp before the end of a week.

They can only hunt walrus successfully at Depot Island with a southerly wind to hold the ice-pack to the floe. Seals are hunted with dogs to find the blow-hole of amog-low, or seal igloo, which, often covered with loose snow, is hidden from the hunter. When found, a wall of snow is built as a protection against the wind, while the hunter waits for hours, and sometimes for days, until the seal comes up to blow, when he is struck through the hole in the ice with a spear and held by a line attached to the boat. It is necessary for this style of hunting that the weather should be such that one can see at a short distance, or on the trackless waste of smooth ice the hunter is apt to get lost. Most of the time we were here it was blowing so that land could not be seen at one hundred yards' distance. It might be well to explain here that, when the wind blows, the dry snow fills the air so that it is thicker than the severest snow-storm in the temperate zone. The Inuits call this condition of affairs "pairk-se-uk-too", and one can witness it almost daily during the winter.

It was the eighth day after our arrival before the storm abated sufficiently to let the hunters out with any prospect of success. The wind was still from the north, and it was very provoking that they could see plenty of walrus and seal on the pack, but far beyond their reach. Affairs were getting desperate now. In the last five days we had but one meal a day, composed at first of about a quarter of a pound of walrus or seal meat, but lately of "kow"—that is, the thick hide of the walrus, with a thin cover of short hair on it, such as is seen on the old fashioned seal-skin trunks. As the hunters got nothing, we were without even our "kow" the next day, with the prospect of remaining without food until Eeglee-leock and Nanook got back from Marble Island, where they went for relief from the natives there three days ago. Lieutenant Schwatka went with them in order to try to get some food for us from the ship. All they had to eat on the way down was walrus blubber, and so great was their anxiety for us that Lieutenant Schwatka and Eeglee-leock left the sled behind at Chesterfield Inlet with Nanook, and walked one day and night without resting, reaching Marble Island at six o'clock in the morning, after a walk of about seventy-five miles.

One of the women in our camp died this day, her death

hastened by privation. She was the wife of Te-wort, or "Papa," as he is universally called, not only by the white visitors to Hudson's Bay, but by his own people. The benignant Inuit custom that allows a plurality of wives to those that desire it, leaves him not altogether comfortless in his old age; but "Cockeye" was his first favorite wife, and the mother of the great majority of his children. The funeral ceremonies covered four days, and the morning of the fifth "Papa" visited the grave, and after his return there was nothing to prevent the usual course of events which the burial and mourning customs had interrupted. Even the dogs could be fed if there was anything to give them to eat.

It was a mournful camp after the hunters got in, Friday night, the 12th of the month, empty handed. They all felt the danger that again threatened them, as it had done twice before during the winter, when they had to kill and eat some of their starving dogs. People spoke to each other in whispers, and everything was quiet, save for the never-ceasing and piteous cries of the hungry children, begging for food which their parents could not give them. Most of the time I stayed in bed, trying to keep warm and to avoid exercise that would only make me all the more hungry. It was impossible to keep warm this night, and my aching limbs drove sleep from my eyes.

The closing ceremony was a most touching one. After "Papa" had returned from the grave, Armow went out of doors and brought in a piece of frozen something that it is not polite to specify further than that the dogs had entirely done with it, and with it he touched every block of snow in a level with the beds of the igloo. The article was then taken out of doors and tossed up in the air to fall at his feet, and by the manner in which it fell he could joyfully announce that there was no liability of further deaths in camp for some time to come.

The wind was from the east Saturday, and a little better for hunting, so the men were off bright and early. About noon there was a joyful sound in camp. The women and children ran into our igloo shouting "Iviek seleko" (walrus killed), and fairly jumped up and down in their joy. I think the veriest stoic would have at least smiled. I know I laughed and said "good," though I tried to look dignified and unconcerned. Thank God, the danger was over, for the present at least, and I should be able to start for Marble Island in a day or two. It was not until the 17th, however, that I got away at last, as no sledges could move or the dogs be fed during the four days succeeding the death of "Papa's" wife. According to the Inuit belief, an infringement of this custom would cause a fearful mortality that I did not care to become responsible for, and had to wait patiently until the gods of the walrus and seal were satisfied that due respect had been paid to the memory of the departed.

The first day of my march to Marble Island I met Ikomar coming with relief for our camp, and took from his sled one of two boxes containing hard bread and some pork, molasses, and tobacco, sending another box and the remainder of the food to Henry and Frank, who would come down to Marble Island when Ikomar returned. I found a note from Lieutenant Schwatka, in which I read that a bottle of whiskey was among the stores sent; but in the excitement of the occasion and my interest in some papers of 1879, I forgot to look for it. My surprise and disappointment can therefore be imagined that night, when Toolooah dragged the bottle forth from the bottom of the bread box, and asked what it was. We each drank some of the contents, and I noticed, on pouring it into a tin cup, that it was of the consistency of thick syrup, and the cup absolutely froze to my lips, at the same time burning them as if with a red-hot knitting-needle. I had often before heard of a bottle of whiskey freezing to a person's lips, but until that moment I had regarded the assertion as a base effort to deceive and to divert the mind from the actual cause of a too prolonged hold of the bottle. I found the whiskey a great comfort on the trip to Marble Island, and could not help feeling that our long winter journey would have been made much more comfortable by some form of ardent spirits, probably diluted alcohol, to be partaken of in small quantities each night on arriving in camp, or after unusually fatiguing work and exposure.

I reached the ship 'George and Mary' at midnight of Saturday the 21st, and found every one in bed, except Captain Baker, who received me very kindly, and at once impressed me as a straightforward, generous-spirited man. The cabin of his vessel is exceedingly small and inconvenient, but the officers submitted to much discomfort in our behalf. I found that the crew had been entirely free from scurvy, which had so seriously afflicted the crews of the fleet at Marble Island the previous winter. The entire freedom from this disease seems to be attributable to Captain Baker's excellent management, and the constant feeding of fresh reindeer, walrus, or seal meat to the crew, as well as to those in the cabin.

He had, however, lost one man, George Vernoi, a Canadian, who died of consumption, with which he was suffering when he shipped at New Bedford, and one officer, Mr. Charles A. Lathe, of Swansea, Mass., first mate, who froze to death while on a hunting expedition to the main-land during the previous fall. He, together with Mr. Gilbert, the third officer of the vessel, and some Kinnepatoo Inuits, went ashore on the 1st of October to secure fresh meat for the crew. In five days they had killed seven reindeer, and started to return to the ship; but a gale prevented their working to windward, and, their sail torn from the mast, they drifted during the night to a small barren island, where in the morning their boat was broken and their provisions washed away. They were suffering extremely from thirst, having neglected to bring water with them from the shore, and found none on the island. A day was spent in endeavoring to repair the boat, and after another bitter night on the island, without water, they got away at nearly nightfall of the day following and reached another island where they found water and spent the night.

Mr. Lathe had already suffered extremely with the cold, as well as with hunger and thirst, and next day, after walking in a snow-storm about twenty miles toward the Kinnepatoo village, on the main-land, he gave up entirely and lay down to die. Mr. Gilbert urged his companion to make another effort, but to no purpose, and had finally to abandon him, though still alive, for the Inuits were nearly out of sight, and as they would not wait for him his own life depended on keeping them in view. Arrived at the Kinnepatoo camp, which was about ten miles from where his companion fell, Mr. Gilbert was much exhausted. The natives then treated him very kindly and supplied him with dry clothing, but no persuasion or promises of reward could induce any of them to go back and look after Mr. Lathe, whom they said would be dead before they found him. Mr. Gilbert remained here for more than two months, when the arrival of some of the tribe from the north brought the joyful news that the ice bridge had formed between Marble Island and the main-land, and then they were willing to conduct him to the ship, where he arrived on the 23d of December, long after all on board had given them both up as dead.

During the year that we were absent from the verge of civilization, as the winter harbor of the whalers may be considered, we had travelled 2,819 geographical, or 3,251 statute miles, most of which was entirely over unexplored territory, constituting the longest sledge journey ever made, both as to time and distance, and the only extended sledge journey ever accomplished in the Arctic, except such as have been made through countries well known and over routes almost as thoroughly established as post-roads. Our sledge journey stands conspicuous as the only one ever made through the entire course of an Arctic winter, and one regarded by the natives as exceptionally cold, as the amount of suffering encountered by those remaining at Depot Island attested, and further confirmed, as we afterward learned, by the experience of those who wintered at Wager River, where many deaths occurred, attributable to the unusual severity of the season. The party successfully withstood the lowest temperature ever experienced by white men in the field, recording one observation of -71 degrees Fahrenheit, sixteen days whose average was 100 degrees below the freezing-point, and twenty-seven which registered below -60 degrees Fahrenheit, during most of which the party travelled. In fact, the expedition never took cold into consideration, or halted a single day on that account.

During the entire journey its reliance for food, both for man and beast, may be said to have been solely upon the resources of the country, as the expedition started with less than one month's rations, and it is the first in which the white men of an expedition voluntarily lived exclusively upon the same fare as its Esquimau assistants, thus showing that white men can safely adapt themselves to the climate and life of the Esquimaux, and prosecute their journeys in any season or under such circumstances as would the natives of the country themselves. The expedition was the first to make a summer search over the route of the lost crews of the 'Erebus' and 'Terror', and while so doing buried the remains of every member of that fated party above ground, so that no longer the bleached bones of those unfortunate explorers whiten the coasts of King William Land and Adelaide Peninsula as an eternal rebuke to civilization, but all have, for the time being at least, received decent and respectful interment.

The most important direct result of the labors of the expedition will undoubtedly be considered the establishing of the loss of the Franklin records at the boat place in Starvation Cove; and as ever since Dr. Rae's expedition of 1854, which ascertained the fate of the party, the recovery of the records has been the main object of subsequent exploring in this direction, the history of the Franklin expedition may now be considered as closed. As ascertaining the fate of the party was not so gratifying as would have been their rescue or the relief of any member thereof, so is it in establishing the fate of the record of their labors. Next in importance to their recovery must be considered the knowledge of their irrecoverable loss.

It may be needless to say here that to Lieutenant Schwatka's thorough fitness for his position as commander of such an expedition may be attributed its successful conduct through all the various stages of its experience. The thinking public will place the credit where it so well belongs, and he will soon find the reward of success in the approval not only of his countrymen, but of all interested in the extension of geographical knowledge and scientific research. It is not too much to say that no man ever entered the field of Arctic labors better fitted for the task, physically or by education and habits of life and mental training, than Lieutenant Schwatka. He is endowed by nature with robust health and a powerful frame, to which fatigue seems a stranger. A cheerful disposition that finds amusement in the passing trifle, and powers of concentration that entirely abstract him from his surroundings, keep him free from "ennui" that is not the least disagreeable feature of life in this wilderness. And he possesses a very important adjunct, though to the uninitiated it may seem trifling, a stomach that can relish and digest fat. The habit of command gives him a power over our Inuit allies that is not to be disregarded. "Esquimau Joe" says he never knew them to mind any one so strictly and readily as they do Lieutenant Schwatka. With all these qualifications for a leader, and the prestige of success following close upon his heels, it would not be too much to predict for him a brilliant Arctic career in the near future.

His excellent management secured his entire party from many of the usual misfortunes of those in the field, and deprived the expedition of the sensational character it might have assumed in less skilful hands. All our movements were conducted in the dull, methodical, business-like manner of an army on the march. Every contingency was calculated upon and provided for beforehand, so that personal adventures were almost unknown or too trival to mention.

CHAPTER XV

ESQUIMAU HOME-LIFE

We had, of course, had abundant opportunities to study the habits of the people among whom we had lived so long. The government among the Inuit tribes, where they have any at all, is patriarchal, consisting of advice from the older and more experienced, which is recognized and complied with by the younger. Parental authority is never strictly enforced, but the children readily defer to the wishes of their parents—not only when young, but after reaching man's estate. The old people are consulted upon all matters of interest. The authority of parents in their family, and of the chief, or ish-u-mat-tah, in his tribe, is enforced without fear of punishment or hope of reward.

When a person offends the sentiment of a community, or inflicts injury upon a neighbor, the matter is talked over among those interested, and reparation may be demanded in the shape of payment, not in money, for they have none, or anything that represents it, but in goods, such as a knife, a sled, a dog, gun, fish-hooks, walrus line, or, indeed, anything that comes handy. There the matter ends; or, if the offender declines to settle, the case may be referred to the ish-u-mat-tah, who will probably insist that payment be made. And yet should the delinquent still prove contumacious and refuse to pay, the matter rests there—there is no punishment for his offence. The well-behaved will talk to the refractory one and say, "ma-muk-poo-now" (no good), but that is all. Should he be hungry or his family unprovided for, the others will all assist him just the same as if he did well and obeyed their laws and customs. He can come into their igloos and chat with them upon the topics of the day, or join in the meal that is under discussion, and the stranger would never know but that the utmost harmony existed among them. If you were one for whom the community had respect, they might privately inform you that "so and so" was "no good," but you would never suspect it from their actions toward him.

So it is in the treatment of their children. Punishment for wrong-doing is almost unheard of, and as for striking a male child, all would recoil from such a thought with horror. The male child, and especially the heir, is a prince in his own family circle. Everything is deferred to his wishes unless he can be persuaded to surrender it. With female children it is different. They must submit to every act of tyranny on the part of their brothers at once, or feel the weight of a parent's hand. Nothing would seem more abhorrent to an Esquimau mind than the thought of striking a man or boy; but to strike a woman or girl is, on the contrary, quite proper, and, indeed, laudable. And when one of those powerful savages strikes his wife it is no gentle love tap, but a blow that might stagger a pugilist. I remember once seeing an Esquimau for whom I entertained the greatest respect, strike his gentle and affectionate young wife, the mother of two fine children. He struck her upon the head with an an-out-ah (a stick made for beating the snow off of fur clothing, and in form and weight like a policeman's club). Two blows fell in quick succession upon that devoted head, and made the igloo ring again. I was undressed and in my sleeping bag at the time, but it was with the greatest difficulty that I could restrain myself from jumping up and interfering to prevent the outrage. It required all the nerve I could muster. I thought I would never respect my friend again; but after a while I began to look upon it more calmly, and in the light of his early training and daily experience for years and years I thought better of him, though not of the act.

They say it is a proper thing to whip women, "it makes them good," and they might add, "it is so perfectly safe". I have often talked with them about it and tried to explain that it was regarded by white people as cowardly to strike a defenceless creature, but this was utterly beyond their comprehension. They could understand that it would be wrong to strike a male, but a female—that was an entirely different thing. Their system of government in regard to both families and communities seems to produce good results. Children are obedient and attentive to their parents, either natural or adopted, and there is but little occasion for governmental interference in the concerns of the people.

Whenever difference of opinion gives rise to difficulty and their intercourse, their usual method of settling the dispute is for those immediately concerned to assemble in some igloo, with several of the old men, and talk the matter over until some definite plan of settlement is reached. This usually proves effectual. I have seen several of these talks, and though I could not understand much of what was said, unless I knew beforehand about what it would be, I could see that the spirit of conciliation manifested itself. All seemed disposed to do what was right, not from fear of punishment for doing wrong, but simply because it was right. They are not given to ceremony on such occasions, or, in fact, upon any other occasion. All the women retire from the igloo or tupic where the talk is to be held when the men come in. Then some raw meat is produced, if there is any to be had, and after eating pipes are lighted and the subject for discussion is approached, conversation gradually drifting in that direction. Esquimaux never do anything in a hurry, and these long-winded roundabout chats are exceedingly congenial to their tastes. So imbued do they become with this idea that even "Joe," notwithstanding his long residence with civilized people, could not shake it off.

For instance, Lieutenant Schwatka would say:—"'Joe,' I wish you would tell the hunters that for the present they must save the saddles of the reindeer they kill to go upon the sleds, and feed the remainder of the carcasses to the dogs." "Joe" would invariably say, "Yes, to-night we will all get together and talk it over." "There is no necessity for talking it over, 'Joe;' just tell them what I say." But, nevertheless, "Joe" would have his powwow, and his feed and his smoke, even upon less important matters than the one mentioned in illustration.

The Esquimaux are polygamists, no distinction whatever being placed upon the number of wives a man shall have. I have never, however, known of any instance of one having more than two at a time. This is very common, however, especially among the Iwilliks and Kinnepatoos, where there is a surplus of women. At least half of their married men have two wives. Every woman is married as soon as she arrives at a marriageable age, and whenever a man dies his wife is taken by some one else, so that with them old maids and widows are unknown.

Instances of polygamy are not so common among the Netchillik nation, for the reason, it is said by the tribes in their vicinity, that they have a custom that prevents the accumulation of women to be taken care of. Their neighbors say that they kill their female babes as soon as born. The first is usually allowed to live, and one other may stand some chance, but that ends the matter. I cannot vouch for the truth of the assertion from my personal knowledge. I can only say that there were more unmarried young men among the Netchilliks and Ookjooliks whom we met than in any other tribe, and but few men with two wives. Among the children there were plenty of boys and but few girls. I understand that the mothers often would be willing to rear their daughters; but the fathers, who have supreme control in their families, insist upon getting rid of useless mouths and choke their infant babes to death, the mothers readily acquiescing. Equeesik, one of our hunters on the sledge journey, who is himself a Netchillik, denies this charge of female Herodism. He told me that it used to be the custom with his people, or some of them at any rate, but that they do not do so any more. I know he has two daughters, one of which was born within a few days' march of Depot Island, on our return trip, and has no son.

The custom of giving away their children is very common among all tribes, and a young wife who loses her first-born has seldom any difficulty in getting a substitute from some one better supplied. Infants are never weaned. I have seen children four and five years old playing, out doors, stop once in a while to run in to their mothers, and cry until they received their milk.

There is very little regard for life manifested by any of the Esquimaux. Several instances of sudden and strange deaths occurred among the infant children at Depot Island and vicinity while we were encamped there. If it were a male child that died, it occasioned some regret, but if it were a female it was considered all right. Even if it were well known that an Inuit had murdered his child, or had killed any one else in cold blood, nothing would be done about it, except that the relatives of a murdered man would probably ask to be paid for the slaughter, and if the request were complied with, that would set the matter at rest. Should it not be complied with, the probability is that the sons or brothers of the victim would embrace some opportunity to kill the murderer and give rise for a demand of payment from the family of the slain murderer, and in case of non-fulfilment a vendetta be established, as is the case now in the tribe that dwells on the coast of Baffin's Bay, near the entrance to Eclipse Sound.

Just before we left Depot Island, in the summer of 1880, there arrived several families from that section of the Arctic, who came, I as informed, to get rid of the vendetta. It seems that the present cause of trouble was a young man, quite small in stature, but very active and energetic, of whom the refugees were very much afraid. Some of their relatives had killed this young man's father, and when they refused to pay for it he took occasion to kill the murderer, for which, as is the custom, they in turn demanded payment. He refused satisfaction, and one night about a year ago some of these people went to his igloo while the family were in bed, and through a small hole that had melted through the snow, they pointed a rifle, and, as they supposed, killed their enemy, of whom they were so much afraid. Unfortunately for them they found they had made a mistake, as instead of killing him they had killed his oldest son, who lay alongside of him in bed. The father said nothing, but reached for his gun, which he had always convenient for an emergency, and shortly after the shot was fired, when the murderer returned to peep through the hole and see the effect of his aim, the father shot him dead. Then it was that the remaining members of the family found that this business was getting to be a nuisance and concluded to leave. As they told me when speaking of the matter, "So much shooting is no good."

Their method of carrying on this sort of warfare is not at all like the duello of Christendom. They don't stand up and fight it out, facing each other; but, on the contrary, appear to be good friends all the time, until the aggrieved one finds what he considers to be the propitious moment, and acts accordingly. They never do anything on the spur of the moment. It takes them a long time to make up their minds, and whatever they do they do deliberately. The rapid and just retribution that followed the killing of the child alluded to in this illustration is the only instance of the kind I know of, though I know of a number where a few weeks or years intervened, the enemies associating like the others and eating in common.

There are no wedding ceremonies among the Esquimaux, and hardly anything like sentiment is known. The relation of man and wife is purely a matter of convenience. The woman requires food, and the man needs some one to make his clothing and to take charge of his dwelling while he is hunting. Marriages are usually contracted while the interested parties are children. The father of the boy selects a little girl who is to be his daughter-in-law, and pays her father something. Perhaps it is a snow-knife, or a sled, or a dog, or now, that many of them are armed with firelocks, the price paid may be a handful of powder and a dozen percussion caps. The children are then affianced, and when arrived at a proper age they live together. The wife then has her face tattooed with lamp-black and is regarded as a matron in society. The method of tattooing is to pass a needle under the skin, and as soon as it is withdrawn its course is followed by a thin piece of pine stick dipped in oil and rubbed in the soot from the bottom of a kettle. The forehead is decorated with a letter V in double lines, the angle very acute, passing down between the eyes almost to the bridge of the nose, and sloping gracefully to the right and left before reaching the roots of the hair. Each cheek is adorned with an egg-shaped pattern, commencing near the wing of the nose and sloping upward toward the corner of the eye; these lines are also double. The most ornamented part, however, is the chin, which receives a gridiron pattern; the lines double from the edge of the lower lip, and reaching to the throat toward the corners of the mouth, sloping outward to the angle of the lower jaw. This is all that is required by custom, but some of the belles do not stop here. Their hands, arms, legs, feet, and in fact their whole bodies are covered with blue tracery that would throw Captain Constantinus completely in the shade. Ionic columns, Corinthian capitals, together with Gothic structures of every kind, are erected wherever there is an opportunity to place them; but I never saw any attempt at figure or animal drawing for personal decoration. The forms are generally geometrical in design and symmetrical in arrangement, each limb receiving the same ornamentation as its fellow. None of the men are tattooed.

Some tribes are more profuse in this sort of decoration than others. The Iwillik, and Kinnepatoos are similar, and as I have described; but the Netchillik, Ookjoolik, and Ooqueesiksillik women have the designs upon their faces constructed with three lines instead of two, one of them being broader than the others. The pattern is the same as that of the Iwilliks and Kinnepatoos, with the addition of an olive branch at the outside corners of the eyes and mouth.

Marriage with them is not the sacred institution of civilization, but exchanges are very common. If a man who is going on a journey has a wife encumbered with a child that would make travelling unpleasant, he exchanges wives with some friend who remains in camp and has no such inconvenience. Sometimes a man will want a younger wife to travel with, and in that case effects an exchange, and sometimes such exchanges are made for no especial reason, and among friends it is a usual thing to exchange wives for a week or two about every two months. Unmarried men who are going on a journey have no difficulty in borrowing a wife for the time being, and sometimes purchase the better half altogether.

It might be supposed that in such a state of society there would be no romances, no marrying for love; but that would be a mistake, for there have been several romantic little episodes that came under my observation during my residence in North Hudson's Bay. There is a poor old man dwelling with the Iwilliks, near Depot Island, named Iteguark, who had two very attractive and useful wives, or Nu-lee-aug-ar, as is the native term. The old man had been a good hunter, but a few years ago met with an accident that resulted in his right knee becoming stiffened, and his hunting days were over. He can still hunt seals through the ice, but cannot work up to them on top of the ice, nor can he chase the reindeer and musk-ox on his native hills. Then it was that Oxeomadiddlee looked with envious eyes upon the youngest and fairest of Iteguark's wives, and induced her to come and live with him. She knew that her new lover was strong and active, and better able to support her than her old love, and listened to the voice of the tempter.

Iteguark was not disposed to submit meekly to this treachery on the part of his friend Oxeomadiddlee, so one morning while the truant wife and her new husband were sleeping in their igloo, Iteguark entered and sought to take the life of the seducer with a hunting knife. But Oxeomadiddlee was on his guard, and being a man of immense strength, he caught his adversary by the wrist, and by the sheer force of his grip compelled him to drop the weapon on the floor. He then released his hold, and Iteguark rushed out to his own igloo and got his bow and

209

quiver; but his enemy was still watchful, and took the bow and arrows away and destroyed them. Here ended hostilities. Oxeomadiddlee paid the old man for his wife, and that settled it forever. Presently another Inuit, named Eyerloo, fell desperately in love with poor old Iteguark's remaining wife, and with his arts and blandishments won her away from her husband. There was no fight this time. The poor old man gave up completely, and said the world was all wrong, and he only waited for his summons to leave it and mount the golden stairs.

A few years ago an Igloolip Inuit named Kyack won the affections of one of Ikomar's wives and this brought on a duel in which Kyack came very near leaving Mrs. Kyack a widow. Ikomar got the head of his enemy in chancery, and tightened his arm around his neck until Kyack dropped lifeless upon the snow. He gradually recovered, and would have returned the stolen wife, but Ikomar refused to take her back, and demanded payment instead. This was tendered to him, and being appeased by the offer further trouble was avoided.

Punnie, one of Armow's daughters, was, in her youth, affianced to Sebeucktelee, but when she reached a marriageable age became the wife of Conwechungk, her adopted brother. The pretext for this new arrangement was that Sebeucktelee's father had not made payment at the time he made the wedding contract, and that Punnie loved Conwechungk better anyhow, and would take advantage of the omission of the intended father-in-law. It made no difference that Conwechungk had another wife—in fact, it was all the better on that account, for he would have one for himself and another to loan around to his neighbors. When I left Depot Island I noticed that he had not only loaned his first wife away, but had traded his dearly beloved Punnie for Tockoleegeetais' wife for an indefinite period, while Sebeucktelee had taken to his bosom Netchuk, the discarded wife of Shockpenark. But life is altogether too short to allow of a complete and reliable record being made of the social gossip of an Esquimau village. Intermarriages are common, and everybody is related to every one else in the most intricate and astonishing manner. I once read of a man who married a widow, and his father, subsequently marrying the daughter of this same widow, was driven insane by trying to ascertain the exact relationship of their children. Such trifles have no effect upon the Inuit brain, or the entire nation would long ago have become raving maniacs.

The natives of Hudson's Strait dress very much like the others, the difference being in the women's hoods, which, instead of being long and narrow, are long and wide, and provided with a drawing string. Instead of the long stockings, they wear a pair of leggings that reach about half-way up the thigh, and trousers that are much shorter than those of the western tribes. The Kinnepatoos are by all odds the most tasteful in their dress, and their clothing is made of skins more carefully prepared and better sewed than that of the others, except in occasional instances.

The bedding of all these Esquimaux is made of reindeer-skins—thick untanned skins of the buck forming what corresponds with the mattresses, and a blanket to cover them is made of well-tanned doe-skins, sewn together so as to be wide at the top and narrowing into a bag at the feet. All sleep naked, winter and summer, a single blanket formed of three doe-skins covering a father, mother, and all the children.

It would astonish a civilized spectator to see how many people can be stowed away to sleep in one small igloo and under one blanket; but the proverbial illustration of a box of sardines would almost represent a skirmish line in comparison. Each one is rolled up into a little ball, or else arms, legs and bodies are so inextricably interwoven, that it would be impossible for any but the owners to unravel them. And these bodies are like so many little ovens, so that, no matter how cold it be, when once within the igloo, the snow-block door put up and chinked, and all stowed away in bed, Jack Frost can be successfully defied.

Esquimaux Building a Hut.

As probably many people know, an igloo is usually built of snow. The word, however, means house, and as their houses consist of a single room, it also means room. Sometimes at points that are regularly occupied during the winter months igloos are built of stones, and moss piled up around and over them, so that when covered by the winter snows they make very comfortable dwellings. This is the case at Igloolik, which means the place of igloos, and also near Tulloch Point, on King William Land, where the ruins of these underground houses were quite numerous. They had been built a great many years ago by the Ookjooliks, when they occupied the land before the Netchillik invasion. A long, low passage-way leads into each dwelling, so constructed as to exclude the wind from the interior, though ventilation is permitted by leaving open the door. This, by the way, is an Inuit custom. Even in the coldest weather the door is open, except when the occupants are asleep, and it is only closed then to keep the dogs from making a raid on the igloo. If the door faces the wind, a shelter is erected outside to cut off the wind, so that the door need not be closed. The coldest day I ever saw, when the thermometer was seventy-one degrees below zero, the door of our igloo was open all the time we were not asleep. A snow igloo is made of snow-blocks about three feet long by eighteen inches wide and five or six inches thick.

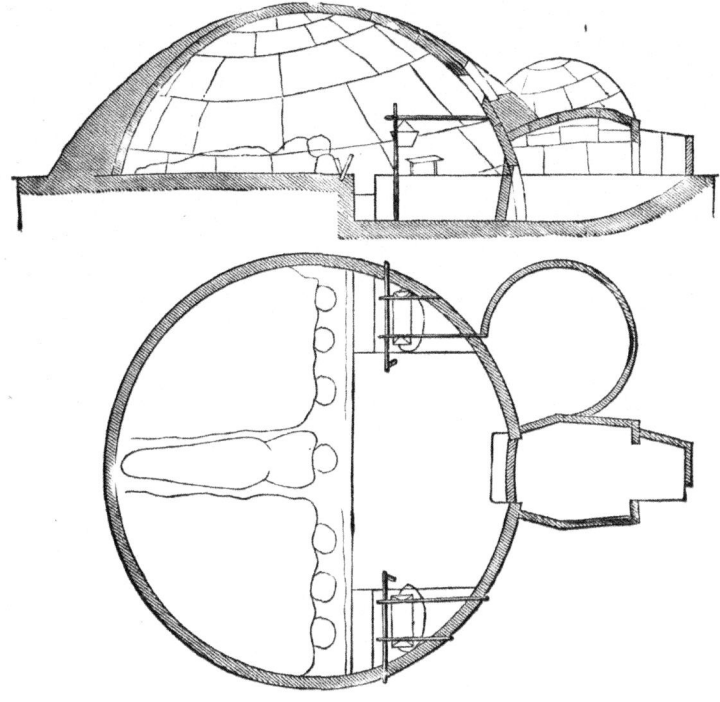

Section and Plan of Esquimau Hut.

The snow-knife is simply a large thin-bladed knife, like a cheese-knife of the grocery stores, with a handle made large enough to be conveniently grasped with both hands. Before iron and knives became so plentiful as at present, snow-knives were made of bone and reindeer or musk-ox horn, but such knives are quite rare now. The Netchillik, Ookjoolik, and Ooqueesiksillik tribes are still quite deficient in iron weapons and implements, and many of their knives are marvels of ingenuity. I saw several made of a little tip of iron, perhaps an inch square, mounted on a handle two feet long, and so shaped that the iron would do most of the cutting and scratching, and the handle acted merely as a wedge to assist the operation. I also saw a man making a knife by cutting a thick piece of iron with a cold chisel, afterward to be pounded out flat and ground down on stones. The entire operation would probably take about three or four weeks with the poor tools at their disposal.

The builder selects snow of the proper consistency by sounding a drift with a cane, made for the purpose, of reindeer horn, straightened by steaming, and worked down until about half an inch in diameter, with a ferule of walrus tusk or the tooth of a bear on the bottom. By thrusting this into the snow he can tell whether the layers deposited by successive winds are separated by bands of soft snow, which would cause the blocks to break. When the snow is selected, he digs a pit to the depth of eighteen inches or two feet, and about the length of the snow-block. He then steps down into the pit and proceeds to cut out the blocks by first cutting down at the ends of the pit, and then the bottom afterward, cutting a little channel about an inch or two deep, marking the thickness of the proposed block.

Now comes the part that requires practice to accomplish successfully. The expert will, with a few thrusts of his knife in just the right places, split off the snow-block and lift it carefully out to await removal to its position on the wall. The tyro will almost inevitably break the block into two or three pieces, utterly unfit for the use of the builder. When two men are building an igloo, one cuts the blocks and the other erects the walls. When sufficient blocks have been cut out to commence work with, the builder marks with his eye, or perhaps draws a line with his knife describing the circumference of the building, usually a circle about ten or twelve feet in diameter. The first row of blocks is then arranged, the blocks placed so as to incline inward and resting against each other at the ends, thus affording mutual support. When this row is completed the builder cuts away the first and second blocks, slanting them from the ground upward, so that the second tier resting upon the edges of the first row can be continued on and around spirally, and by gradually increasing the inward slant a perfect dome is constructed of such strength that the builder can lie flat on the outside while chinking the interstices between the blocks. The chinking is, however, usually done by the women and children as the building progresses, and additional protection secured from the winds in very cold weather by banking up a large wooden snow shovel, the snow at the base often being piled to the depth of three or four feet. This makes the igloo perfectly impervious to the wind in the most tempestuous weather. When the house is completed, the builders are walled in. Then a small hole about two feet square is cut in the wall, on the side away from where the entrance is to be located, and is used to pass in the lamps and bedding. It is then walled up and the regular door cut, about two feet high, and nitched at the top. It would bring bad luck to carry the bedding into the igloo by the same door it would be taken out. Before the door is opened the bed is constructed, of snow-blocks, and made from one to three or four feet high, and occupies about three-fourths of the entire space. The higher the bed and the lower the door, the warmer the igloo will be.

The house being built, passes into the care of the women, who arrange the beds and put up the lamps for lighting, warming, and cooking. The woman's place in the igloo is on either side of the bed, and next to the wall. In front of her she arranges her lamp, which is a long, shallow basin of soapstone, the front edge straight and the back describing an arc. The wick, which is composed of pulverized moss, is arranged along the front edge, and kept moistened by the oil that fills the lamp by tilting it forward—the lamp being delicately poised, with this end in view, upon three sticks driven into the snow beneath it. If there be two women, they occupy both ends of the bed, each with her lamp in front of her. Over each lamp is constructed a frame upon which to dry stockings that have become moistened by perspiration during the day's exercise, and from which depends the kettle for melting snow or ice to make water or to cook. The distinctive Esquimau kettle (oo-quee'-sik) is made of soapstone and is flat bottomed. It is made long and narrow, so as to fit the flame of the lamp, and to derive all the benefit possible therefrom. It has the advantage over the iron and copper kettles, that have come into use through trade with the whalemen and Hudson Bay Company's posts, of cooking more rapidly and of not being injured if left over the flame without water.

Esquimau Woman Cooking.

216

It is the duty of the women to attend constantly to the lamps, to melt water for drinking and cooking, and to cook the food. They also turn the wet shoes and stockings inside out and dry them at night. A "good wife" is one who sleeps but little after a hard day's march, but attends constantly to the articles upon the drying frame, turning them over and replacing the dry with wet. When one frame full of clothing has been dried, she places the articles under her in the bed, so that the heat of her body will keep them warm and dry, and replaces them upon the frame with other articles. She gets up long before any one else is awake and looks carefully over all the clothing to see what mending is required. Her position, when not asleep, is with her bare feet bent under her in Turkish fashion, and there she sits all day long before her fire, engaged in making clothing, cooking, or other household duties, and is seldom idle. When at work she lifts up her voice and sings. The tune lacks melody but not power. It is a relief to her weary soul, and few would be cruel enough to deprive her of that comfort, for her pleasures are not many. She is the slave of her children and her husband, and is treated to more abuse than affection.

CHAPTER XVI

HOMEWARD

Notwithstanding the natural anxiety to return again to our native land after so long an absence, it was with genuine regret that we parted from our poor savage friends on Depot Island to embark upon the vessel that was to carry us home. Nor was the sorrow to us alone, for these simple children of the ice have warm hearts. Some of the old women embraced us tenderly, while the salt tears cut deep furrows through the dirt upon their faces. The younger ones exclaimed, and evidently with truth, "Watcheow oounga keeieyoot amasuet" (By and by me cry plenty).

"Papa," Armow, and Ishnark—better known as "Jerry," or "Jelly," as they pronounce it—held our hands as if reluctant to let go, and gazing wistfully into our faces said, "Shoogarme watcheow tukko" (I hope by and by to see you). It is impossible to translate exactly their meaning in this short sentence, but it is more as if they would say, "Surely it seems impossible that we shall never see you again."

That they were in earnest in the expression of their grief I have every reason to believe, for they had shown their kindly interest and affection at a time that if ever one's affection is put to the test theirs was. They had, so to speak, adopted us as their children. Not merely had they divided their last morsel of food, but had given to us and their children, and had gone without themselves. It was merely some walrus hide that had been saved to make soles for their shoes, but nevertheless it was literally their last mouthful, and when that was gone we all went hungry until the long-continued storm abated and an opportunity was afforded to kill a walrus, which appeased our hunger for the time being. Is it unnatural that we should absolutely love these kind friends, or was it a thing to be ashamed of that theirs were not the only tears that fell at parting? Of all savages—I was going to say of all people—commend me to these simple-hearted Esquimaux, with all their dirt and gluttony, for genuine, self-sacrificing hospitality. As we were being rowed out to the ship by an Inuit crew at ten o'clock on the night of the 1st of August, our faces were turned toward the land, where the sky was still brilliant with the light of a gorgeous sunset. Lieutenant Schwatka sat beside me in the bow of the boat, and neither of us had spoken since we left the shore, until he turned to me and said, "I was not prepared for this."

"Prepared for what?" said I.

"I was not prepared to feel the pain of parting from these people and this country as I feel it now. Even the near prospect of getting back to civilization, and of meeting friends and hearing news scarcely ameliorates the pang at this moment. But it will soon be over, I suppose."

At last we were all on board the ship, and when the men began to weigh anchor, merrily singing over their work, the three boat-loads of Inuits put off hastily, though they paddled around the vessel and seemed loath to depart.

"Where is Toolooah—did he bid you good-by, governor?" said I to Lieutenant Schwatka.

"No," he replied, "but you can see him here;" and stepping up to the side of the ship I saw our Toolooah seated in the bow of Armow's boat, his head bent down and his face buried in his hands.

"I can understand his feelings exactly," said the governor. "He dare not trust himself to go through the ordeal, poor fellow. He knew he would break down when it came to that, and I am glad he didn't, for I am afraid I should too."

Until the morning that we left, it had been confidently

expected that Toolooah and his family, consisting of his wife and two children, would accompany us to the United States. It had been the great ambition of his life to visit the wonderful white men's country, and Lieutenant Schwatka had promised to take him home, provided he could obtain the consent of the captain of the vessel in which we returned. Captain Baker had already given his consent, and there seemed nothing to interfere with their plans. Toolooah and his wife were busy in securing suitable clothing in which to appear abroad when occasion should arise for wearing it, and the faithful services he had rendered on our sledge journey were to be recompensed in the United States, from which he would take home an outfit that should last as long as he lived. But the last day we were on shore some of the old men came to Lieutenant Schwatka, and begged he would not be angry if they said that a long and anxious consultation had resulted in the conclusion that it would be running too great a risk for Toolooah to go to the United States. No man of their tribe had ever been to a civilized country but "Esquimau Joe," who, by the bye, had also made up his mind to remain in the Arctic a year or two longer. He had told them of the great mortality attending those of his people from Cumberland Sound who had gone to England and America, and they were afraid. I think that Toolooah, personally, would have willingly encountered the risk; but with these people, such government as they have is patriarchal, and the young men submit with the best grace to the decision of their elders. It was a matter of regret both to Lieutenant Schwatka and myself that we did not have an opportunity to bestow the attention upon him in our own land that his constant care for our safety and comfort in his country entitled him to at our hands.

The anchor soon swung at the bow of the 'George and Mary', and her yards were squared for Marble Island, where we were to take on board water for the homeward-bound voyage. Our Inuit friends shouted their last farewells, and we were actually "en route" home.

Fortunate was it for us that there was a kind-hearted whaler in Hudson's Bay, or we would have been compelled to spend at least one more winter in the polar regions. But Captain Baker treated us with the greatest consideration not only while we were his guests during the spring at Marble Island, but when we returned to Depot Island he gave us such provisions from his stores as he could spare, and without this assistance we would have suffered considerably, for twice again after our return the natives were entirely without food for several days. But instead of our starving with them, we were enabled to save these poor people much suffering by sharing our slender stock with them. We left the ship in her winter quarters on the 3d of May, and on the 11th pitched our tent on the highest rock on Depot Island. The natives soon came from their igloos on the ice about a mile away, and gathered around us. Whenever they killed a walrus or a seal they brought us some of the meat, for which we paid them, as usual, with powder, caps, or lead. But from the 22d of May, when they killed two walrus, until the 7th of June, when the ship hove in sight from her winter quarters, the weather had been such that they had killed nothing but two small seals. The consequence was that for several days they were without food, and our provisions were gone the day before, so that when the ship was seen we were waiting patiently until the Inuits returned from the pursuit of some walrus that were seen on the ice, in order to break our fast. It was not only a joyful sight to see the ship at this time, but an additional pleasure to note the cloud of thick black smote that hung over her deck, denoting that they had killed a whale and were boiling out the blubber. This was good luck for the officers and crew, and fortunate for us, because the black skin of the whale is exceedingly palatable and wholesome food, and there would in all probability be enough of it on board to keep us and our Inuit allies from hunger for a long time, at least until they could secure food by hunting.

We were pleased to learn that the whalers had killed the only whale they saw, which augured a successful season for them. It eventually proved, however, that the augury was delusive, for from that time forward they did not see another whale, though they cruised the bay until the 9th of August. Subsequently we learned that the whales had all gone out of Hudson's Bay through the strait in the early spring, owing to the entire absence of whale food, which had probably been destroyed by the intense severity of the winter. The natives living near North Bluff and Hudson's Strait had seen plenty of whales passing eastward early in the season, when the ice was still thick, or, as one of them told me, "when the young seal are born," which is in the latter part of March and early in April. They had killed three large whales and struck two others that escaped. We went into North Bay and found these Inuits encamped on the mainland, about fifteen miles from the mouth of the bay, and Captain Baker bought from them a head of whalebone, which they said was at Akkolear, which was still further up the bay, or strait, as it proved to be.

Mr. Williams, first officer of the 'George and Mary', went with two boats and some Inuit guides, sailing directly up the bay toward the north-west until it debouched again upon Hudson's Strait, about fifty miles above where we were anchored, or about sixty-five miles north-west of North Bluff. Here he found the whalebone as described by the natives, and brought it on board after an absence of four days.

The large island, or, in fact, two islands that are thus formed, as there is another passage into the sea about twenty-five miles north of North Bluff, are called by the natives "Kigyuektukjuar," in view of their insular character. Kigyuektuk means island, and especially a large island, King William Land being thus distinguished by them as the island. A "small island" is Kigyuektower, and "long island" Kigyuektukjuar.

The land on the north and east of North Bay is called Queennah, which means "all right," and was given to it in view of the fact that in winter it is filled with reindeer, who can go no farther south in their migration, and spend the winter on the Meta Incognita of Queen Elizabeth, or the Queennah of the Esquimaux. Akkolear means a narrow passage or channel, where the land is visible on both sides as you pass through. The natives we met here are more cleanly in their persons and dress than any others we saw on the Arctic, but there their superiority ends. They are most persistent beggars, and indeed require watching, or they will sometimes steal, a vice to which the Esquimaux as a nation are little given. I saw two of their women, while sitting in our cabin, comb their hair without discovering a single specimen of the genus pediculosum; while, should any one of the other tribes we met have done the same thing, the result would have been most overwhelmingly satisfactory. But though they are dirty they will neither lie nor steal, except in rare instances. The natives of the north shore of Hudson's Strait were spoken of by the early explorers of the present century—Parry, Back, and Lyon—as rude, dirty, and unreliable, and they have not improved much since that day, except in regard to dirt. They are certainly more cleanly—one good trait they have learned from association with white people, to counterbalance many vices thus acquired. But never was I more confounded than when an old woman, who brought a pair of fine fur stockings to Captain Baker, asked for a pack of cards in exchange. The captain had brought her to me to act as interpreter for him, but though the word she used sounded familiar to me I could not for the life of me remember what it meant in English until she made motions of dealing cards and said, "Keeng, kevven, zhak." Then the light burst upon me, but nothing had been further from my mind than playing-cards as an article of trade.

Three of these women wore calico skirts, but they looked as much out of place on them as they would on the men, and I came to the conclusion that it does indeed require some art to look well in a "pinned back." These women, when their skirts were in the way of climbing up the side of the vessel, either gathered them up out of the way or took them off and passed them up separately. Their clothing was complete without this civilized inconvenience, which had no more to do with their costume than the buttons on the back of a man's coat. The temperature in Hudson's Strait was much lower than in the bay, and we felt the cold intensely. I began to imagine that my acclimatization had not been complete, until I noticed that the Inuits who came on board complained of the cold as much as we did. Indeed, I believe that one feels the cold in an Arctic summer much more disagreeably than in the winter. The low temperature in the strait is in all probability attributable to the ice that is constantly there, either local ice or the pack brought down from Fox Channel by the wind and current. The great Grinnell Glacier, on Meta Incognita, which Captain Hall estimated to be one hundred miles in extent, must also have considerable effect upon the climate. As we passed down toward Resolution Island we could see this great sea of ice from the deck of the vessel in all its solemn grandeur, surrounded by lofty peaks clad in their ever-enduring mantles of snow.

I did not go on shore while our vessel lay at anchor in North Bay, for I had no anxiety to encounter the mosquitoes which abound there, though not to the extent that makes life such a burden as upon the eastern shores of Hudson's Bay. While our water-casks were being filled at Marble Island in the early part of August, Captain Baker and I went in one of the ship's boats to the main-land, about fifteen miles to the south-west, to secure a lot of musk-ox skins and other articles of trade at a Kinnepatooan encampment there, and though we spent but one night on shore, I never before endured such torture from so small a cause as the mosquitoes occasioned us. Indeed, my hands and his for a month afterward, were swollen and sore from the venom of these abominable little pests. They are not like civilized mosquitoes, for no amount of brushing or fanning will keep them away. Their sociability is unbounded, and you have absolutely to push them off, a handful at a time, while their places are at once filled by others, the air teeming with them all the time. The natives keep their tents filled with smoke from a slow, smouldering fire in the doorway, which is the only plan to render them habitable at all; but the remedy is only one degree better than the disease, as Captain Baker remarked to me, with his eyes filled with tears. The only relief from these torments is a strong breeze from the water, which carries them away; but even then it is not safe to seek shelter in the lee of a tent, for there they swarm and are as vigorous in their attacks as during a calm. The men wear mosquito-net hoods over their heads and shoulders while in camp or hunting, and women and children live in the smoke of their smouldering peat fires.

The shores of Hudson's Bay are low and barren, and abound in lakes of every size and shape. They are too low to produce glaciers, but are just right for the production of the finest crop of mosquitoes to be found in the world, as has previously been remarked by Franklin, Richardson, Back, and, indeed, all the explorers of this territory. After leaving Marble Island we sailed toward Depot Island, Cape Fullerton, and Whale Point, so that we might see any other ships that had come in this season and get some news from them. We found plenty of ice in Daly Bay and the entrance to Rowe's Welcome, the ice bridge still extending from near Whale Point to Southampton Island.

On Sunday the 8th of August, while moving slowly through the ice-pack off Cape Fullerton, we saw a she-bear and cub asleep on a large cake of ice about a quarter of a mile from the ship, and one of the boats was lowered to go in pursuit. Lieutenant Schwatka, Mr. Williams, and I went in the boat, and quite enjoyed the exciting chase. Before the boat was lowered the bears seemed aware of the presence of danger, and took to the water, the old one in her motherly anxiety for the safety of her cub carrying it on her back most of the time. When they found the boat gaining upon them, and close at hand, they left the water and stood at bay on a cake of ice. A bullet from Lieutenant Schwatka's rifle broke the mother's backbone and she dropped, when Mr. Williams gave her the "coup de grace" with a bullet through her head at close range. We were quite anxious to capture the little fellow alive, but found it difficult to kill the mother without wounding him, as he clung to her poor wounded body with the most touching tenacity. It was heartrending to see him try to cover her body with his own little form, and lick her face and wounds, occasionally rising upon his hind legs and growling a fierce warning to his enemies. At this juncture Lieutenant Schwatka got out upon the ice, and, after several ineffectual attempts, at last succeeded in throwing a rope over the head of the cub, which put him in a towering passion. Nevertheless he was towed alongside the ship and hoisted on deck, together with the carcass of his mother, but he never ceased to growl and rush at every one who approached him. We would gladly have brought him alive to the United States, for he was a handsome little rascal, but the vessel was small and devoid of conveniences for that purpose; so the captain ordered him killed, and his fate was, consequently, sealed with a bullet from Mr. Williams's pistol.

We met the whaler 'Isabella' in Fisher's Strait, and the 'Abbott Lawrence' near Charles Island, and from both got some later news, but no letters from either. We learned from them that the 'Abby Bradford' had gone in already, and must have passed us in Fisher's Strait the day before we met the 'Isabella', in a thick fog that prevailed. We were sorry not to have met the 'Abby Bradford' also, for we felt pretty certain that she must have letters for us; but it seemed scarcely worth while to go back in search of her. The 'Isabella' and 'Abby Bradford' had been in company for twenty-seven days from Resolution Island to Nottingham Island, surrounded by ice all the time and narrowly escaping destruction. The 'Isabella' was carried by the current right upon a large iceberg, which would most certainly have wrecked the vessel; but, when just about to strike, the eddy swept them around and past the berg, though they had entirely lost control of the ship. They were both "nipped" by the ice several times, and on one of these occasions the 'Abby Bradford' suffered such a severe strain that her timbers creaked and groaned terribly, and her deck planks were bowed up. So imminent did their peril appear that the boats and provisions were got out upon the ice preparatory to abandoning the vessel, when, just as it seemed as if she must succumb, the pressure was relaxed and the crew returned to their ship. We had head winds before reaching Resolution Island, but after passing Cape Best the winds were fair, and we made a fine run of six days to the latitude of St. John, N. F. We saw a brig off Hamilton Inlet, evidently trying to beat into that harbor; but saw no more vessels until the 2d of September, when we saw a heavily laden bark some distance ahead of us making toward the west. We changed our course so as to endeavor to head her off, but though we gained upon her considerably, could not overtake her before dark. On the 3d we saw a number of vessels, including one steamer, all, except one large merchantman, bound eastward.

A little humpback whale that came playing around our ship, as if trying to get a harpoon in him, prevented our heading off the steamer and getting some late papers. But as soon as a boat was lowered into the water the fishy representative of King Richard thought it began to look too much like business at this time, and hastened off to look for his mother. We saw quite a large school of humpbacks during the same afternoon, but there was too much wind, with the near prospect of a gale, to render it worth while to hunt them. We had some pretty heavy blows on our way home, and on the last day of August we were struck by a squall that gave us a very good idea of what a gale would be like should it have continued for a day or two; but within twenty minutes of the time it struck us it had passed off, the sun was shining brightly, and we were making sail again, with nothing to indicate what had just taken place save a few barrels of immense hailstones that still covered the deck like so much coarse salt and a chilliness in the atmosphere that made you shiver in spite of yourself. It was fearful, though, while it lasted; the lightning and thunder crashes were almost synchronous, indicating a most unpleasant proximity. Since the night of the

2d of September we had been cut off by southwest winds and enveloped with fogs of varying density. Everything on deck was as wet as if a heavy rain-storm had just passed over, and great drops of water kept dropping from the sails and rigging, making it very unpleasant to venture beyond the cabin.

During the morning of the 7th the fog lifted a little and showed us three fishing-smacks anchored about a mile away, and we directed our course toward them, with the hope of getting some fresh fish as well as some fresh news. Mr. Gilbert, second officer of the 'George and Mary', took me in his boat on board the schooner 'Gertrude', of Provincetown, Mass., whose master, Captain John Dillon, extended a hearty welcome. In answer to our first question he told us who were the Presidential candidates. Captain Dillon prevailed upon me to recount some of the incidents of our sledge journey. He seemed very much interested in the recital, brief as it necessarily was, and hospitably pressed us to dine with him, as it was just about his dinner hour. Desiring to impress upon his steward the importance of his guests he said:—"Steward, it is a great treat to see these gentlemen. You ought to take a good look at them. They have had one of the toughest times you ever heard of. They have just come down from—where?" (aside to me). "King William's Land," said I, scarcely able to retain my composure. "King William's Land," he repeated, "and were looking for Franklin." The doubt in his mind as to who this mythical "Franklin" was seeming to add much to the interest that invested us.

We had a substantial meal of fried haddock, which was particularly enjoyable, in the absence of fresh meat on board our ship since the reindeer meat was exhausted. In the laudable pursuit of information I felt interested in seeing how they lived on board these fishing schooners, and had accepted the kind invitation to dinner as much on that account as for the sake of the fresh fish I anticipated. I saw that the cabin was too small to accommodate a dining-table, but had four very wide bunks in it, one of which was the captain's, and the others occupied by two men each. There is not the same amount of discipline on board these vessels, which are out for so short a time, as upon merchantmen or whalers, and all hands eat at the same table. We found the feast spread in the forecastle, which was also used as the galley, and was consequently oppressively warm to us from the north, in this thick, sultry weather. On each side of the forecastle I observed three large bunks, each of which accommodated at least two men. This was their second voyage this summer, they having been fortunate enough to fill up before their first three months had expired. The crews are usually shipped for three months, and receive about $50 compensation for the voyage. If they get full before the time is up, that is their gain. Sometimes, however, they have an interest in the voyage the same as whalers, but usually, I understand, are paid from $40 to $75 for a season, which means three months unless sooner filled. The men do not fish from the deck of the vessel, but from little flat-bottomed dories, each man paddling his own boat and changing its location to suit his whim. When brought on board the vessel the fish are immediately cleaned, split open and salted right down in the hold, without the formality of putting them in barrels or casks. After they are landed on shore they are dried and assorted according to size and sold by the quintal of 112 pounds, though 100 pounds is estimated as a quintal from the hold of the smack. The 'Gertrude' had already 175 quintals on her second cargo the day we were on board, but the captain seemed much more desirous of hearing of our strange adventures than of imparting the information that I sought. He appeared much impressed with the circumstance that we were "worth looking at," as he said, and dwelt much upon the fact that this summer was a good season for him to see strange things.

"On my first voyage this summer," said he, "that little dory, thirteen and a half feet long, in which two young men are going around the world, came alongside my vessel, and I gave them some water and lucky cake, and now I meet you gentlemen from—where?" (addressing me). "King William's Land," said I.

"Oh, yes, King William's Land. Let me have some fish put into your boat before you go." And the kind-hearted fisherman gave us about a barrel of fine fresh cod and haddock, besides a fifty-fathom line and some hooks. He also gave us three late newspapers; and we sent him in return a copy of Hall's "Life Among the Esquimaux," and some other reading matter, besides a pair of sealskin slippers, and a fine walrus skull with the ivory tusks in it. This was a present from Mr. Gilbert. Just as we were about leaving I turned to Mr. Gilbert and said, "The Governor will be glad to hear the news."

"What!" said the surprised skipper, "have you got a real Governor on board?" And then I had to explain that it was merely a title we had bestowed upon Lieutenant Schwatka in view of the faithful care he took of his people, though, I believe, the youngest in the party. The incident was only amusing as showing that the captain had heard so many strange things this morning that he was prepared to believe anything, no matter how absurd it might appear.

The day following our visit to the fishing schooner was still foggy and without a breath of wind stirring. We therefore availed ourselves of the opportunity to use our fish-lines, and succeeded in securing about fifty fine cod and haddock, besides one huge dogfish, which snapped ferociously when hauled into the boat, and had to be despatched with a boat-hook. We experienced considerable squally weather about the middle of September, interspersed with head winds and calms. On the 15th there were several vessels in sight, and a large iron bark came so near that we concluded to send aboard for newspapers. The waist boat was cleared away and the second mate started to intercept the stranger, but scarcely had the boat been lowered into the water when a squall came up and the sea became very rugged, so that in passing to the leeward of the bark, though he shouted out that it was only papers that he wanted, the captain did not hear him, and luffed up into the wind to deaden his headway. But even then the bark drifted ahead so rapidly that it was hard work for our boat to catch it by rowing in such a heavy sea. The stranger then lowered his top-gallant sails and hauled his foreyards aback, and in about twenty-five minutes Mr. Gilbert was alongside. He sprang lightly up the side of the big vessel, and, standing before the captain, with all the characteristic politeness of the French people, presented Captain Baker's compliments and asked for some late papers. The captain of the bark was a splendid old Scotchman who had grown gray battling with stormy seas for many years. But when he found out that all we wanted was newspapers, he was so completely overpowered with surprise that all he could say was, "Well—I'll—be—blanked." This he kept repeating all the way to his cabin as he went to gather some late copies of the 'New York Herald'. When he again came upon deck he had recovered his accustomed composure, and asked where we were from and where bound. He said his vessel was the bark 'Selkirkshire', of Glasgow, from New York the night of the 12th inst., and then turning again to Mr. Gilbert said, "And is that all you wanted? And a fair wind? Why, man, you'll be home to-night. Well—I'll—be—blanked." Never before in all his experience had he known a vessel within two or three days' sail of home, with a fair wind, take so much trouble to stop another merely for the purpose of getting some newspapers. It was rather "a stunner," that is a fact, but at the same time was unintentional. The squall came up after our boat was lowered and prevented Mr. Gilbert doing what he had intended, which was merely to go alongside, get a few papers thrown overboard and drop back, without causing more than five minutes' detention, if any. But the wind prevented their hearing him, when he shouted to them that he only wanted papers, and for them to go ahead, as they missed getting close enough when they passed; so when he saw them taking so much trouble to stop he felt it his duty to pull up and explain on board. Captain Anderson, of the 'Selkirkshire', recovered his equanimity sufficiently to send his best respects to Captain Baker, with the very welcome papers—fresh for us, as there were some as late as the 'Herald' of the Saturday previous. I have no doubt, though, that every time he recalls the episode on his voyage to England he will say to himself, "Well, I'll be——"

Saturday, the 18th, we were becalmed on the George's Bank, about a quarter of a mile from another large bark, bound the same way as we were; and as it is so excessively monotonous at sea, especially in a calm, and knowing that we could not be causing any delay this time, we lowered a boat, and Captain Baker, Lieutenant Schwatka and I paid a visit to Captain Kelly, of the bark 'Thomas Cochrane', of St. John, N. B., fifty-seven days from Gloucester, England, bound for New York. We found Captain Kelly a genial, whole-souled sailor, who received us very cordially, and three hours slipped away most pleasantly in his society. He had his family on board, and said he would have been exceedingly comfortable had he not run short of provisions in such an exceptionally long voyage between the two ports. On the Banks of Newfoundland he had encountered a Norwegian bark loaded with grain, to which he sent a boat with an explanation of his necessities. The captain returned word that he was short himself, but sent a bag of wheat, which he remarked would sustain their lives for some time. Captain Kelly received the wheat graciously, and the next day met an old friend, who sent him stores sufficient to carry him home. Captain Baker told him he could supply him with ship's stores if he desired it, but he said he was all right now and did not require further assistance.

Tuesday noon, "Land, ho!" was shouted from the masthead, and soon the low, white shore of Nantucket was plainly visible. A strong head wind kept us out until Wednesday morning, when we took on board a pilot, and before night were ashore in New Bedford. During the entire trip Captain Baker had done everything in his power to promote the comfort of his passengers, and earned for himself their lasting gratitude.

CHAPTER XVII

THE GRAVES OF THE EXPLORERS

I will briefly bring this record to a conclusion. The map that accompanies it will give the reader an opportunity to more clearly understand the nature of the search conducted by Lieutenant Schwatka over the route of the retreating crews of the 'Erebus' and 'Terror', and by it he can also trace the sledge journey to and from King William Land as well as the preliminary sledge journeys in the winter of 1878 and 1879. The location of each spot where skeletons of the brave fellows were found is marked, and everywhere cenotaphs were erected to their memory. Owing to the length of time that has elapsed since this sad event, it was not always possible to tell the exact number of individuals represented in a pile of bones that we would gather sometimes from an area of nearly a half mile. The skeletons were always incomplete. Sometimes nothing but a skull could be found in the vicinity of a grave, and, again, often the skull would be missing. At one place we could distinguish four right femurs, and could therefore be positive that at least four perished here. This was at the boat place marked on Erebus Bay.

A number of natives whom we interviewed in the Netchillik country asserted most positively that there were two boat places in Erebus Bay, about a quarter of a mile apart; and Captain C. F. Hall obtained the same information while at Shepherd's Bay, in 1869. We therefore made a most careful search for another, after finding the first wreck of a boat at that portion of the coast, but without success. It seemed to us quite important to establish so interesting a fact, but nevertheless the effort was fruitless.

We obtained from the natives wooden implements which were made from fragments of each boat, but the wood from one must have been entirely removed previous to our visit. Whether or not this is the same boat seen by McClintock is a matter that can be ascertained, for we have brought home the prow containing the inscription spoken of by him. He, however, saw portions of but two skeletons, while the collection of bones buried by us here were distinctly of four persons.

North of Collinsen Inlet we found but one grave—that of Lieutenant Irving. We, however visited the sites of several cairns, whose positions are marked upon the map. Although the route to and from Cape Felix is marked by a single line only, it should be remembered that our search extended inland so as to make a broad sweep about five miles from the coast. The point marked as the grave of an officer, between Franklin Point and Erebus Bay, is one of especial interest. The care with which the grave had originally been made seems to indicate the popularity of the individual and that the survivors had not yet exhausted their strength to such a degree as to be the cause of neglect. In fact, there were no evidences anywhere that they had ever neglected showing marked respect to the remains of those of their comrades who perished by their side; but, on the contrary, it is probable that all who died on the march were decently interred. A very significant fact in this connection is recognizable in the appearance of a grave which had been opened by the Esquimaux near Tallock Point. It was made of small stones, while larger and more appropriate abounded in the vicinity, showing the reduced physical condition of the party at the time. It was, indeed, a most touching indication of their devotion to each other under these most adverse circumstances that the grave had been made at all. The graves east of this point presented the same general appearance. This might be considered as an evidence that the boat in Erebus Bay had drifted in after the breaking up of the ice there, while these poor fellows were on their way back to the ships in search of food now known to have been there. It is not likely that the sick or dead would have been deserted by their comrades unless in the direst extremity.

The point marked as the location of the hospital tent is the place spoken of by Ahlangyah, where so many dead bodies were seen by her party after they had spent the summer on King William's Land in consequence of failing to get across Simpson Strait before the ice broke up. Where she met the starving explorers is also indicated. On the mainland the place is marked where the old Ookjoolik Esquimau saw the footprints of the last survivors of the 'Erebus' and 'Terror' in the spring snows of the year 1849. Also, near by is where he and his friends unwittingly scuttled the Northwest Passage ship—the Dangerous Rapids near the mouth of Back's River, the home of the Ooqueesiksillik Esquimaux, and the spot where we loaded our sleds with provisions on our way home. The route down Back's River, as we found its course, is put down, while dotted lines show how it is mapped on the Admiralty charts. It is not discreditable to Back's survey that an error should be made in tracing the course of the river, for it is probable that bad weather hid the sun from his observation at that portion of the river where he could travel very swiftly; while upon our return trip we were moving along this river by stages of not more than from five to nine miles a day. Our course up the river could not have been toward the southwest when we saw the sun rise to the right of our line of march almost daily. The place where the records were destroyed may be seen to the west of Point Richardson.

Among the most important relics of the expedition are two medals. The larger one, found at Lieutenant Irving's grave, is of solid silver; and the neat, cleanly cut edges which are as sharp to-day as if just from the die, indicate the value placed upon it and the care taken of it by its owner. It was buried with his remains at a spot about four miles below Victory Point, on King William's Land, and evidently remained undisturbed until the grave was found by Esquimaux who visited the vicinity some time after McClintock's search, more than twenty years ago.

From its position when found by Lieutenant Schwatka it would appear that it had been taken out of the grave by the natives and laid upon one of the stones forming the wall of the tomb while they were seeking for further plunder, and was subsequently overlooked by them. The remains which were thus identified were sent to grateful relations in Scotland, and buried with due honor in a graveyard of Lieutenant Irving's native town.

The other medal, which was found at Starvation Cove, is of pewter, and may be described as a token commemorative of the launch of the steamship 'Great Britain', by Prince Albert, in July, 1843. The obverse bears a portrait of His Royal Highness, around it inscribed the words:—

PRINCE ALBERT, BORN AUGUST 26, 1819.

The inscription on the reverse reads as follows:—

THE GREAT BRITAIN.
LENGTH 322 ft; BREADTH 50 ft. 6 in.
DEPTH, 32 ft. 6 in.
WEIGHT OF IRON, 1,500 TONS.
1,000 HORSE POWER.
LAUNCHED, JULY 19, 1843,
BY H. R. H. PRINCE ALBERT.

The vessel was built entirely of iron, and was the largest ever constructed at the time of the launch. On that occasion a great banquet was given, and one of the guests carried away the medal, which was destined to be found so many thousand miles away.

Lieutenant Irving's remains were the only ones that could be sufficiently identified to warrant their removal. Had there been others we would have brought them away.

It was a beautiful though saddening spectacle that met our eyes at the only grave upon King William's Land, where the dead had been buried beneath the surface of the ground. Near Point le Vesconte some scattered human bones led to the discovery of the tomb of an officer who had received most careful sepulture at the hands of his surviving friends. A little hillock of sand and gravel—a most rare occurrence upon that forbidding island of clay-stones—afforded an opportunity for Christian-like interment. The dirt had been neatly rounded up, as could be plainly seen, though it had been torn open and robbed by the sacrilegious hands of the savages; and everywhere, amid the debris and mould of the grave, the little wild flowers were thickly spread as if to hide the desecration of unfriendly hands. The fine texture of the cloth and linen and several gilt buttons showed the deceased to have been an officer, but there was nothing to be seen anywhere that would identify the remains to a stranger. Every stone that marked the outline of the tomb was closely scrutinized for a name or initials, but nothing was found. After reinterring the remains, which were gathered together from an area of a quarter of a mile, and erecting a monument, Lieutenant Schwatka plucked a handful of flowers, which he made into a little bouquet, and brought home with him as a memento.

APPENDIX

INUIT PHILOLOGY

Perhaps no branch of Arctic research is of more interest to the scholar than the language of the people who inhabit that region. A careful comparison of the dialect of the different tribes is of great value in ascertaining their history, the origin of the race and the gradual extension of their journeyings to the remotest point from their native land yet reached by them. It is generally admitted that the North American Esquimaux are of Mongolian extraction; that at some period the passage of Behring Strait was affected and the immigrants gradually extended their migration to the eastward and finally occupied Greenland, where the mighty ocean headed them off and brought their wanderings in that direction to an abrupt termination. During what period of the world's history the exodus from Asia occurred is not known. There are those who believe it to have taken place when what is now known as Behring Strait was an isthmus, the shallowness of the water throughout that channel indicating the physical change to have been of comparitively recent date. This opinion was upheld by Lutke in his "Voyage Autour du Monde," vol. 2, page 209, and Whymper, in his work upon Alaska, page 94, alludes to the shallowness of Behring Strait and also of the sea so named, as permitting the whalers to ride at anchor in their deepest parts. Peschel in "Races of Man", page 401, prefers to believe that the transfer was made while Behring Strait still held its present character.

There are not wanting authorities who seek to show that the entire Western Continent was thus peopled by immigration from Asia, and similarity of feature with the Mongolian is traced even to the most southern tribes of South America. The close connection between the "medicine men" of the Indians, the arng-ke-kos of the Esquimaux, and the shamans of Siberia and Brazil, are also quoted to show the probability of one origin. It is, however, in the language of the hyperborean races of America and Asia that the strongest proofs of a like origin is found. The Tshuktshi of Northern Asia, the Esquimaux of America, and the Namollo, all bear a very close relationship, especially in linguistic characteristics.

In common with all the aboriginal languages of America, the Esquimaux language is agglutinative, though, for the accommodation of the white strangers who visit their shores, they separate the words and use them in a single and simple form. In its purity it employs suffixes only for the definition and meaning, though complex sentences are often formed of a single word—that is, it is a polysynthetic in character. No philologist familiar with the whole territory has ever made a comparison of the dialects of the polar tribes, probably because no philologist is familiar with all the dialects spoken there. Everything therefore that would tend to throw any light upon the subject or to place before the scholar material by which to prosecute such philological studies must be regarded as of importance.

The long residence of the Danes in Greenland and their intermarrying with the native Esquimaux, has led to a more thorough acquaintance with the language of the aborigines of that continent, than any other portion of the polar regions. In fact, as long ago as 1804 a complete dictionary of the Greenland tongue was published by Otho Fabricius, the translation being in the Danish language. With the exception of a few fragmentary vocabularies, this is the only work upon which the traveller or the student of the languages of the Polar regions can depend.

Mr. Ivan Petroff, the Alaskan traveller, has taken some pains to compile a vocabulary of the various dialects of the Pacific races with whom he has sojourned, which, when published, will form another link in the chain by which the scholar may trace the spread of the Asiatic tribes along the northern seaboard of America. With the publication of the subjoined vocabulary, in continuation of the philology of the central or Iwillik tribes, the chain may be considered complete.

With these people many of the familiar sounds of the civilized languages are found, as, for instance, the child's first words, an-an-na (mother), ah-dad-ah (father), ah-mam-mah (the mother's breast), ah-pa-pah (little piece of meat, either raw or cooked). Then there is the very natural expression for pain or sickness—ah-ah. Many words seem to indicate the meaning by imitating the action or sound to be described, as the motion of the kittewake when it swoops down toward you with its petulant cry, is well described by the word e-sow'-ook-suck'-too and the vibratory motion of a swinging pendulum by ow-look-a-tak'-took.

The superlative degree is expressed by the suffix adelo—as amasuet (plenty) and amasuadelo (an immense number); also tapsummary (long ago) and tapsumaneadelo (a very long time ago). Examples could be multiplied, but are not necessary. The suffix aloo has somewhat of a similar meaning, or as "Esquimau Joe" translated, it signifies "a big thing;" thus, ivick (walrus), ivicaloo (a big walrus); shoongowyer (beads), shoongowyaloo (big beads), etc. Persons are named usually after some animate or inanimate object, and in repeating to you their own or some one else's name they usually affix the word aloo, as ishuark is a black salmon and also a man's name, but in mentioning the name they always say Ishuark-aloo, though such ceremony is not indulged in on ordinary occasions.

Igeark-too signifies spectacles, and because Lieutenant Schwatka always wore eye-glasses he was known to the natives as Igeark-too-aloo. His companion, the 'Herald' correspondent, was known by a less dignified appellation. A similarity between his name, as they pronounced it, and the English word "mosquito,"—or, as they called it "missergeeter"—led them to distinguish him by the Innuit name for that little pest, keektoeyak-aloo—as "Joe" would translate it "a big mosquito." They make no distinction in gender, often the same name being applied to men and women. There were a man and a woman at Depot Island each named Shiksik (ground squirrel), and you had to distinguish which one you intended when you spoke of either.

They seldom take the trouble to make explanations, and a singular mistake occurred once at Depot Island in that way. On one of the small islands, near the mainland and Hudson Bay, Lieutenant Schwatka saw, in the fall of 1878, a very fine looking dog, called E-luck-e-nuk, and asked its owner's name. He was informed that it belonged to Shiksik, and, as the old woman of that name was in the camp and he knew of none other, he offered to buy it from her for his dog team. She consented to the proposed transfer very readily, and said it was a very fine dog indeed, she had no doubt it would give entire satisfaction. Some time during the winter, after the hunters had all returned from the reindeer country, a little old man offered to sell Lieutenant Schwatka a very fine large dog for one pound of powder and a box of caps, and, when requested to produce his dog, brought in E-luck-e-nuk. The Lieutenant recognized the animal at once by a broken ear and a loose-jointed tail, and, smiling graciously, told the would-be dog seller that the dog already belonged to him by purchase from Shiksik for a similar price, to her in hand paid about six weeks prior to the present occasion. The old man did not seem to understand the matter very clearly and went out for an interpreter, whom he found in "Esquimau Joe." The latter then stated that the dog in question belonged to the person then present, and when Lieutenant Schwatka indignantly asserted that every one in camp declared the dog belonged to Shiksik at the time of purchase, Joe remarked, "At's all right; he name Shiksik, too." As an example of the simplicity of the

Innuit character, it should be remarked that when the purchase was originally made, all the people looked complacently and admiringly on without a word of explanation, though they well knew the mistake, merely remarking the unexampled generosity of Igeark-too-aloo. Under such adverse circumstances does the barterer ply his traffic with the Esquimaux.

It is exceedingly difficult to secure a good interpreter among these people. Even "Esquimau Joe," who travelled so long with Captain Hall, and lived so many years in the United States and England, had but an imperfect knowledge of the English language, though he had been conversant with it almost from infancy. There was, however, at Depot Island, a Kinnepatoo Innuit, who came there from Fort York in the fall of 1878, who spoke the English language like a native—that is to say, like an uneducated native. He would prove almost invaluable as an interpreter for any expedition that expected to come much in contact with the Esquimaux, as all their dialects were understood by him. His father had spoken English and was Dr. Rae's interpreter upon many of his Arctic journeys. This young man had also accompanied that veteran explorer upon his voyage up the Quoich River, and from Repulse Bay to Boothia, at the time he ascertained the fate of the Franklin expedition. In translating from the English to the Innuit language he usually employed the Kennepatoo, his native dialect, which at first was quite confusing, the accentuation of the words being so peculiar to one familiar with the Iwillik tongue only. From him much information concerning the language was derived, and through him one who would give careful consideration could secure much valuable matter, especially concerning the structure of the language.

In one instance, at least, the Innuit language has an advantage over the French. They have a word for "home." You ask an Innuit, Na-moon'? or Na-moon,-oct-pick (Where are you going?) and he may reply, Oo-op-tee'-nar (Home—that is, to my igloo, or my tent, as the case may be). There is an expression that sounds familiar to ears accustomed to the English tongue, but which has another meaning in their language—Ah-me or ar-my'. This is not an exclamation of regret, but simply means, "I do not know."

In the higher latitudes sounds are conveyed to a long distance, owing partially to the peculiar properties of the atmosphere, the comparative evenness of the surface and to the absence of other confusing sounds, for under other conditions they would not be transmitted to any unusual distance. It used to be the custom in the early summer of 1880 for those who had been hunting upon the mainland to come to a point on the shore nearest the Depot Island and to call for the boat to be sent to ferry them over. This nearest point was by triangulation two miles and a half distant. When, however, the distance would be too great for conversation, or the wind would be in the wrong direction, a few signals were used that could be distinguished a great way off. The signal to "come here" is given by standing with your face toward the party with whom you desire to communicate and then raising your right arm to the right and moving it up and down like a pump handle. The effect can be increased by holding a gun or your hat or anything that can be seen at a greater distance in the moving hand. The signal "yes" is made by turning your side to the party and bowing your body forward several times, forming a right angle at the waist.

The Esquimaux language, though comprising but few words, is one that is difficult for foreigners to acquire and equally difficult to write, owing to the existence of sounds that are not heard in any of the civilized tongues and not represented by any combination of the letters of the English alphabet. Though somewhat gutural it is not unmusical, and for the sake of euphony final consonants are often omitted in conversation. As for instance, the Inuit name for Repulse Bay, Iwillik, is more frequently called, "Iwillie," a really musical sound. And so with all such terminations. It is not difficult for a stranger to acquire a sufficient knowledge of the language to enable him to converse with the natives who inhabit the coasts and are in the habit of meeting the whalers who frequent the nothern waters in the pursuit of their avocation. There is a kind of pigeon English in use in these regions that enables the strangers to communicate with the natives and make themselves understood, though they would understand but little of a conversation between two natives. As an illustration, the word "notimer" means "where," and "ki-yete" is used for any form of the verb "to come;" therefore "notimer ki-yete" would be understood by them to mean "Where do you come from?" Now one native addressing another would not use that form at all, but would say "Nuke-pe-wickt," which bears no resemblance to the words used in the whalers' language. Also, take the same word "notimer" and follow it with "owego," which is used for any form of the verb to go, and you have "Notimer owego," "Where are you going?" The native, however, would say "Namoon-ock-pict," or perhaps "Nelle-ock-pin" (which way are you going?). Still they would readily understand the expression familiar to the whalers and traders, as the words are really Esquimaux words, but used in a free, broad sense; as, for instance, the reader would understand a foreigner who used the word "speak" instead of the other words expressing the same thought, as "tell," "ask," "talk," &c. "Speak Charles come here" would convey intelligence to your mind and be understood as well, though not so readily until accustomed to it, as "Tell Charles to come here."

There are also words that neither belong to the Esquimaux nor any other language, but are very valuable and expressive. "Sel-low" has been used for so long a time to express the idea "sit down," and the application of the latter term is so broad, that "sel-low" has been incorporated into the language and was understood even by the natives of the interior whom we met on our sledge journey and who had more of them never before seen a white man. As, for example, you would ask, "Emik sellow cattar?" (Is there any water in the pail?) and be thoroughly understood, though a native would say, "Cattar, emik ta-hong-elar?" Another useful word adopted from the unknown is "seliko," which means to kill, shoot, break, bend, scratch, destroy or any kindred thought. "Took too, seliko, ichbin?" (Did you kill any reindeer?) The old fashion way of putting it is, "Took too par?" But that would only be understood by the natives.

Our interpreter, Ebierbing (Esquimau Joe), says that the language has undergone considerable change since the advent of white men, and even since his early boyhood, and sometimes would tell me of meeting strangers, who came into camp, from the interior who spoke "old fashion," as he called it. This, he said, was especially the case with the inhabitants of Southampton Island, called by the natives "Sedluk." Though situated directly in the line of travel of the whalers in Hudson Bay, all of whom pass directly along its rocky coast, it is an almost unknown territory. It is known to be inhabited, but its people are seldom seen. The head of the island is far from Iwillik, and the frozen straits that separate the two countries would afford an admirable route of communication. The island is said to be well stocked with game and the inhabitants are comparatively comfortable. While our party was in Hudson Bay a whaler was wrecked on the western coast of Southampton, north of cape Kendall, and the crew easily secured a reindeer the day they landed. They remained there but two days and then sought the other shore of Rowe's Welcome, so as to be in the course of the other whalers then in the bay in order that they might be picked up by them. They said, however, that if compelled to remain on the island they had no doubt of their ability to secure plenty of game to maintain them, or at least to keep off scurvy. Last year the captain of the wrecked vessel visited the island of the scene of the wreck in order to save as much as possible from destruction. He went in a whale boat with a crew of Iwillik Esquimaux, and while there met with a party of the natives. I subsequently had a talk with the captain's Iwillik crew and inquired about the people of Sedluk. They told me that their language was "old-fashioned" and that their arms and implements were mostly of the obsolete pattern of the Stone Age.

Though living so near together there had been no communication between the nations; and only once before, about three years previous to my visit to Hudson Bay, when a whale had gone ashore on Sedluk, an Iwillik native on board the vessel that killed the whale went with the crew to claim the carcases and brought news of the foreign country and its people. I was told that the language of these people of Sedluk was similar to that spoken by the fathers and grandfathers of the Iwillik tribe. They had evidently the same origin, and while one became improved by intercourse with foreign nations and adopted words from foreign tongues, the other remained as it was in the past, unimproved by interchange of ideas. I have never seen anything like a full glossary of the Esquimaux language, and believe that at this time, when Arctic affairs are attracting so much attention everywhere, a list of the most important words used in communicating with the natives, and the method of uniting them, would prove quite interesting. My experience was that though we at first found it difficult to talk with the interior tribes they soon caught the idea and conversation became easy. Innukpizookzook, an Ooqueesiksillik woman who with her husband joined our party on Hayes River, learned the method of communication in two weeks, so that it was as easy to hold conversation with her as with any of those who came with us from Hudson Bay and had been accustomed to the peculiar language since their birth. In fact, as a general thing, we found the women much brighter than the men, not only in acquiring language but in understanding the descriptions of wonderful things in the white men's country.

It used to be an endless source of amusement to the men, women, and children in the Arctic regions to look at the pictures in the illustrated books and journals. Colored maps were also very attractive to them, and the large type in advertisements apparently afforded them great pleasure. They were not at particular to hold the pictures right side up; side-wise or upside down seemed quite as satisfactory. Though admiring pictures exceedingly, I did not find them very proficient draughtsmen, and yet nothing seemed to give them more pleasure than to draw with a lead pencil on the margin of every book they could get hold of, and my Nautical Almanac and "Bowditch's Epitome" are profusely illustrated by them. Their favorite subjects were men and women and other animals, always drawn in profile and with half the usual number of feet and legs visible.

GLOSSARY

The following glossary comprises all the words in general use in conversation between the natives and traders in Hudson Bay and Cumberland Sound, and a thorough knowledge of it would enable the student to make himself understood throughout the entire Arctic, with the assistance of a few signs which would naturally suggest themselves at the proper time:

A

Arrow—Kok'-yoke.
Arm—Tel'-oo.
Another—I-pung'-er.
All night—Kuee-en'-nah.
Angry—Mar-me-an'-nah.
All—Ter-mok-er-mingk.
Autumn—Oo-ke-uk'-shark.
Afraid—Kay-pe-en'-nah.
A little while ago, to-day—Wateh-eur'.
Ask—O-kow-te-vah'-vor.
Antlers—Nug'-le-you.
Axe—Oo'-lee-mar.
Aurora Borealis—Ok-sel-e-ak-took, ok-shan'-ak-took.
Air—Ar-ne-yung'-ne-uk.
After, or last—O-puk'-too.
After (to carry)—Ok-la-loo'-goo.
After (to bring)—I'-vah.
Always—E-luk-o-she'-ar.
Alone—In-nu-tu-a-rk'.

249

A game (like gambling)—Nu-glu-tar.
A herd—Ah-mik-kok'-too.
Act of medicine men—Suk-ki'-u.
Apples (dried)—Poo-wow'-yak.
Ankle—Sing-yeung'-mik.
Arm—Ok-sek'-too.

B

Bear—Nan'-nook.
Bear (cub)—Ar-took'-tar.
Bullet—Kok'-yoke.
Bow—Pet-e'-chee.
Bird—Tig'-me-ak.
Boots—Kum'-ming.
Blood—Owg.
Black—Muk'-tuk.
Belch—Neep'-shark.
Brother—An'-ing-er.
Bones—Sow'-ner.
Bag—Ik-pe-air'-re-oo.
Book—Muk-pet-toe'-up.
Belt—Tep'-shee.
Blubber—E-din-yer'.
Bashful—Kung-we-shook'-pook.
Blue—Too-mook'-took.
Breastbone—Sok'-e-djuck.
Backbone—Kee-mik'-look.
Belly—Nong'-ik.
Brain—Kok'-i-tuk.
Beard—Oo'-mik.
Beads—Shoong-ow'-yah.
Blanket—Kep'-ig.
Break—Sel'-li-ko.

Bark—Oo-we-uk'-too.
Boil—Kul-ak'-pook.
Bite—Kee'-wah, O-kum-wik'-poo.
Breathe—Ar-nuk-ter-re'-uk.
Build snow house—Ig-loo-le'-yook.
Burn—Oon-ok'-took.
Big river—Koog-ooark'.
Brass headband—Kar'-roong.
Butcher knife—Pee'-low.
Before (or first)—Kee'-sah-met, Oo-tung-ne-ak'-pung-ar.
Bring (verb)—Tik-e-u-dje'-yoo.
Body—Kot'-e-jeuk.
Black moss—Kee-now'-yak.
Big lake—Tussig-see'-ark.
Berries (like red raspberries)—Ok'-pict.
Berries (small black)—Par-wong.
Berries (large yellow)—Kob'-luk.
Bill (of bird)—See'-goo.
Button—See'-ah-cote.
Buttonhole—See-ok-wahk'-pe-ok.
Blubber—Oke-zook.
Blubber (oil tried out)—Tung'-yah.
Bitch—Ahg'-neuck.
Ball of foot—Man-nook'-kok.
Bend (verb)—Ne-yook'-te-pook.
Break (verb)—E-ling-nuk'-poo, Nok'-ok-
    poe, Noo-week'-pook, Kow'-poo.
Beat (as a drum, verb)—Moo'-mik-took.
Beat (snow off of clothing, verb)—Tee-look'-took-took.
Beat (with club, verb)—Ah-now-look-took.
Boots (deerskin)—Ne'-u, Mit-ko'-lee-lee.

C

Caps—See'-ah-dout.
Cheek—Oo-loo'-ak.
Codfish—Oo'-wat.
Come here—Ki-yeet', ki-low', ki-ler-root'.
Clothing—An'-no-wark.
Clear weather—Nip-tark'-too.
Cold—Ik'-kee.
Cup—E-mu'-sik.
Cairn—In-nook'-sook.
Clam—Oo-wil'-loo.
Child—Noo-ter-ark'.
Cloud—Nu'-yer.
Chief—Ish-u-mat'-tar.
Cook—Coo-lip-sip'-too.
Canoe—Ky'-ak.
Coat (inside)—Ar-tee'-gee.
Coat (outside)—Koo'-lee-tar.
Cloth—Kob-loo-nark'-tee.
Child, or little one—Mik'-ke
  (abbreviation of mik-e-took-e-loo, little).
Cask—Kah-tow-yer.
Cry (verb)—Kee-yie'-yook.
Cap, or hood—Nah'-shuk.
Carry (verb)—Ok-lah-loo'-goo.
Chew (verb)—Tum-wah'-wah.
Cut (verb)—Pe-luk'-took.
Cross-eyed—Nak-oon-i'-yook.
Copper—Kod-noo'-yer.
Calf (of leg)—Nuk-i-shoong'-nuk.
Crawl (verb)—Parm'-nook-took.
Cough (verb)—Coo-ik-suk'-took.
Come (verb)—Tee-kee-shark'-took-too.
Commence (verb)—Ah-too-ik-now'-ook-took.

D

Dog—Ki'-mak, King'-me.
Doe (old)—No-kal'-lee.
Doe (young)—Nu-ki'-etoo.
Day, or to-day—O-gloo'-me.
Day after to-morrow—Oo-al-e-an'-nee.
Day before yesterday—Ik-puk-shar'-nee.
Duck—Me'-ah-tuk.
Dangerous—Nang-e-yang-nak'-took.
Dog harness—Ar'-no.
Dead—Tuk'-ah-wuk.
Dark—Tark, ta-ko'-nee.
Down—Tow'-nau-ee.
Dawn—Kow-luk'-poo.
Door—Mat'-dor, par, koo-tuk.
Daughter—Pun'-ne.
Dress—Au-a-wark'-took.
Drown—Ki-yar'-wuk.
Drink—E'-mik-took.
Dream—See-muk'-took-pook.
Do you like?—U-mar'-ke-let-it-la?
Dripping water—Ko-duk'-too, Kush-e-koo'-ne.
Do (verb)—I-u-met'-u.
Dried Salmon—Pe-ip'-se.
Deerskin drawers—E'-loo-par.
Deerskin trousers—See'-lah-par.
Dive (verb)—Me'-pook.
Dislike (verb)—Pe-u-wing-nah-lah'-yar.

E

Ear—See'-a-tee.
Eyes—E'-yah.
Ermine—Ter'-re-ak.
Elbow—E-quee'-sik.
East—Tar'-wan-ne.
Early-Oo'-blah.
Every day—Kow'-ter-man.
End for end—Ig-loo'-an-ar.
Entrails—Ein'-er-loo.
Egg—Mun'-nik.
Eat—Ner-ee-uk'-took-too.
Empty—E-mah'-ik-took.
Everything or every one—Soo-too-in'-nuk.
Every night—Ood'-nook-ter-mock'-er-mingk.
Eye tooth—Too-loo'-ah-el'-lek.
Enough—Te-ter'-par.

F

Fox—Ter-re-ar-ne'-ak.
Fire—Ik'-o-mar.
Fish—Ik'-kal-uk.
Fur—Mit'-kote.
Foot—Is'-se-kut.
Face-Kee'-nark.
Finger ring—Mik-e-le-rar'-oot.
Female—Nee-we-ak-sak.
Far—Oon-wes'-ik-poo.
Farewell—Tare-wow'-e-tee.
Finished—In-nuk'-par.
File—Ag'-e-yuk.
Flipper—Tel'-ar-rook.

Faster—Ok-shoot'.
Fork—Kok-e-jerk.
Fringe—Ne'-ge-ver.
Feather—Soo'-look.
Fingers—Arg'-ite.
Finger (index)—Tee'-kee-ur.
Finger (second)—Kig-yuck'-tluk.
Finger (third)—Mik-ke-lak.
Finger (little)—Ik-ik-ote.
Full—Put-tah'-took.
Fly—E-sow-ook-suk'-too.
Fight—Neng-nik-par'.
Feel—Tep-sik-ak'-took.
Freeze—Keegk-e-yook'.
Forget—Poo-yuk'-too.
Find (verb)—Nin-e-va'-ha.
Finish (verb)—In-nuk'-par, Koo-lee-war'.
Fall (verb, neuter)—E-yook-ar'-took.
Fall (verb, a person)—Pard'-la-took.
Float (verb)—Pook-tah-lak'-too.
Fetch (verb)—I-ik-sek'-took.
Finger-nail—Kook'-ee.
Fore arm—Ah'-goot.
Follow (verb)—Toob-yok'-she-yook.
Fish (verb)—On-le-ak'-took.
Feed dogs (verb)—Kig-me-ar'-re-ook.
Fold (verb)—Pir'-re-pook.
Forehead—Kow'-roong.
Frozen (or frost)—Quark.

255

G

Gun—Suk-goo'-te-gook.
Goose—Ne-uk'-a-luk.
Gloves—Po'-ah-lo.
Good—Mah-muk'-poo.
Glad—Kuyan'-a-mik.
Gone—Peter-hong'-a-too.
Go—Owd-luk'-poo.
Give me—Pel'-e-tay.
Grave—E-le'-wah.
Green—Too-me-ook'-took.
Gun cover—Powk.
Give (verb)—Na-look'-ze-yook.
Ground squirrel—Shik'-sik.
Gravel—Too-wah'-pook.
Get (verb)—Shoo-mig'-le-wik.

H

Here—Una, Muk'-kwar.
Hole—Kid'-el-look.
Handkerchief—Tuk-ke-o'-tee.
Halo—Ka-tow'-yar.
Hiccough (verb)—Neer-e-soo-ock'-took.
Home—Oo-op'-te-nar.
Hot—Oo-oo'-nah Hard (verb)—Se-se-o-ad'-elo
Hunt (verb) reindeer—Ah-wak'-took.
Hunt (verb) musk ox—Oo-ming-muk'-poo.
Howl (verb)—Mee'-ook-took.
Hang (verb)—Ne-wing-i'-yook.
Hurry—Too-wow'-ik-took, Shoo-kul'-ly.
Help—E-see-uk'-par.

256

Herring (peculiar to King William Land
and vicinity)—Cow-e-sil'-lik.
Here (or there)—Tap'-shoo-mar.
Hammer (of gun)—Ting-me-ok'-tar.
Heel—King'-mik.
Hand—Puk'-beeg.
Hair—New'-yark.
Hand—Ar'-gut.
Husband—Wing'-ah.
Hard bread—She'-bah.
How far?—Karn'-noo-oon-wes'-ok-ik-te'-vah.
Half—E-lar'-ko.
Hate—Took-pah'.
He—Una.
How many—Kap-shay'-ne.
Hard—See'-see-yoke.
Hand me—Ki-jook.
Hill—King-yar'-ko.
Hungry—Kahk-too.
Hear or understand—Too-shark'-po.
Handle—E'-poo-ah.
How—Kon'-no.
Heart—Oo'-mut.

I

Ice—Se'-ko.
Iron—Sev'-wick.
I, me, mine, etc.—Oo-wung'-ar.
Ice chisel—Too'-woke.
Instep—Ah-look.
It is better, OR, is it better—Pe-e-uke'.
Island—Kig-yeuck'-tuck.
Island (small)—Kig-yuk-tow'-ar.

Inside—E-loo-en'-ne.
Intestines—Ein'-er-loo.
Indian—Ik'-kil-lin.

J

Jack knife—O-koo-dock'-too.
Jump (verb)—Ob-look'-took.
Jump—Ob-look'-took.
Just right—Nah-muck-too.

K

Kettle—Oo-quee'-zeek.
Kidney—Tock'-too.
Kill—To-ko-pah'-hah.
Knee—Nub-loo'-te.
Knuckles—Nub-we'-yan.
Kiss (rub noses)—Coon'-e-glew.
Kittewake—E-muk-koo-tar'-yer.
Kill (verb, reindeer)—Took'-too-par.
Kill (verb, bear)—Nan-noo'-me-owd.
Keep (verb)-Pah'-pah-took.

L

Little river—Koog-ah-lar'.
Lose (verb)—I-see'-u-wuck.
Lower jawbone—Ah-gleer'-roke.
Like (verb)—Pe-u-we'-we-yook.
Lungs—Poo'-wite.
Long ago—Tap-shoo-man'-ne.

Lead—Ok'-ke-gook.
Lip (upper)—Kok-tu'-we-ak.
Lip (lower)—Kok'-slu.
Leg—Ne'-yoo.
Loon—Kok'-saw.
Look—Tuk'-ko.
Large—An'-no-yoke.
Love—Kou-yah-e'-vah-vick.
Liver—Ting'-you.
Lake—Tus-sig.
Light—Ood'-luk, oo'-blook.
Laugh—Ig-luk'-too.
Lift—Kee'-wik-took.
Leak—Arng-mi-yook.

M

Musk-ox—Oo'-ming-munk.
Midnight—Oo'-din-wark.
Moon—Tuk'-luk.
Man—Ang'-oot Mouth—Kang'-yook.
Medicine man—Arng'-ek-ko.
Male—Nu-kup'-e-ak.
Much—Am-a-suet'.
Meat—Neer'-kee.
Meat cooked—Oo-yook'.
My son—Ear'-ken-ear-ar.
Marrow—Pat'-ak.
Musquito—Keek-toe'-yak.
Make—Mix-uk'-too.
Moss (running)—Ik-shoot-ik.
Moss (spongy)—Mun'-ne.
Mix (verb)-Kar'-te-took.
Milk—Ah-mar'-mik-took.

Milkbag—E-we-eng'-ik.
Match—Ik-keen'.

N

Never—I-pung'-ar.
Now—Man'-na.
Nail—Kee'-kee-uk.
Navel—Col-es'-ik.
Nostrils—Shook'-loot.
Night—Oo'-din-nook.
Needle—Mit'-cone.
Nose—Tling'-yak.
Neck—Koon-wes'-ok.
Near—Kon-e-took'-ah-loo.
No—Nok'-er, nok-i'.
Noon—Kig-yuk-kah'-poo-kik-ah.
Naked—Ar-noo-wi-lee-ak'-took.
Nest—Oo'-blood.
Narrow—Ah-me'-too.

O

Old—Oh'-to-kok.
Outside—See-lah-tau'-ne.
Oar—E-poot.
Old man—Ik-tu'-ar.
Old woman—Ah'-de-nok.
Over there—Ti'-mar.
Out doors—See'-lar-me.
Observation of sun—Suk-a-nuk'-ah-yook.

P

Pencil—Titch'-e-row.
Pemmican—Poo'-din-ik.
Pant (verb)—Arng-ni-u-ak'-took.
Pup—King-me-ak'-yook.
Pour (verb)—Koo'-we-yook.
Promise—Pee-da-go-war'-ne.
Place anything in its sheath—E-lee-wah'.
Put down (verb)—E-leeg'-yoke.
Place (verb)—Im'-in-ar.
Play (verb)—Kik'-it-toon.
Powder—Ok'-de-ur.
Pretty—Mah-muk'-poo.
Promise—Pe-dah-go-wah'-nah.
Paper—Al-le-lay'-yook.
Ptarmigan—Ok-ke-ge'-ah.
Pan—Ah-wap'-se-lah.
Pail—Kat'-tar.
Pin—Too-be-tow'-yer.

Q

Quickly—Shoo-kul'-ly.

R

Round—Pang'-ar, Arng-mar-look'-too.
Reside (verb)—Noo-mig'-e.
Row (verb)—E'-poo-too.
Runners of sled—See'-woong-nar, We-ung'-nuk.
Roll (a bundle)-E-moo'-war.
Rest (verb)—Noo-kung-ah'-took.

261

Rot (verb)—Shoo-yook'-too, E-vood'-nok.
Reindeer—Took'-too.
Reindeer (big buck)—Pang'-neuck
Reindeer (young buck)—Nu-kar-tu'-ar.
Reindeer (fawn)—No'-kark.
Ramrod—Kok'-dook-sook.
Red—Owg.
River—Koog.
Rabbit—Oo-kae'-ut.
Rock—We-ar'-zook.
Rain—Mok'-uk-too.
Raven—Too-loo'-ah.
Rapids—E-tem-nark'-zeack.
Ribs—Too-lee-med'-jit.
Run—Ood-luk-too.
Ride—Ik-e-mi'-yuk.
Resemble—Ar-djing'-er.
Remember—Kow-ye-mu'-wuk-er.

S

Sledge—Kom'-mo-tee.
Seal—Net'-chuk.
Seal (large)—Ook'-jook.
Seal (bladder nose)—Nets-che'-wuk.
Seal (fresh water) Kosh-e-geer'.
Seal (jumping)—Ki-o-lik.
Snow—Ap'-poo.
Stockings (long)—Ah-luk'-tay.
Stockings (short)—E-king'-oo-ark, e-nook-too.
Sun—Suk'-e-nuk.
Star—Oo-bloo'-bleak.
Skin—Am'-ingk.
Swan—Coke'-jeuk.

Sea or salt—Tar'-re-o.
Salmon—Ek'-er-loo.
Salmon (black)—Ish'-u-ark.
Stone—We'-ark.
Snow knife—Pan-an'-yoke.
Small—Mik-e-took'-e-loo.
Some—Tah-man'-ar-loo.
Swim (verb)—Poo'-e-mik-took, Na-'look-took.
Sink (verb)—Kee'-we-wook.
Smile (verb)—Koong'-ik-kook.
Spit (verb)—Oo-e-ak'-took.
Stare (verb)—E e-e'-yook.
Shake (verb)—Oo-look'-took.
Stretch (verb)—Tesh-ik-ko'-me-yook.
Slats of sled—Nup'-poon Screw—Kee-gee-ar'-lee.
Snow drift or bank—O-que'-che-mik.
Squid (whale food)—Ig-le'-yahk.
Spyglass—King'-noot.
Strong smell—Tee-pi'-e-took.
Shin—Kuh'-nok.
Shoulder—Ke-es'-ik.
Swap (verb)—Ok-ke-la'-yook.
Sharpen—Kee-nuk'-took, Air-e-yook'-took.
Sing (men)—Pe'-se-uk.
Sing (women)-Im'-nyick-took.
Sweat—Ar-mi-yok'-took.
Sneeze—Tug-e-yook'-took.
Squint—Kahn-ing-noo'-yook.
Scare—Kock-se-tek'-poong-ar, Ik'-see-book.
Starve—Pik'-lik-took, Pig-le-rark'-pook.
See anything coming far off—Og-le-luk'-pook.
Spinal cord—Kitch-e'-ruk.
Seal spear—Oo-nar'.
Sealskin slippers—Pee'-nee-rok.
Sealskin boots (short)—E'-keek-kuk.

Sorry—Ah-kow'-mit-u.
Stomach—Neer-u'-ker.
Shot (discharge of a gun)—Suk-ko'-eet.
Sealskin—Kis'-ingk.
Saw—Oo'-loot'.
Spotted—Oo-kee-leur-yere', Ar-glark'-took.
Svuare—Se-nar'.
Soft—Ah-kut-too-ah'-loo.
Strong—Shung-e'-yook.
Snake—Ne-meur'-e-ak.
Scratch another thing (verb)—Ah-guk'-took.
Stumble (verb)—Pard'-look-took.
Snore (verb)—Kom-noo'-we-ook.
Swear (verb)—O-kah-look'-took.
Suck (verb)—Tum-woi'-yook.
Swallow (verb)—E'-wah.
So—Ti'-ma-nar.
Summer—Ow'-yer.
Shirt—Ar-tee'-gee.
Spring—Oo-ping'-yark.
Same—Ti'-ma-toe.
Sister—Nur-year'-ger.
Scraper—Suk'-koo.
Snow stick—An-owt'-er.
Snow-block—Ow'-ik.
Spectacles—Ig-eark'-too.
Spoon—Al'-lute.
Sinew—Oo-lee-ute'-ik.
Sick—Ah'-ah, Ar-ne-ok'-took.
Scissors—Kib-e-ow'-te.
Smoke—E'-shik.
Stranger—Ahd'-lah.
Sunrise—Suk-ah-ne-uk'-poke.
Sunset—Ne-pe'-woke.
Sit down—Ing-e'-tete.

Stand up—Nik-e'-we-tete.
Steam—Poo'-yook-took.
Sand—See'-ah-wark.
Snowing—Con'-nuk-too.
Snow shovel—Po-ald'-er-it.
Speak—O-kok'-po.
Sleep—Sin'-nik-poo.
Ship—Oo'-me-ak.
Smoke (verb)—Pay-u'-let-tee.
Scratch—Koo'-muk-took.
See—Tak'-ko-wuk.
Smell—Tee'-pee.
Steal—Tig'-lee-poo.
Show—Tuk-o-shu-ma'-uk-too.
Sweetheart—E-veuck'-seuck.

T

To-morrow—Cow'-pert, Ok'-ar-go.
Two or three days ago—Ik'-puk-shar'-nee.
Tallow—Tood'-noo.
Teeth—Ke'-u-tee.
Tongue—Oo'-guark.
Tent—Tu'-pik Thunder—Kod'-ah-look.
Thunderstorm—Sel'-ah-look.
Trousers—Kok-ah-leeng'.
There—Ta'-boir.
Thanks—Quee-en'-nah-coo'-nee.
These people—Ta'-ma-quar.
Those people—Tuk'-o-quar.
Then—Oo-bah'.
Thread—Eve'-er-loo.
Tusk—Too'-rok.
Tenderloin—Oo-lee-oo-she'-ne.

Tail—Pam'-e-oong'-gar.
There (in the distance)—Tite'-quar.
Track—Too'-me.
Tired—Too-ki'-yoo.
Thumb—Koo-bloo'.
Thick weather—Tock-se-uk'-too.
Thirsty—E-me-rook'-too.
Thick—Eb-zhoo'-zhook.
Thin—Sah'-took.
Tatoo—Tood-ne'-uk.
Think—Ish-u-mi'-yuk.
Tell—Kow'-you-yor.
Trace—Ok-zu-nar'.
That will do—Ti'-mar-nar.
Think—Ere-kert-sert'-ro.
Take—Pe-e-ock-i'-re.
Tear (verb)—Al'-ik-pook.
Trigger—No-kok-tah.
Toe (big)—Po'-to-wok.
Toe (first)—Tee'-kee-ur.
Toe (middle)—Kig-yuck'-tluck.
Toe (third)—Mik'-e-lak.
Toe (little)—Ik'-ik-ote.
Thread (verb)—Noo-wing-yok'-par.
Thigh—Kok-too'-ok.
Throat—Too-koo-ed'-jik.
This person—Tab'-shoor mar.
Throw (verb)—Me-loo-e-ak'-took.

U

Ugly—Pe'-ne-took.
Understand or hear—Too-shack'-poo.
Up or north—Tap-an'-ny.

Upset (verb)—Koo'-e-yook.
Upset a kyack and inmates—Poo'-she-pook.
Undress—We-ze-tk'ook.

V

Vibrate (verb)-Ow'-look-a-tak'-took.

W

Will you?—E'-ben-loo.
Why?—Shu.
What?—Shu'-ar.
Who, which, what?—Kee'-nar.
What is the matter?—Kon-ah-we'-pin.
Wolverine—Cow'-bik.
Weak—Shung-e'-took.
Whistle—Oo-we-nyack'-too.
Wake up (verb)—Too-puk'-poo.
Work (verb)—Sen-uk'-suk-too.
Walrus—I'-vick.
Water—E'-mik.
Wood—Ke'-yook.
Woman—Ah'-de-nok.
Woman's boat—Oo'-mi-eu.
Whale—Ok'-bik.
White man—Kob-lu-nar.
Wife—Nu-le-ang'-er.
Whalebone—Shoo'-kok.
Walrus hide—Kow.
White gull—Now'-yer.
Wind—An'-no-way.
White—Kowd'-look, Kok'-uk-too

When—Kong'-er.
Wait—Watch'-ow.
Where—No-ti'-mer.
What is—Kish-oo'.
Winter—Oke'-e-yook.
Window—E'-o-lar.
Warm—O'-ko.
Wolf—Ar-mow.
Whip—Ip-pe-row'-ter.
What—Shoo'-ar.
Wing—E'-sar'-ro.
Wide—Se-lik'-too.
Wrist—Nub-gwok.
Walk—Pe-shook'-too.
Write—Titch-e-ruk'-kut.
Whisper—E-shib-zhook'-took.
Wake up—Too-pook'-poo.
Want—Tah-oom-ar-wung'-ar.
Work—Sen-uk-euck'-too.
Wink—Kob-loo-shook'-too.
West—Tar'-wan-ne.

Y

Yesterday—Ip-puk'-shur.
Young man—Nu-ku-pe-air-we'-nee.
Young woman—Nu-le-uk-sar-we'-nee.
Yes—Ar'-me-lar. You—Ich'-bin.
You and I—Oo-bah-gook'.
Year—Ok-ar-ny.
Yawn (verb)—I-ter'-uk-poo.
Yell (verb)—Ko-ko-ok'-took.

PHRASES

Go ahead—At-tee'.

What is the name of—I-ting'-er.

What are you making?—Shu-lah-vik'.

Who is it?-Kee-now'-yer.

Where are you going?-Nah-moon-okt'-pict.

Where do you come from?—Nuk ke-pe'-wict.

I have found it—Nin-e-vah'-hah.

Is it good?—Pe-e-uke'.

I don't know—Am-e-a'-soot.

Shut the door—Oo'-me-yook.

Open the door—Mock'-tere-yook.

Do just as you please—Is-you-muk-e-yang'-ne.

I guess—Shu'-a-me.

Give me a light—Ik-ke-de-lung'-ar.

Give me a drink—Im'-ing-ar

Give me a smoke—Pay-u'-let-e-de-lung'-ar.

I don't know anything about it—Kow-you-mum-e-mum'-me.

Where does it come from?—Nuk-ke-nu'-nar?

Come in—Ki-low'-it. Right here—Muk'-ko-war.

Who is it?—Kee-now-yer.

I am not sure—Shu'-ah-me.

Is the meat done?—Oo-par'?

Too much—Pee-lo-ak'-poke.

Too little—Mik-ke-loo-ak-poke.

Which way?—Nel-le-ung'-nook?

A poor thing—Nug-a-leen'-ik.

NUMERALS

1 (One)—An-tow' zig.

2 (Two)—Mok'-o, Mud'-el-roc.

3 (Three)—Ping'-ah-su-eet.

4 (Four)—See'-tah-mut.

5 (Five)—Ted'-el-e-mut.

6 (Six)—Ok'-bin-uk.

7 (Seven)—Ok'-bin-uk-mok'-o-nik.

8 (Eight)—Ok'-bin-uk-mok'-a-sun-ik.

9 (Nine)—Ok'-bin-uk-see'-tah-mut.

10 (Ten)—Ko'-ling. 20 (Twenty)—Mok'-ko-ling.

They have little idea of numbers beyond the number of their fingers, and such as they can borrow by calling attention to their neighbors' fingers. Any sum that calls for more than that is to them amasuet (many) or amasuadelo (a great many).

NO IDEA OF
LENGTH OF YEARS

It is not at all singular, then, that they have no idea of their ages when they get beyond the number of years that the mother can keep upon one of the wooden or ivory buttons that hold her belt in place. It is impossible, therefore, to tell whether they are a long-lived race. There are many among them who bear the marks of advanced age, but such may have resulted more from hardships and exposure than from the accumulation of years. There is a gray-haired old dame with the Iwillik tribe at Depot Island who was a grown woman at the time of Sir William Edward Parry's visit there in 1821, and remembers the circumstances with all the distinctness that marks the early reminiscences of the old in every country. There was another woman there apparently as old, but there was no early event by which her age could be traced except that she told 'The Herald' correspondent that she remembered having seen Parry on board of a ship in Baffin's Bay when she was a little girl.

Printed in Great Britain
by Amazon

15087141R00161